THE BIBLE
BLUEPRINT

A GUIDE TO BETTER
UNDERSTANDING
THE BIBLE FROM
GENESIS TO REVELATION

THE BIBLE BLUEPRINT

A GUIDE TO BETTER UNDERSTANDING THE BIBLE FROM GENESIS TO REVELATION

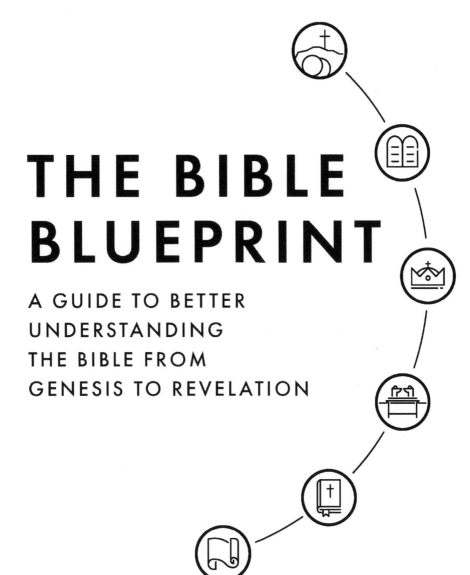

ROSE SPILLER & CHRISTINE PAXSON

Ambassador International
GREENVILLE, SOUTH CAROLINA & BELFAST, NORTHERN IRELAND

www.ambassador-international.com

The Bible Blueprint

A Guide to Better Understanding the Bible from Genesis to Revelation
©2021 by Christine Paxson and Rose Spiller
All rights reserved

ISBN: 978-1-64960-040-0
eISBN: 978-1-64960-041-7

Cover Design by Joshua Frederick
Typesetting by Dentelle Design
Editing by Katie Cruice Smith

AMBASSADOR INTERNATIONAL
Emerald House
411 University Ridge, Suite B14
Greenville, SC 29601, USA
www.ambassador-international.com

AMBASSADOR BOOKS
The Mount
2 Woodstock Link
Belfast, BT6 8DD, Northern Ireland, UK
www.ambassadormedia.co.uk

The colophon is a trademark of Ambassador, a Christian publishing company.

ACKNOWLEDGMENTS

First and foremost, we would like to thank God, Who is Sovereign over everything, for bringing us together and allowing us to do what we both love best—studying, writing, and teaching His Word! We would also like to thank all of our family and friends who have prayed for us, encouraged us, and helped us in so many ways! Thanks, too, to Gordon Conwell Theological Seminary, Reformed Theological Seminary, and Biblical Training for making seminary-level online programs and classes available. Finally, a big thank you to Dr. Sam Lowry for again putting his confidence in us; to Katie Cruice Smith, our amazing and patient editor; and to the rest of the Ambassador staff! You guys are awesome!

DEDICATIONS

*To my husband and best friend, Ed, whose constant love
and support made this endeavor possible. I love you!
To my sons and sons-in-law—Matt, Shawn (Bo), Jeff, and Kevin—and to my
daughters and daughter-in-law—Michelle, Nicole, and Laura. Your support
and encouragement mean more than you know! I love you all so much!
To my grandchildren: Julia, Lily, James, Olivia, John, Emma,
Landon, and Logan. You are all the loves and joy of my life!*

~ Rose

*To my husband, John, the love of my life. Thank you for
showing Christ's love to me in so many ways.
To Ian and Zach, I love you so much. Being your
mom has brought me great joy.
To the best parents and parents-in-law in the world, I love all
of you very much. Thank you for always being there.*

~ Chris

TABLE OF CONTENTS

GOD WROTE A BOOK!

Have you ever thought about the Bible as a book written by God? It is; and every Christian needs to read it! The Bible was written by approximately forty different authors over the course of fifteen hundred years. (A few of the books have unknown authors, so an exact number is impossible to know). The Bible is God's Word without error. God literally breathed out His Word using human authors who were guided by the Holy Spirit as they wrote. Every word in the Bible included in the thirty-nine books of the Old Testament and twenty-seven books of the New Testament are equally inspired. The Bible is our final authority and is a trustworthy source of absolute truth. The Bible is God's story of redemptive history. It answers the fundamental questions all humans have:

- Who am I?

- Where did I come from?

- Where am I going?

- What is my purpose?

The Bible is meant for every Christian to read! It is not just for theologians, pastors, and Bible teachers. With some basic knowledge about the big picture and the structure of the Bible, almost anyone can begin to get an understanding of what God has told us about Himself, ourselves, and the world around us.

Whether you're a new Christian or have been one for years, reading the entire Bible for the first time can seem like a daunting task. Not only is it a rather large book to read, but it's also made up of several different genres and uses both literal and symbolic texts that can be confusing and complex. Because of this, Christians who start out reading the Bible often either skip entire passages and books in it or end up putting it aside and reading another book altogether! Even if that other book is a good commentary on the Bible, it still isn't the Bible!

While it may sound strange for one of the "other books" to point this out, the idea for *The Bible Blueprint* is to equip you to start reading and studying your Bible in its entirety. This book is not meant to take the place of Bible. Instead, it is an overview to help you see the big picture of what God has been and is doing throughout history. As we go through each of the sixty-six books, we will summarize the themes and main ideas of each book, help unlock some of the more complex passages, decode some of the symbolism, and, ultimately, show how every word in Scripture points to Jesus! We have purposely left out large parts because it would be impossible to include everything and because we want you to hunger to fill in the gaps for yourself!

Good commentaries and supplemental books are an excellent resource when you are studying your Bible, but there is nothing that compares to reading the actual pages of what God divinely inspired the writers to write! No other book has the saving, life-giving, life-transforming message of the Bible. It is our prayer that you will soon find yourself immersed in His Word daily. You will find that no matter how many times you read a passage, there is always another truth to unlock in it. The Bible never gets boring, no matter how many times you read it!

PART 1

THE FOUNDATION
GENESIS AND JOB

Whether you're building a house, learning how to read and write, or making your favorite soup recipe, getting it right at the start is the key to having success. When you learned to read and write, the first thing you needed to grasp was a firm understanding of the sound that each letter makes. Without knowing that, you would not be able to sound out words nor write the letters in proper order to communicate what you wanted to say to someone. As every cook or chef knows, the ingredients that are the backbone of any recipe can either "make it" or "break it." Starting out with a homemade stock or broth and fresh ingredients for your favorite soup is much different than using only bouillon cubes and canned vegetables. One is likely to leave you with people asking for your recipe, and the other, while still fine to eat, will likely just leave you with a higher sodium count in your body! How we start from the beginning has significant impact on the outcome.

While these two examples show the importance of how we begin something, laying the foundation for a house is probably the best analogy for building a strong foundation for understanding the Bible. When a builder plans to construct a house, he takes into account the size of the house and the conditions of the location underneath where the house is going to sit. From there, he plans the type of foundation that will support the needs for bearing the weight and style of the house so that it doesn't collapse. It's got to have the right support underneath so that it can stand even in the worst of conditions.

It is no different with understanding the Bible when it comes to both your salvation and your life here on Earth. Without a proper understanding of God, His sovereignty, and His redemptive plan of history, human beings are left tossing on the waves of the ups-and-downs of living in a fallen world and left to crash on the shore at any given moment. Your spiritual life will feel the same. A strong theological foundation, coupled with a true understanding of Scripture, will set your feet on solid ground and allow you to stand firm, even in those times when you fall on your knees before the Lord weeping.

Chapter 1

THE DOCTRINE OF THE TRINITY AND BIBLICAL COVENANTS

To begin our foundational knowledge, we have to start at the beginning with something that has no beginning—God! God is an eternal Being. This means He has always existed and always will. God is one God, Who exists eternally as three Persons: the Father, the Son, and the Holy Spirit. To put it a different way, God is one in essence and three in person. The Father, Son, and Holy Spirit are distinct Persons. The Bible speaks of the triune God in that way.

For instance, we see the Father as God in **Philippians 1:2**—*"Grace to you and peace from God our Father and the Lord Jesus Christ."* We see Jesus as God in **Titus 2:13**—*"Waiting for our blessed hope, the appearing of the glory of our great God and Savior Jesus Christ."* And we see the Holy Spirit as God in **Acts 5:3-4**—*"But Peter said, 'Ananias, why has Satan filled your heart to lie to the Holy Spirit and to keep back for yourself part of the proceeds of the land? While it remained unsold, did it not remain your own? And after it was sold, was it not at your disposal? Why is it that you have contrived this deed in your heart? You have not lied to man but to God.'"*

These are not just three different ways of looking at God, nor are they just different roles played by God at different times in the way that a person could be described by using three different titles. For example, many women are daughters, mothers, and sisters. To think of the Trinity in that way is a heresy called "modalism."

The truth that there are three different Persons of the Trinity also means that the Father is not the Son; the Son is not the Holy Spirit; and the Holy Spirit is not the Father. We see this in the way that the Persons of the Trinity refer to Themselves and Each Other when they say "I" or "You" or when Jesus prays "to the Father." It's also important to point out that God the Father did not turn into Jesus, and Jesus did not turn into the Holy Spirit! All three Persons have existed eternally, co-equally together, and we see evidence of that since all Three were there at Creation in **Genesis 1:26-27**—*"Then God said, 'Let us make man in our image, after our likeness. And let them have dominion over the fish of the sea and over the birds of the heavens and over the livestock and over all the earth and over every creeping thing that creeps on the earth.'"*

Each Person of the Trinity is fully God in and of Themselves and by Themselves, yet are not three different Gods, but one God.

There is only one God. Scripture is clear that there is only one God. Although we cannot fully understand everything about the Trinity, we need to accept this doctrine as true. Wrong understanding of this doctrine can easily lead to misunderstanding truths in Scripture and can possibly lead to heresy.

While we're on the subject of God, there are some attributes of His that will be helpful to know about as we start exploring the Bible.

GOD'S SOVEREIGNTY AND PROVIDENCE

It's important to understand right from the beginning that God is sovereign over every single thing that happens—everything, including salvation! **Ephesians 1:3-5** says, *"Blessed be the God and Father of our Lord Jesus Christ, who has blessed us in Christ with every spiritual blessing in the heavenly places, even as he chose us in him before the foundation of the world, that we should* *be holy and blameless before him. In love he predestined us for adoption to himself as sons through Jesus Christ, according to the purpose of his will."*

Nothing can happen, and nothing does happen, without God ordaining or allowing it to. This is because He is the Ruler over all! Nothing catches God off-guard. He is providentially working all things out according to His plan, both for our good and for His glory. There is absolutely no such thing as coincidence, chance, luck, karma, or something "just happening." God is, has always been, and will continue to be completely sovereign over everything and everyone. **Acts 17:26** tells us, *"And he made from one man every nation of mankind to live on all the face of the earth, having determined allotted periods and the boundaries of their dwelling place."* The Trinity planned out all of the days of the Earth and all of the days of every person who has ever lived, or will ever live, before the creation of the world.

Nothing can thwart His plans. Everything that happens that seems "good" from our earthly perspective, as well as "bad" from our perspective, is part of God's plan, as we'll see toward the end of Genesis in the life of Joseph when he tells his brothers, *"As for you, you meant evil against me, but God meant it for good, to bring it about that many people should be kept alive, as they are today"* **(Gen. 50:20).** This is one of the most important things for a Christian to understand and fully believe. Whatever happens in our lives— whether it's the devastation of a tornado that strikes our house, the joy of a new birth, the loss of a job, or the good news of a promotion—is not based on a struggle between two equal forces of good and evil; it's not a struggle between God and Satan to see who will win. Satan, just like all of the angels, is a created being. Satan, who is a fallen angel, can do absolutely nothing without God's permission. God is totally, one hundred percent in control of all of the universe, down to every minute detail. Every molecule would blow apart without His constant upholding of it.

This is not "fatalism," where our choices don't affect the future. Because we don't know God's preordained plan, we freely make choices every day—choices about work, where to eat, morality, and the like. These choices include how we pray, how we treat others, and even whether we choose to commit sin or not, which is what makes us morally responsible for our sin. God is never the Author of sin. Although He uses our sin to work out plans that He made from eternity, we are free moral agents and, therefore, responsible for our sin. He does not cause us to sin; He doesn't have to because we're sinful by nature. We'll delve into this more later in the chapter.

GOD IS OMNIPOTENT, OMNISCIENT, AND OMNIPRESENT

Aside from His sovereign and providential care, God reigns over everything. His *omnipotence* means that He has "infinite power."[1] This power includes power over nature, nations, disease, the devil, and death—to name only a few. God is in control of *everything* in the whole universe.

God is also *omniscient.* Omniscience means "infinite knowledge of."[2] Therefore, God knows everything past, present, and future! And one more important thing to know about God that is true of *no one* else, including Satan, is that God is *omnipresent.* The word *omnipresence* means "universal presence of."[3] God is present everywhere all the time. God's nature is spiritual, as we see in **John 4:24**—"*God is spirit, and those who worship him must worship in spirit and in truth.*" He is not limited by space or time. This should be a comfort to the believer because, as J. I. Packer puts it, "One thing that is clear, however, is that he is present everywhere in the fullness of all that he is and all the powers that he has, and needy souls praying to him anywhere in the world receive the same fullness of his undivided attention."[4]

---

1   *The New Strong's Exhaustive Concordance*, Nashville, TN: Thomas Nelson Publishers, 1990, 149.
2   Ibid.
3   Ibid.
4   J.I. Packer, *Concise Theology: A Guide to Historic Christian Beliefs*, Chicago: Tyndale House Publishers, 1993.

THE REVELATION OF GOD

God reveals Himself in two ways—general revelation and special revelation. General revelation is God making Himself known to *all* people through nature. Believers, though, receive special revelation as the Holy Spirit enables them to understand Scripture. The Bible is God's message to His people, telling them all that He desires them to know about Himself, His glory, our salvation, and how we are to live this life.

Although we can know God through both nature and Scripture—and while there is much we can comprehend—our finite minds cannot possibly understand all the things of God. There is no way we mere humans can grasp the infinite knowledge of God completely! There are some biblical truths that we can't totally wrap our minds around, explain in totality, or grasp entirely. That in no way makes them untrue. We must believe everything in the Bible is true, even if we have to acknowledge there's some mystery to it that we can't fully explain.

MAN'S PURPOSE

As we've said before, God has always existed in all three Persons of the Trinity. He does not need, nor has He ever needed, anything. In light of that truth, it is wrong to believe that God created man because He "needed" him. **Acts 17:24-25** tells us, *"The God who made the world and everything in it, being Lord of heaven and earth, does not live in temples made by man, nor is he served by human hands, as though he needed anything, since he himself gives to all mankind life and breath and everything."* He did not need mankind for love, a relationship, or because He was lacking anything. The three Persons of the Godhead do not need us!

We are told in **Isaiah 43:7** that we were created for His glory. We were created to display His glory and to enjoy making His glory evident as we go through life. Everything we do in life is to be done in a way that is

God-glorifying. **First Corinthians 10:31** commands us, "*So, whether you eat or drink, or whatever you do, do all to the glory of God.*" God created mankind in the world He made so that we would carry out His eternal plan of the ages. We are to shine His glory and greatness to the world, basking in the enjoyment of being a child of God as we do it.

BIBLE COVENANTS

Throughout the Bible, the word "covenant" is used frequently, so it's helpful to have some general knowledge about it before delving in. A covenant is an agreement between two parties. The covenants we find in the Bible are important because Christianity is based on having a relationship with God. God's covenants with humanity unify the teachings of the entire Bible, Old Testament through New Testament. To understand what that relationship between God and His people is supposed to look like and how it is to function, God uses covenants that are linked together throughout the Bible. Understanding them will help us understand what God is doing throughout history.

The Bible covenants (except for the Covenant of Redemption) are covenants between God and humans. God is the "greater party" in the covenant, and humans are the "lesser party." Thus, humans are not in a negotiating position in the covenants in any way.

The covenants throughout the Bible build on one another; they do not replace one another. There is continuity throughout them in the way that God deals with His people. God did not have a "Plan A," and when that didn't work, came up with "Plan B," and so on, and so on, thus always changing how He deals with humanity throughout history. To believe that God changes His plans would leave us with a God Who is always reacting to humans and unable to be counted on because He's always changing how He deals with people! God is immutable, which means He does not change. He does not change as if tossed by the waves or like shifting sand that's unable to be trusted to stand on. We can always depend on Him to act according to how He has revealed Himself and His will in the Bible. As we're also told in **Numbers 23:19**, *"God is not man, that he should lie, or a son of man, that he should change his mind. Has he said, and will he not do it? Or has he spoken, and will he not fulfill it?"*

There are several covenants we'll touch on as we go through the Scriptures, but the three main covenants in the Bible are:

- **Covenant of Redemption**—This is the only covenant that is not made between God and humans; it was made between the three Persons of the Trinity. This covenant is the foundation for all of the others. This is the agreement made amongst the Trinity to bring a chosen remnant of people to salvation. It was made before the time of creation, and we see the work of each Person of the Trinity in regard to our salvation throughout the Bible. For example, the Father electing those to be saved is seen in **2 Thessalonians 2:13**. We then see Him giving the elect to the Son as an inheritance in **John 17:2, 6**. The Son consents to do the work necessary to save the elect in **Philippians 2:7-8** and **John 10:17-18**. And the Holy Spirit agrees to apply the work of Christ to us, sealing us forever into His salvation in **John 14:16-17** and **15:26**. All of this is also seen in **Ephesians 1:3-14**.

- **Covenant of Works**—This is the agreement between God and Adam in which Adam was put in the land of the Garden of Eden and told to be fruitful and multiply. He was promised blessings and life upon obedience to the terms of the covenant and curses and death should he disobey the terms of the covenant. This covenant was broken when Adam and Eve disobeyed God by eating of the fruit from the Tree of the Knowledge of Good and Evil, also known as The Fall of Man. Every human from that point on has been tainted with an inherited sin nature that is hostile to God and which makes them enemies of God. No one can be good enough to earn the salvation of *a perfectly holy* God. From this point on, everyone who is to be saved will need a *perfectly holy Substitute* to be their Savior.

- **Covenant of Grace**—This covenant was entered into with Adam directly after the Fall, when God promised to send the Seed of the woman (Christ) to crush the head of the Serpent (Satan). All of the rest of the covenants fall under this category because everyone who is saved will be saved by God's grace alone (Sola Gratia).

THE OVERARCHING STORY OF THE WHOLE BIBLE

The Bible needs to be looked at and studied as one whole book. There is a "big picture" to the Bible. Many people miss the big picture or go into studying the Bible without this knowledge. What is that big picture? It is what we saw in the Covenant of Redemption—that from before the foundations of the world, God has had a plan to work through human history to redeem a people for Himself through Jesus.

THE OLD TESTAMENT

The Old Testament lays the foundation for everything in the New Testament. The whole Old Testament points to Christ. The Old Testament is still just as relevant today as the New Testament is. In fact, you cannot properly understand the New without the Old! You'll see the need to study both in some of the theological things we point out in this book!

Everything in the Old Testament happened before the birth of Christ. There are thirty-nine books in the Old Testament. We begin with the first book of the Bible, Genesis. Genesis and the four subsequent books (Exodus, Leviticus, Numbers, and Deuteronomy) are called the Pentateuch. They are also referred to as the Books of Moses, or the Law, as it is most often referred to in Scripture. They're also known as the Torah in Judaism. All five were written by Moses during the time of Deuteronomy in 1445-1440 B.C.

All of the dates for much of the Old Testament are approximate because dating is very difficult for this early part of history. The dates used in this book are from the Discovery Bible: Biblehub.[5]

---

5   Rich Valkanet and Discovery Bibles, "Bible Timeline," Bible Hub.com. https://biblehub.com/timeline/ (accessed January 22, 2019).

Chapter 2

GENESIS

The book of Genesis is the first book in the Bible. It contains fifty chapters that give us the history of the beginning when God in all three Persons of the Trinity created the universe as we know it, through the time of the patriarchs (Abraham, Isaac, and Jacob), to what would eventually be known as the heads of the twelve tribes of Israel arriving in Egypt. The book of Genesis lays the foundation for everything that is to come.

Right from the beginning, we are introduced to the Triune God, and we see Him creating everything. God created the universe *ex nihilo*, which is Latin for "out of nothing."[6] Everything He created was good. At creation, God took what was formless and empty and made it into something; He took something that was uninhabitable and made it habitable. He did this sometime before the year 4000 B.C.

Based on the original Hebrew and the way the same word is used in other texts, it's likely that the creation days were six 24-hour periods of time. Because God is God, He can create anything He wants in any way He wants. He can create a mature tree, as well as the seed; He can create a grown man from the dust of the ground. Therefore, for these reasons and others, we will leave other arguments about the creation days out and look at these as normal days as we now know. The things that are written in the Bible would have made sense to the people to whom they were written. Therefore, when Moses

6   *Merriam-Webster*, s.v. "ex nihilo" accessed June 27, 2019, https://www.merriam-webster. com/dictionary/ex nihilo.

wrote "days," the Israelites would have been thinking in terms of what they knew a "day" to be. Even if they weren't thinking in terms of twenty-four-hour periods but, more simply, just "evening and morning," it's not likely they would not have been doing mental gymnastics wondering if a day really meant tens of thousands of years or something completely different.

After God made the heavens and the earth and all plants and animals, He created Adam out of dust and Eve out of Adam's rib, something you can read more about in Genesis chapter two. God made humans "in His image." This doesn't mean that we physically resemble God. It means we were to be His representatives in the world, living to reflect His glory in a perfect way.

When all of creation was finished, God rested on the seventh day. Did God, Creator of the universe, need to rest? Of course not! He did this to show us, by example, that we are to rest weekly because unlike Him, we do need it! But we need something more than rest; we need God. So, God not only rested from His work, He also blessed the seventh day and made it holy. In other words, He gave us a holy sabbath rest to worship Him and get to know Him better, something He knew was as crucial to our life as food and water.

Our first parents were given a beautiful place to live called the Garden of Eden. They were put in charge of and had dominion over all of the animals and creatures of the Earth, as well as plant life. They were supposed to be benevolent caretakers, ruling kindly and thoughtfully over all the Earth. They had work to do, but it was pleasant and productive. Adam even got to name each of the animals.

As the first man and woman, Adam and Eve were the parents of the whole human race. Their genealogy is recorded in the Bible. Life was harmonious between the two of them, God and them, and the animals and them. God gave Adam and Eve the job of "filling the earth and subduing it." Think about this mandate when we get to the story of the Tower of Babel later in Genesis!

For some amount of time which we don't know the length of, life went on this way. Not only was their life harmonious, but there was no death for any living creature! As long as they obeyed God, they lived in this perfect world. Even though they were naked, they felt no guilt or shame in front of each other or in front of God. Adam and Eve were living under the Covenant of Works that we talked about earlier. They had the ability to *not* sin. They could keep their harmonious, death-free life and have an unbroken relationship with God forever—as long as they obeyed Him. They could (in effect) "work" for their salvation by obeying and continue to enjoy God's blessings. God had given them one command—not to eat fruit from the Tree of the Knowledge of Good and Evil, and it had a consequence for not following it—they would die. The curse that came with disobeying was death.

One day while Adam and Eve were in the Garden, Satan showed up in the form of a serpent, and worse yet, a talking one! Satan tempted Eve by twisting God's words and making her doubt God's goodness. Satan then went further and lied to her and told her the exact opposite of what God had said—that if they ate the fruit, they wouldn't die. **Genesis 3:4-6** says:

> *But the serpent said to the woman, "You will not surely die. For God knows that when you eat of it your eyes will be opened, and you will be like God, knowing good and evil." So when the woman saw that the tree was good for food, and that it was a delight to the eyes, and that the tree was to be desired to make one wise, she took of its fruit and ate, and she also gave some to her husband who was with her, and he ate.*

This act in human history is referred to as "the Fall" or "original sin." At this moment, harmony is completely destroyed. This was not just an act of eating some forbidden fruit. Our first parents made a conscious decision that they did not want to be ruled by God. They shirked His authority, thumbed their noses at Him, and did as they pleased. Adam and Eve's desire to be like God, to be autonomous and rule themselves instead of submitting to their Creator's authority, changed everything. Death and decay, toil and hardship have now entered the world. Not only humanity but also all of creation would suffer the effects of their sin. The apostle Paul tells us this in **Romans 8:19-23**:

> *For the creation waits with eager longing for the revealing of the sons of God. For the creation was subjected to futility, not willingly, but because of him who subjected it, in hope that the creation itself will be set free from its bondage to corruption and obtain the freedom of the glory of the children of God. For we know that the whole creation has been groaning together in the pains of childbirth until now. And not only the creation, but we ourselves, who have the firstfruits of the Spirit, groan inwardly as we wait eagerly for adoption as sons, the redemption of our bodies.*

Why such drastic changes for eating a forbidden piece of fruit? Because God is perfectly holy. When we sing the hymn "Holy, Holy, Holy," we are not just repeating the word *holy* for no reason! Remember this when you get to **Isaiah 6:3**, which tells us, *"Holy, holy, holy is the LORD of hosts; the whole earth is full of his glory!"* The word "holy" is used three times to signify that God is perfectly holy in all of His attributes! His holiness is so pure and morally perfect, that it cannot tolerate any form of sin.

First John 1:5 says, *God is light, and in him is no darkness at all."* Therefore, He must also be perfectly holy in justice. Hence, He does not and cannot overlook sin. He cannot "wink" at it and pretend it never happened. There is a penalty for sin that must be paid.

It's pretty safe to say that all Christians would agree that God is good, kind, loving, gracious, and merciful; and they should agree because He is. This is something that we should be very thankful for because if God was all-powerful, and all-knowing, and perfectly just without also being gracious and merciful, we would all have reason to be terrified! These attributes of God also mean that He is not evil, that He hates sin, and that He demands justice. This is an important distinction to the way many Christians think about God being loving, kind, gracious, and merciful. Many want to believe God ignores His justice. They want to believe in a God Who never punishes evil, One Who lets sin slide and only looks at our "good behavior." They want a God Who is going to open Heaven to all people but the "worst of the worst." But God cannot overlook sin . . . not any of it. It would be against His nature to do that. And it wouldn't be very loving, or kind, to do so.

Not only was Adam and Eve's relationship with God broken, their sin "infected" all of humankind from that moment on. Since then, every person has been born with an inherent sin nature that is hostile to God, thereby putting everyone under His wrath and curse. People are not born innocent like the world tells us they are. **Romans 3:10-18** tells us:

> *"None is righteous, no, not one; no one understands; no one seeks for God. All have turned aside; together they have become worthless; no one does good, not even one." "Their throat is an open grave; they use their tongues to deceive." The venom of asps is under their lips." "Their mouth is full of curses and bitterness." "Their feet are swift to shed blood; in their paths are ruin and misery, and the way of peace they have not known." "There is no fear of God before their eyes."*

We are not sinners because of the individual sinful acts that we commit. We are sinners because we are born that way. The Bible says we are actually *dead* in our sinful state: *"And you were dead in the trespasses and sins in which you once walked, following the course of this world"* **(Eph. 2:1-2a)**. Just as a dead man can't reach out his hand for help unless someone restarts his lifeless heart, humans in their sinful state are spiritually dead and cannot change that unless God first regenerates their heart.

Adam and Eve are now under the curse of being dead; and for the first time, they feel guilt and shame. They realize they are naked and try to cover themselves with inadequate garments made out of fig leaves. Not only do they feel vulnerable being naked in front of each other, but also their shame and guilt make them hide from God. Mercifully, God intervenes and makes them adequate coverings out of animal skin. He sacrifices one of the beautiful animals that up until then had been freely enjoying the

Earth. This is the first instance we see of the shedding of blood to cover sin, and it's also the first death. This death to cover sin is a picture of our need for a Redeemer, Someone to pay the ransom price in our place. You'll see this pictured over and over again in the Bible. It's also a glimpse that God is the One Who provides the sacrifice for us. He does the saving work Himself from start to finish. Adam and Eve's feeble attempt at covering their nakedness with fig leaves did nothing, and our good deeds—our "works"—can't cover our sin either.

God gives Adam and Eve and all humanity hope in the Messianic prediction in **Genesis 3:15**: *"I will put enmity between you and the woman, and between your offspring; he shall bruise your head, and you shall bruise his heel."* These words to the serpent are a promise that Christ, the seed of the woman, would crush Satan's head. God, solely by His grace, would save a people for Himself.

As we move further into Genesis, we see the depth of sin and its vastness in chapters four through eleven. Sometime before the year 3000 B.C., Adam and Eve had two sons—Cain and his younger brother, Abel. Both sons brought an offering to God, and Abel's was accepted, while Cain's was not. Why did God only accept Abel's offering? Purely by God's electing choice. While it seems that Abel's offering was what made him acceptable to God, the text doesn't say that. Abel *and* his offering were "respected" or "regarded" by God, while the opposite was true of Cain. This is evidence of God's election in salvation. It's evidence that God regenerated Abel's heart. John Calvin says this about the passage:

> *God is said to have respect unto the man to whom he vouchsafes his favor. We must, however, notice the order here observed by Moses; for he does not simply state that the worship which Abel had paid was pleasing to God, but he begins with the person of the offerer; by which he signifies, that God will regard no works with favor except those the doer of which is already previously accepted an approved by him.*[7]

---

7   John Calvin, Verse 4 in "Calvin's Commentary on the Bible: Genesis 4," www. studylight.org/commentaries/cal/genesis-4.html. 1840-57.

Abel had a heart that desired to please God; and since the Fall, the only way a sinful human can have that is to have it regenerated by the Holy Spirit. This is an act of God, not something man can ever do himself.

Cain was mad that he was rejected, and he took it out on his brother by killing him. After Cain killed Abel, God cursed him and sent him away. He would have to live the rest of his life as an outcast. He was sent away to a land in the East, where he eventually married his sister. We know it was his sister because Scripture traces all of humanity back to Adam and Eve.

Adam and Eve gave birth to another son named Seth. The godly line would come through him, which included a man named Noah, who had three sons named Shem, Ham, and Japheth. Eventually, physical death came to Adam.

THE CLEANSING FLOOD

By 2500 B.C., sin was rampant on the Earth; it was so bad that God decided to wipe all living creatures out with a flood. **Genesis 6:2** gives us an example of just how bad things were: *"The sons of God saw that the daughters of man were attractive. And they took as their wives any they chose."* We aren't told who these "sons of God" were, but there are a few possibilities. Because they are mentioned in regard to the wickedness on Earth, it's possible they're wicked rulers of dynasties, but this is probably the most unlikely idea. It's also possible that they were men from the godly line of Seth who chose to intermarry with the ungodly line of the people—something we see later was forbidden. There is a good possibility linguistically that they were fallen angels, demons who took human form, at least for a time. No matter which is correct, the point is that because God is perfectly holy, He must judge sin!

God planned to destroy the human race—along with all the animals and all living things—with a worldwide flood. However, God saved the human race as well as the animals and other creatures from extinction by choosing Noah and his family to go into an ark, along with pairs of all living creatures and a few extras for sacrifice offerings after they've resettled on land. Noah "found favor" with God, and he was called "a righteous man," but Noah was not without sin. God chose to save Noah and his family *solely by His grace*, not because Noah did anything to earn it. Furthermore, out of Noah's three sons, God chose Shem to continue the godly line.

Noah built the ark just the way God told him to. It took Noah 120 years to build the ark according to God's specific instructions. Noah and his family and pairs of all the animals got in the boat and were saved from the flood. The waters receded; they left the ark; and Noah and his family worshipped God.

God makes a covenant we call the *Noahic Covenant,* and it's found in Genesis chapters eight and nine. Like the covenant made with Adam, it's a covenant made with all of humanity, but also with all living creatures. In it, God swears to never destroy the Earth again by flood, and He pledges to preserve the stability of the Earth.

> *And when the LORD smelled the pleasing aroma, the LORD said in his heart, "I will never again curse the ground because of man, for the intention of man's heart is evil from his youth. Neither will I ever again strike down every living creature as I have done. While the earth remains, seedtime and harvest, cold and heat, summer and winter, day and night, shall not cease" (Gen. 8:21-22).*

By saving Noah and his family, God gives us a glimpse of the Covenant of Grace by showing that He will save a remnant.

God didn't leave them without a sign of hope that He would keep His promise. He set the rainbow in the sky so that when the rains came, they could look to it and remember that He would not forget His promises to them. Noah and his family were given the same mandate as Adam and Eve—to be fruitful and fill the Earth. This is also the point in history when the animals started to fear and dread man, something stronger than just man's having dominion over them, and one reason is because man's diet was increased by God to include meat.

Sometime after this, Noah planted a vineyard, got drunk, and lay uncovered in his tent. His son Ham *"saw the nakedness of his father and told his two brothers outside"* **(Gen. 9:22)**. "Saw the nakedness of his father" could have many meanings based on what it means elsewhere in the Bible. It could be anything from thinking it was funny and telling his brothers, to voyeurism, to sex with his father, or even sex with his mother. Whatever it was, when Noah found out what Ham did, he cursed him by declaring that Ham's descendants would be slaves of his brothers Japheth and Shem, who was in the godly line, later to be known as the people of Israel. Ham became the father of the Canaanites, who would be known for their terrible spiritual degradation. This laid the ground for Israel's later conquest of Canaan.

INCOHERENT CHATTERING TOWER BUILDERS

Adam and Eve weren't the only humans in history with a desire to be like God. Sometime before 2100 B.C., a group of people migrated east toward the town of Shinar and decided to settle there. At this point, everyone spoke the same language.

With a desire to *"make a name for [themselves] lest (they) be dispersed over the face of the whole earth"* **(Gen. 11:4)**, they decided to build a city with a tower that reached to Heaven, and they started to do it using homemade bricks and tar for mortar, possibly thinking that using tar would help keep them safe if there's another flood.

What's the big deal about people building a city to live in? First of all, they were doing it for their own glory. Secondly, they were doing it so they wouldn't be scattered over the whole Earth. Remember earlier in this chapter when we told you to keep in mind God's mandate to "fill the earth and subdue it?" These tower builders were doing something in direct opposition to God's mandate! There are other things wrong, too, including the idea of a tower reaching to Heaven and the pagan shrine that topped most of this type of tower in the pagan nations.

This story ends with God intervening and scattering them over the face of the whole Earth. And not only that! He also confused their speech so that they couldn't understand each other. From then on, man has spoken different languages.

When we get to the New Testament at Pentecost, we get a small picture of a reversal of Babel. At Pentecost, when the Holy Spirit came upon the Church, people spoke in tongues, which means they could supernaturally communicate in foreign languages of other people groups, languages they didn't know prior to that. This was done so that all the people in Jerusalem at the time could hear the Gospel message in their own language and believe. We'll talk more about that later when we get to the New Testament!

FATHER ABRAHAM

In the year 2091 B.C., God called a man named Abram, a descendant from the godly line of Noah's son, Shem, to leave his country and travel to the land of Canaan, a land that God would give His people and would be called the Promised Land. God promised, *"And I will make of you a great nation, and I will bless you and make your name great, so that you will be a blessing. I will bless those who bless you, and him who dishonors you I will curse, and in you all the families of the earth shall be blessed"* **(Gen. 12:2-3)**. Abraham is known as the first patriarch of the faith.

Abram is from the Ur of the Chaldeans; and although his lineage is from the godly line, Abram is from a pagan-worshipping family, as we're told in **Joshua 24:2**, *"And Joshua said to all the people, 'Thus says the LORD, the God of Israel, Long ago, your fathers lived beyond the Euphrates, Terah, the father of Abraham and of Nahor; and they served other gods.'"* God used Abram to fulfill His purpose, despite the idol worship. The fact that Abram was a pagan worshiper whom God called is further proof of God's election in salvation. Like Noah, God chose Abram by His grace. God *called* them; neither man went looking for God.

Abram obeyed God and left with his wife, Sarai, his father, Terah, and his nephew, Lot. They traveled to a place called Haran, where they stayed for a while and then eventually moved on to Canaan like God had instructed. After being in Canaan for a while, sometime around the year 2085 B.C, Abram and his nephew Lot separated so that the land could support all of their livestock. It's after this that God furthered His promise to give Abram land and numerous offspring. There's just one problem—it had been six years since God's promise to make him into a "great nation," and Sarai seemed to be barren.

A few years later, about 2081 B.C., God made His covenant with Abram, which we call the Abrahamic Covenant. The Abrahamic Covenant is found in Genesis chapter fifteen and reiterated again in chapters seventeen and twenty-two. In it, God swore on oath to Abram to give him and his descendants the land he's living on known as the Promised Land. It had been ten years since the initial promise to be made into a great nation, four years since the promise of "offspring," and there was still no child. At this point, Abram was afraid his servant would be his heir. But God had different plans. He told him, "'This man shall not be your heir; your very own son shall be your heir.' And he brought him outside and said, 'Look toward heaven, and number the stars, if you are able to number them.' Then he said to him, 'So shall your offspring be'"* **(Gen. 15:4-5)**.

The ceremony performed to ratify this covenant is an amazing picture of God's salvation. In those days when two kings were making a covenant or agreement, often they would kill some animals and split them in half, leaving a path down the middle of the two halves. Then they would walk *together* down the path, signifying that if one of them should break the covenant, then that person should become like the dead animals that were on either side of them. God had Abram prepare the animals the same way, but the rest of the ceremony was done totally differently. God put Abram into a deep sleep, and **Genesis 15:17** says, *"When the sun had gone down and it was dark, behold, a smoking fire pot and a flaming torch passed between these pieces."* God was not only going to be the One to keep the covenant, He would also be the One to take the punishment for Abram and his offspring breaking the covenant. And that's exactly what He did through Jesus. Humans do not keep God's law; we can't. But Jesus not only kept the law perfectly so that He could be the perfect sacrifice, but then He went to the cross and suffered the wrath of God that we deserved as the real covenant breakers. We sing about God being amazing because He truly is!

Abram believed God's promises by faith, and it was credited to him as righteousness. It's from this text we know that we are saved by faith alone. Righteousness comes *by faith alone* (Sola fide), and not by works—*"Abraham believed God, and it was counted to him as righteousness"* **(Rom. 4:3)**.

The point of the text is not telling us we can have anything we want or that we can achieve anything we want if we just "have enough faith." Abraham's faith didn't give him a child; his faith in God gave him salvation. This text is about salvation coming by faith alone. For the Christian, that faith needs to be in what Jesus accomplished on the cross—paying the penalty for our sin and reconciling us to God.

Within about a year, Sarai got tired of waiting for the promised child and decided to take matters into her own hands. She decided to give her maid, Hagar, to her husband to sleep with in hopes to produce offspring. This was common practice in the day. Any offspring produced by the maid would be considered Sarai's. This was important in an age where childbearing was highly important for continuing the family line and to not leave widows destitute. Hagar got pregnant, and as you can imagine, trouble ensued between the women. In 2080 B.C., Hagar bore a son to Abram. His name was Ishmael, and he became the father of Islam.

Thirteen years later, Sarai still hadn't born a child herself. At this time, God made a covenant with Abram again to instruct him to circumcise all the males in his household, including himself. From this time on, all of the males in the household, both slave and free, were to be circumcised at eight days old. This would continue as his future generations became the nation of Israel. Circumcision is a sign showing that they are people living in a covenant relationship with God. It is a sign that separates them from the other nations and people groups. In the New Testament times, baptism replaced circumcision, and that's why many churches do infant baptism today. However, circumcision did not signify they were all saved, nor does baptism. They are both signs of being set apart, but the sign has no saving power itself. It only sets them apart, giving them the benefits of living in this covenant community.

Three more things happened in this meeting with God: Abram's name was changed to Abraham; Sarai's name was changed to Sarah; and God reiterated His promise of a son through Sarah. Abraham was one hundred years old by this time. Abraham asked God for the blessing to come through Ishmael, but God told him that Ishmael is not the child of the covenant. God's everlasting covenant would come through the child of Sarah, and he would be named Isaac.

There is more going on here than the results from disobedience and impatience in not waiting for the Lord to give Sarah a child. There is a theological concept here that's expounded on in the New Testament. Ishmael was the son of the slave woman. He would never share in the inheritance of the son of the promise. In fact, when Abraham and Sarah did have a son, Sarah wanted Hagar and Ishmael to leave, and the Lord agreed with her and told Abraham to send them away. What's going on here?

Galatians 4 gives us the answer. Abraham's son by the slave woman was born according to the flesh, while Sarah, the free woman, bore the son of the promise. **Galatians 4:24-26** says, *"These women are two covenants. One is from Mount Sinai bearing children for slavery; she is Hagar. Now Hagar is Mount Sinai in Arabia; she corresponds to the present Jerusalem, for she is in slavery with her children. But the Jerusalem above is free, and she is our mother."* Galatians expounds more from there, but the point is that those who have put their trust in Jesus' death on the cross as payment for their sin are saved. They are free and have an inheritance of eternal life with God forever. But those who are not saved are living under the Law. They will not share in the inheritance of those who are in Christ. In other words, they will not spend eternal life in Heaven but will be condemned to hell.

THE WICKED CITIES

We segue to a story about Abraham's nephew Lot, who came with them from Ur of the Chaldeans. He made a bad judgement call and moved his family close to the cities of Sodom and Gomorrah. Not too long after, they moved inside the city, despite its wickedness.

One day, while Lot was sitting at the gate of Sodom, two angels came to the city, and Lot invited them to his house for the night so that they didn't have to lodge in the town square. This was considered proper hospitality among the nations who lived in the area. Just before bedtime, the men of the city—*all of them*, both young and old—surrounded the house and demanded that Lot bring the two men who were his guests outside. The Bible tells what transpired after that in **Genesis 19:5-10**:

> *And they called to Lot, "Where are the men who came to you tonight? Bring them out to us, that we may know them." Lot went out to the men at the entrance, shut the door after him, and said, "I beg you, my brothers, do not act so wickedly. Behold, I have two daughters who have not known any man. Let me bring them out to you, and do to them as you please. Only do nothing to these men, for they have come under the shelter of my roof." But they said, "Stand back!" And they said, "This fellow came to sojourn, and he has become the judge! Now we will deal worse with you than with them." Then they pressed hard against the man Lot, and drew near to break the door down. But the men reached out their hands and brought Lot into the house with them*

and shut the door. And they struck with blindness the men who were at the entrance of the house, both small and great, so that they wore themselves out groping for the door.

After the angels helped Lot get safely back inside, they told Lot to get his whole family out of the city because they're going the destroy it. Lot hesitated, so the next morning the angels seized him and his wife and daughters by the hand and led them out. They were told to run and not look back at the destruction going on. **Genesis 19:24** tells us the city's fate, *"Then the LORD rained on Sodom and Gomorrah sulfur and fire from the LORD out of heaven. And he overthrew those cities, and all the valley, and all the inhabitants of the cities, and what grew on the ground."* Lot's wife couldn't resist the temptation to look back, and she turned into a pillar of salt. Did she look back in amazement or in longing? We aren't told, but the warning not to look back should've been heeded. Both Sodom and Gomorrah were cities full of wickedness, and God brought Divine judgment upon them by totally destroying them.

When we consider the wickedness of these two cities, our minds often think of the sexual sin talked about in this passage. However, that was not their only sin. **Ezekiel 16:49-50** is a passage comparing Israel to Sodom, and as we see here, the wickedness went far beyond what's mentioned in Genesis and includes sin found in many of us, if not in all humanity. *"Behold, this was the guilt of your sister Sodom: she and her daughters had pride, excess of food, and prosperous ease, but did not aid the poor and needy. They were haughty and did an abomination before me [God]. So I removed them, when I saw it."*

God used their punishment as a picture of what will happen to false teachers and unbelievers. *"And He condemned to ruin and extinction the cities of Sodom and Gomorrah, reducing them to ashes [and thus] set them forth as an example to those who would be ungodly"* **(2 Peter 2:6 AMPC)**.

In one of the more disturbing passages of Scripture, after a period of living without their mother to guide them and with no other men living in the vicinity, Lot's two daughters get him drunk so that they can have sex with him in order to conceive. Both daughters give birth to sons. One of Lot's grandsons / sons is the father of the Ammonites, and the other is the father of the Moabites. Both people groups were enemies of Israel. However, one of their descendants—Ruth, a Moabitess—became part of the Messiah's family tree.

THE SON OF THE PROMISE

In the year 2066 B.C., regardless of all human wisdom thinking it was impossible, ninety-year-old Sarah gave birth to Isaac! Isaac is known as the second patriarch. He would be the continuation of the line of God's chosen people. It seems that the story should end here with everyone living happily ever after; but when Isaac is around twelve years old, or somewhere in his early teenage years, God "tests" Abraham, and he is asked to sacrifice Isaac as a burnt offering. Does God really condone child sacrifices here? After Abraham and Sarah had waited all that time, did they really have to sacrifice their son, the one through whom the promises were supposed to come?

If God really did require child sacrifice, as the Creator, He would have every right to do so, but that is not what was going on here. Abraham was told to kill the heir who was supposed to inherit the blessings and who would bless "all the nations." Abraham was willing to go through with it, trusting that God would either bring Isaac back to life or that He would provide a substitute sacrifice. And that's exactly what He did! God did provide a substitute. This was a typological picture of Christ in the Old Testament.

"Tests" are not so that God will find out whether we "pass" or "fail." God already knows everything past, present, and future. So, if God is not waiting to reward us or punish us depending on whether we pass or fail, then why the test? There may be many specific reasons for trials and tests, some of which are mentioned in the following verses:

- **James 1:2-4**: *"Count it all joy, my brothers, when you meet trials of various kinds, for you know that the testing of your faith produces steadfastness.*

And let steadfastness have its full effect, that you may be perfect and complete, lacking in nothing."

- **Deuteronomy 8:16**: *"Who fed you in the wilderness with manna that your fathers did not know, that he might humble you and test you, to do you good in the end."*

Abraham's test was, indeed, special with its theological implications pointing to Christ as the substitute on our behalf. However, like Abraham, we will be called on to go through trials and tests. Also like Abraham, we can trust God to help us stand firm and walk in obedience, relying on Him through the grace He's provided.

TWO NATIONS

By the year 2026, Sarah had died, and it was time for Isaac to get married. But first, they had to find him a wife! This isn't like romance and dating today. Instead, Abraham sent his servant to Sarah's relatives to find a wife for his son. This was important because Abraham did not want him intermarrying the ungodly line. Through prayer and divinely ordered camel watering, the servant had success! The name of this virgin who's about to meet her husband for the first time was Rebekah.

Like Sarah was at first, Rebekah was also barren. However, Isaac handled things much differently than his father. Isaac prayed to the Lord about it, and she became pregnant with twins. She asked God about the "jostling" in her womb, and the Lord told her, "Two nations are in your womb, and two peoples from within you shall be divided; the one shall be stronger than the other, the older shall serve the younger" **(Gen. 25:23)**. God divinely chose the younger over the older.

Two nations did come from her womb. In the year 2006 B.C., the twin boys were born, the younger one named Jacob—who would later be named

"Israel" and whose family would become the nation of Israel—and the older named Esau, who would become the father of the Edomites. These are the twins who are talked about in both **Malachi 1** and again in **Romans 9:11-13**, where we're told, *"Though they were not yet born and had done nothing either good or bad—in order that God's purpose of election might continue, not because of works but because of him who calls—she was told, 'The older will serve the younger.' As it is written, 'Jacob I loved, but Esau I hated.'"* God sovereignly, by His own free grace, not based at all on anything either twin had done or not done, chose Jacob (who is actually a liar and a cheater) to be His people. He rejected Esau, and in the future, He justly lays waste to his descendants, the Edomites.

Jacob would be the continuation of the line of God's chosen people. Along the way, and as crazy as it sounds, Esau sold Jacob his birthright in exchange for some soup, thus despising his birthright. Later, with the help of their mother, Jacob stole Esau's blessing from their nearly blind father, Isaac, by wearing Esau's tunic and goat skin over his body. Esau was left with receiving a curse from their father. The blessings could only be conferred on one person and couldn't be altered. The blessing was for fertility and dominion, and as God's chosen descendant of Abraham, this divinely ordained destiny would carry through.

God said Jacob would be the one to get the blessing. This is an example of God using human sin to affect His purposes. God didn't tell Rebekah and Jacob to take matters into their own hands, and He didn't make them deceive Isaac. All of this happened through the sinfulness of a mother and father who each showed favoritism to one boy over the other and boys who did normal, sinful things—the type of things we all do as we go through life.

BEGINNINGS OF A CHOSEN NATION

To spite his parents, Esau married Canaanite women. Intermarriage with the Canaanites would have been detestable to the Israelites, and Isaac and

Rebekah were horrified. To avoid this with Jacob, he was sent to his mother's relatives to find a wife. On his way to his uncle Laban's house, Jacob had a dream. In it, he saw a ladder, or stairway, going between Earth and Heaven. Angels were ascending and descending on it, and God was standing above it. God gave Jacob basically the same covenant promises He gave to Abraham. The angels and stairway to Heaven indicate an "axis" between Heaven and Earth. This is a picture of Christ, the Mediator between God and man. Jacob named the place Bethel, which means "house of God."

Jacob's uncle Laban, Rebekah's brother, was a liar and a cheater! Sound familiar? Jacob would come to understand his own sinfulness in these areas because of his uncle's dealings with him. His uncle had two daughters, Leah and Rachel. Leah was older and not as attractive; Rachel was younger and beautiful. God providentially had Rachel at the right place to meet Jacob as he came into town. Jacob fell in love with Rachel and asked Laban for her hand in marriage, and Laban agreed to the marriage in exchange for seven years of work first. When the seven years were up, Laban held a wedding feast. Unbeknownst to Jacob, Laban switched his daughters, and Jacob ended up consummating his marriage with Leah, not Rachel! We don't know how Jacob could sleep with Leah thinking it was Rachel. There are lots of ideas, but we're not told in the Bible. After finishing the marriage week with Leah, Jacob also got to marry Rachel with the promise of him giving Laban seven more years of work.

Rachel was barren, but Leah started bearing Jacob children. In order to keep up with her sister's ability to conceive, Rachel gave Jacob her maid servant, Bilhah, to produce offspring for herself, and an intense competition for offspring ensued! Leah did the same with her maid, Zilpah, to produce even more children from her line. One of the women even sold their right to sleep with Jacob for a night in exchange for some fruit!

God eventually opened Rachel's womb, and she gave birth to two children. In the end, Jacob, also known as Israel, had twelve sons and at least one daughter, Dinah, by these four women. From those twelve sons would come the tribes that form the nation of Israel: Reuben, Simeon, Levi, Judah, Issachar, Zebulun, Gad, Asher, Dan, Naphtali, Benjamin, and Joseph's two sons, Ephraim and Manasseh.

The sons born of Leah were Reuben, Simeon, Levi, Judah, Issachar, and Zebulun. Levi was the tribe that Israel's priests came from. Judah was the tribe through whom David, and eventually King Jesus, came.

Rachel had two sons, Joseph and Benjamin. Joseph would be the inheritor of the birthright promises usually given to the oldest son, meaning he would get a double portion of the inheritance. Although Reuben was the oldest, he slept with his stepmother, causing him to lose those promises. Joseph's double portion would be divided between his two sons, Ephraim and Manasseh. That is why Joseph does not have a tribe named after himself—his two sons do. Zilpah gave birth to Gad and Asher, and Bilhah gave birth to Dan and Naphtali.

In 1908 B.C., Jacob left Laban to go back to his homeland, taking his whole family and all of the livestock he'd acquired. On the way, Jacob spent a night wrestling with God, at the end of which God changed his name to Israel. Rachel died in 1903 B.C. while giving birth to their second son, Benjamin.

Because Joseph was the firstborn of Jacob's beloved wife Rachel, Joseph held a special place in Jacob's heart. This caused jealousy and strife with the other sons, and Joseph's brattiness and tattling on his brothers didn't make matters any better. He was given what we are told was a "multicolor coat" by his father, which actually was a long-sleeved tunic given ceremonially and implied some sort of special inheritance.

The brothers talked about killing Joseph, but instead decided to sell him to some slave traders that were passing through the territory. Because they couldn't tell their father what they'd done, they led him to believe that Joseph was dead by tearing his coat apart and dipping it in goat's blood. In reality,

Joseph was taken to Egypt and sold to Potiphar, one of pharaoh's officials. But the brothers had no idea what happened to him. To them, the object of their jealousy was gone, and life went on.

Around this time, Judah left his brothers and went to the land of the Canaanites, where he spent about twenty-two years. While he was there, he got married and had three sons. The first was wicked, and *"the Lord put him to death,"* according to **Genesis 38:7**, sometime after he'd gotten married to a woman named Tamar, but before they had any children. It was the responsibility of the next son to sleep with the wife to produce offspring for the older brother who was no longer living. **Genesis 38:9-10** tells us, *"But Onan knew that the offspring would not be his. So whenever he went in to his brother's wife he would waste the semen on the ground, so as not to give offspring to his brother. And what he did was wicked in the sight of the LORD, and he put him to death also."* Judah's sons were not faring so well, so he decided to send the widow to her father's house until the third son grew up and could be given to her to produce offspring. However, he never did what he said he would do. In the meantime, Judah's wife died, too.

When Tamar realized she wasn't going to be given to the youngest son, she dressed as a prostitute, which included covering her face, and placed herself in the path of her father-in-law. Not recognizing Tamar, Judah slept with her. She wisely kept some of his belongings as a pledge for the payment he didn't have with him at the time. Tamar returned to her father's house with the items Judah left with her. Soon, Tamar and everyone else knew that she was pregnant. When Judah found out, he ordered her to be killed, the normal practice at that time. However, Tamar revealed who the father was when she presented the items she kept from him as a pledge. This made Judah realize how wrong he was to not give her to his youngest son. He said, *"She is more righteous than I, since I did not give her to my son Shelah"* **(Gen. 38:26).** Tamar gave birth to twins—one whose name was Perez—and he was in the Messianic line. Judah did not sleep with her again.

Meanwhile, Judah's brother Joseph had been in Egypt for about twenty-two years, where he eventually rose to second-in-power to the pharaoh. This was not a pleasant rise to power, and it took a lot of time—some of which was spent in slavery, and some of which was spent in jail after being wrongly accused of attempted rape. Sold as a slave by your brothers, falsely accused and put in jail, and being forgotten about for years would get the best of a lot of people; but all the while, Joseph handled himself as if he was working for God. Despite what must have been a great deal of struggle, difficulty, and strife at times, he stayed faithful.

Joseph came to power because God gave pharaoh a dream years beforehand warning that a horrendous famine was coming. Prior to that, God providentially caused Joseph to be in the right place at the right time, where He gave him the interpretation to the dreams of two other men, both of which came true. When he was brought before pharaoh, Joseph gave God all the credit for the interpretation of dreams. Once again, God gave him the interpretation to pharaoh's dream—Egypt was about to experience seven years of plenty, followed by seven years of famine. Not only was he able to tell him the meaning of the dream, but Joseph was also able to give pharaoh a plan of action for preparing for the famine. Because of this, Joseph was made second-in-command of all the land.

When the famine hit, it not only devastated Egypt, but also affected other nearby lands, one of which was Canaan. This forced Jacob to send his sons to Egypt in the hopes of securing food for the entire family. Jacob sent all the brothers to Egypt, except his new favorite, Benjamin. Still believing Joseph was dead, Benjamin had become his favorite, being the only child left who was born of Rachel.

When the brothers arrived in Egypt, they came before Joseph, but they didn't recognize him. Many years had passed, and Joseph was dressed as an Egyptian. Plus, they certainly wouldn't have expected their brother to hold such a high office. But Joseph recognized them and questioned them intensely about their family back home. He "messed with them" a bit, too. He returned their silver to their bags so that it looked like they'd stolen the grain; he made one of them stay behind in jail until they brought Benjamin back; and he sat them at the table in their perfect birth order to eat—just to name a few instances. Eventually, Joseph revealed his identity and had them return home to bring their whole families, along with their father, Jacob, back to Egypt to live. Finally, they had a happy family celebration. The pharaoh gave Joseph's family the best part of the land to live on so that they could shepherd their flocks.

Why did all of these things, both terrible and good, happen to Joseph? This was God's plan being worked out through *secondary causes*. These secondary causes consisted of everyday decisions, some of which were sinful. They were the decisions of a father who loved one son more than his others, some possible arrogance on the part of Joseph at being the favorite, extreme jealousy on the part of the brothers, and a slave caravan that was passing through just when they'd gotten fed up with him.

The secondary causes also consisted of a woman lying about a rape that never happened, causing Joseph to be thrown in jail, where God gave him the interpretation of two men's dreams. They included famine-producing weather and the dreams of the pharaoh. And what exactly was God working out through these secondary causes? He was getting Joseph's brothers, their families, and his father, Jacob (also known as Israel), to Egypt!

God is providentially in charge of both the ends, as well as all the means to the ends. **Proverbs 16:33** shows this: *"The lot is cast into the lap, but its every decision is from the LORD."*

Joseph recognized God's providential hand in everything that happened when he said to his brothers, who were terrified of retribution from him, *"As for you, you meant evil against me, but God meant it for good, to bring it about that many people should be kept alive, as they are today"* **(Gen. 50:20)**. This is an important truth. Everything that happened to Joseph was part of God's plan.

The brothers freely made sinful decisions out of their own wickedness. God didn't have to make them commit these sins. God also did not react to their sinful actions, "cleaning up" the mess they made and "fixing it" to make something good come out of it. From the very beginning, God was working through the sin of the brothers to fulfill His plan—getting Jacob's family to Egypt.

Joseph's family came to Egypt in 1875 B.C., marking the beginning of the nation of Israel. This is where the Israelites would prosper and grow very numerous over the next 430 years. During that time, they fell out of favor with the pharaohs and eventually became slaves for the Egyptian people. Until Moses came along . . . (More about him in Part 2, The Law.)

Chapter 3

JOB

Job's life falls chronologically into the time prior to 2100 B.C., therefore, these events happened around the time of Abram in Genesis. The book of Job is categorized as a wisdom book and is found in the Bible alongside the others of the same genre: Psalms, Proverbs, Ecclesiastes, and the Song of Solomon. It's one of the most important books for understanding God's involvement in human pain and suffering and how a good and loving God can let bad things happen to good people. It also shows us man's insignificance in comparison to God, and it causes us to look forward to something better than this life. The book does this by letting us look through the lens from a heavenly perspective at events in Job's life—an important perspective to keep in mind as we, ourselves, go through the ups and downs of everyday living.

Job's story starts with one of the rare glimpses into the heavenly realms. Angels were presenting themselves before God; and on this particular day, Satan came with them, after he'd been roaming back and forth on Earth. God started the conversation, asking Satan in **Job 1:8**, *"'Have you considered my servant, Job, that there is none like him on the earth, a blameless and upright man, who fears God and turns away from evil?'"* God was baiting Satan to fulfill His purpose of testing and refining Job. Satan took it hook, line, and sinker, asking God, *"'Does Job fear God for no reason? Have you not put a hedge around him and his house and all that he has, on every side? You have blessed the work of his hands, and his possessions have increased in the land. But stretch out your hand*

and touch all that he has, and he will curse you to your face" **(Job 1:9-11)**. God, Who is omniscient, knew exactly how Job would react; Satan, who is not all-knowing, had no idea. God put everything Job had in Satan's hands, except for Job himself. Satan was restricted, at first, from harming Job.

Not only was Job a righteous man, but he was also a rich man who owned thousands of sheep, camels, oxen, and donkeys. He was married and had seven sons and three daughters, and he also had many servants. They were a close-knit family, and the children spent time together eating and drinking. On one such occasion, Job received the news that his oxen and donkeys had been carried off by raiders after killing all his servants who were nearby. Shortly after, another servant came rushing in, telling him a different band of raiding parties had taken his camels and killed all the servants who were with the camels. If all of this wasn't enough misery, the next bit of news Job received was that a wind had struck the house where the children were feasting, and the roof collapsed, killing them all. Then the Bible tells us, *"Then Job arose and tore his robe and shaved his head and fell on the ground and worshiped. And he said, 'Naked I came from my mother's womb, and naked shall I return. The LORD gave, and the LORD has taken away; blessed be the name of the LORD.' In all this Job did not sin or charge God with wrong"* **(Job 1:20-22)**.

But Job's story does not end there. On another day, we get a second glimpse of Heaven, where a conversation took place that was similar to the first one. The difference is that this time, God allowed Satan to afflict Job physically, but he was not permitted to kill him. Things got much worse for Job as he broke out in painful sores from the soles of his feet to the top of his head. Job says in **Job 7:5**, *"My flesh is clothed with worms and dirt; my skin hardens, then breaks out afresh."*

Job's story is about a man who loses almost everything—even, eventually, his health. He wrestled with the question, "Why?" The Bible gives us the full picture of what was going on, but Job had no idea why these things were happening to him. Three of his friends tried to convince him that his suffering was caused by sin in his life of which he needed to repent. Another friend showed up and told him basically the same thing. They had it all wrong.

It was only when God answered Job that Job began to understand. Not that he understood why these things were happening because God never gave Job an answer to why he suffered. What Job came to understand was man's insignificance in light of Who God is. After God gave Job his first rebuke, the conversation goes like this in **Job 40:1-5**: *"And the LORD said to Job: 'Shall a faultfinder contend with the Almighty? He who argues with God, let him answer it.' Then Job answered the Lord and said: 'Behold, I am of small account; what shall I answer you? I lay my hand on my mouth. I have spoken once, and I will not answer; twice, but I will proceed no further.'"*

The sovereignty of God extends over *everything*. Absolutely nothing happens that is outside of His control and the providential working out of His plans. Satan cannot do one, single thing without permission from God. Satan is not responsible for everything that we consider "bad" from our earthly perspective. God is in control of all of it. We see this at the beginning of the book and again toward the end in **Job 42:11**: *"And they showed him sympathy and comforted him for all the evil that the LORD had brought upon him."*

The book of Job also leaves us with no question that the idea of karma is totally wrong. Life is unfair. Bad things do happen to people we consider good, and good things do happen to people we consider bad. Another thing Job teaches us is that "bad" things that happen can't be chalked up to God's punishment for sin.

Despite great pain and suffering to which he's given no answer to his question "why," Job came to the conclusion that God is the Almighty Creator and Sustainer, and in comparison, man is insignificant. No one knows God's ways, and they cannot be thwarted. Through suffering, God opened Job's mind to that fact. We can ask "why," but God does not have to answer anyone. Through suffering, Job learned more about God. Job was transformed by his newfound knowledge. He finally saw his rightful place before God, Who is perfectly holy in all things. God is worthy of worship, no matter what He chooses to do in our lives. Once we really see Who God is and who we are in comparison, we will say, like Job, *"I had heard of you by the hearing of the ear, but now my eye sees you; therefore I despise myself, and repent in dust and ashes"* **(Job 42:5-6)**.

The Christian life is one of repentance. God does not promise believers the worldly version of "the good life." He does not promise health or wealth. He does not promise to fulfill all of your dreams—or even to fulfill one of them. What He *does* promise the Christian is to transform them to be more and more like His Son. Often, that transformation happens through suffering.

For the believer, the suffering endured in this life is not the end. Something better is coming—living in the presence of God in a new Heaven and new Earth. Job's even greater blessings at the end of his life point us to that. The best is yet to come!

> *Who shall separate us from the love of Christ? Shall tribulation, or distress, or persecution, or famine, or nakedness, or danger, or sword? As it is written, "For your sake we are being killed all the day long; we are regarded as sheep to be slaughtered." No, in all these things we are more than conquerors through him who loved us. For I am sure that neither death nor life, nor angels nor rulers, nor things present nor things to come, nor powers, nor height nor depth, nor anything else in all creation, will be able to separate us from the love of God in Christ Jesus our Lord* **(Rom. 8:35-39)**.

PART 2

THE LAW
EXODUS THROUGH RUTH

If you are doing the math, you are probably wondering how we are going to cover sixty-six books of the Bible in six parts when we've only done two books in the first part. So important to understanding the Bible is the foundation of Genesis, that we needed to practically give it its own section. Now, however, we will move a little faster through the books. In this part, entitled The Law, we will cover the books from Exodus through Ruth. Technically, the books of Joshua, Judges, and Ruth are not part of the Law, but they do cover the conquest and early inhabitation of the Promised Land, so they fit well into this section.

THE PENTATEUCH

We begin with the four remaining Books of the Law: Exodus, Leviticus, Numbers, and Deuteronomy. As we said in chapter one, these books, along with the Book of Genesis, make up what is called The Pentateuch, meaning "five books." Moses wrote these books while the Israelites were journeying in the desert after God delivered them out of Egypt. Moses was writing these books to the Israelites and to the foreigners who had converted and joined them. He wrote first to those who he led out of Egypt in the exodus, and then later to a new generation of Israelites who would finally enter the Promised

Land. For both groups, Moses' goal was to help the people understand through their history and through God's commands who they were and Who God is. As we said, not everyone among them were natural-born Israelites, but even for those Jewish from birth, being in the pagan nation of Egypt for 430 years had left their history as God's chosen people often neglected. In addition, Moses, through God, knew that idol and pagan worship would be a continuous downfall for the Israelites. By giving them the foundation of who they were, Who God is, and what God expected of them, Moses was trying to help them avoid being ensnared by this sin.

Having a land or homeland is a basic theme in the Old Testament. Having a land or place to live that God gives you is basic to all of God's people. Throughout these books, we see the beginnings of God giving His people a land of their own, although it doesn't actually come to fruition until the book of Joshua. The Promised Land for the Old Testament believers is a foreshadowing of God giving the ultimate Promised Land—Heaven—to all of His believers.

Exodus opens after the death of Joseph (1806 B.C.), with the last book of the Pentateuch, Deuteronomy, ending just as the Israelites are about to enter the Promised Land for the second time (1406 B.C.). There is a lot of overlapping in these books (laws and covenant promises are repeated, for example). Therefore, while we will look at each book individually, we will also mention where there is overlapping. There are portions of these books that can be a challenge to read. The seemingly endless laws, offerings, and minute descriptions can get tedious. But when we keep in mind that God wrote every Word of Scripture with a purpose, it turns, "What does this have to do with me," into, "What is God telling me though this?"

Chapter 4

FROM EGYPT TO THE PROMISED LAND

EXODUS

The book of Exodus opens with the names of Jacob's sons who settled in Egypt. Exodus means "emigration,"[8] referring to the emigration of the Israelites out of Egypt. This book is the historical narrative of the Israelites' enslavement to Egypt, God delivering His people out of that slavery, and God establishing a covenant with His people. Exodus is what is called a "bifid" book, which just means it has two distinct parts. Chapters one through nineteen recount the most significant event in Jewish history when God delivered Israel out of slavery in Egypt. Chapters twenty through forty tell of the Israelites receiving the Mosaic Covenant from God. This includes instruction on worship, laws, and the construction of the Tabernacle.

After the death of Joseph, his brothers and their families continued to live in Egypt and increase in number. Soon, there was a new pharaoh in town, and Joseph and his family were quickly forgotten. The Hebrews—as the Israelites are called—had multiplied to astounding numbers. Pharaoh became concerned about their increasing population, so he forced them into slave labor as a means of controlling them. Still, they flourished.

---

8   *Merriam-Webster*, s.v. "Exodus," accessed January 26, 2019, www.merriam-webster. com/dictionary/exodus.

To further decrease the population, pharaoh made a decree that the Jewish midwives who were assisting the Hebrew women during birth were to kill any male baby. Girls were allowed to live. The midwives, fearing God, refused to do this.

During this time, there was an Israelite man from the tribe of Levi whose wife gave birth to a son. They hid their boy for three months; but being unable to hide him any longer, his mother placed him in a papyrus basket and sent him floating down the Nile. The baby's sister, Miriam, followed him along the edge of the water. God providentially had pharaoh's daughter standing by the river when the basket floated by. Having pity on the Hebrew baby, she decided to keep him as her own and named him Moses, which means "drew out or pulled out." Miriam offered to get a wet nurse to feed the child for pharaoh's daughter. Unbeknownst to the princess, Miriam gets their mother.

As the grandson of pharaoh, Moses grew up as a prince, while his people continued to serve as slaves. One day, he saw an Egyptian guard beating one of the Israelites. Moses killed the guard and hid him in the sand. After his action was discovered, pharaoh wanted to kill him. (So much for dear, old Grandpa!) Fearing for his life, Moses ran hundreds of miles away, ending up in the desert of Midian.

Moses spent the next forty years shepherding sheep for his father-in-law. One day, the now eighty-year-old Moses led his flock to Mount Horeb. Suddenly, a bush a little way off ignited but didn't burn up. When Moses investigated, he discovered that God was in the bush! More specifically, Jesus was in the bush. (The preincarnate Jesus appeared several times throughout the Old Testament, sometimes in physical form and sometimes spiritually. This phenomenon is called a theophany.) The Lord told Moses He was going to deliver His people out of their slavery in Egypt, and He had chosen Moses to lead them. Understandably, Moses didn't jump at the chance to leave his quiet life and return to Egypt where he may be killed, especially now that he was an old man! God, though, is not One to take no for an answer. God graciously gave Moses a few miraculous signs to show Moses that He would be with him. Moses still protested, saying he was not an eloquent speaker. God, showing compassion, agreed to let Moses take his brother, Aaron, along with him.

LET MY PEOPLE GO!

Moses returned to Egypt. It had been forty years since he was last there. The Israelites did not know him, nor did they appoint him as their leader. It was only through God prompting them and the miraculous signs Moses did for them that they came to accept him as their leader. Moses and Aaron went before pharaoh and told him to let the Israelites go so that they may worship their God, Yahweh. God had forewarned Moses that He would *harden* pharaoh's heart so that pharaoh would not let the Israelites go. The Lord did this so His power could be shown to all, especially to the Jewish people. It was also a way of God showing that He was all-powerful, and the Egyptian gods were useless. Everyone would be left with no doubt that it was only the One true God, Yahweh, Who saved His people while the Egyptians and their gods were powerless to stop Him.

As foretold, pharaoh refused to let the Israelites go. Moses warned him that if he didn't, all the water in the Nile would be changed into blood, and all of the fish would die. Egypt would be left with no drinking water. This was the first of ten plagues that God sent on pharaoh and Egypt. There was a back and forth between pharaoh and Moses eight more times with pharaoh either refusing to let the people go or relenting but then immediately changing his mind.

The second plague was frogs emerging from ponds and streams and covering the land. The third was the dust on the ground turning into millions of swarming gnats. Then, flies infested the Egyptian homes. This plague and all the subsequent ones affected only the Egyptians—there were no flies in the homes of the Israelites. Next came the plague of the livestock, where all the animals died. Then the plagues of boils, hail, and locusts. The ninth plague was a plague of darkness. All of Egypt was plunged into darkness, except in the areas where the Israelites lived. This plague was a direct attack on the Egyptian sun god, Ra. God was showing the Egyptians their phony pagan gods were no match.

Still not willing to set the Israelites free—remember, God had hardened pharaoh's heart—God sent the tenth and final plague, the plague of the firstborn. This time, though, His people were to participate. God instructed the Israelites to go to their Egyptian neighbors and ask for gold, silver, and clothing. And the Egyptians gave it to them! Of course, they had a little help from God, Who predisposed the Egyptians' hearts to favor the Israelites and give them these precious treasures. God also gave His people very specific instructions that they were to take a one-year-old, perfect, male lamb, sacrifice it to God, cook it, and eat it. Then, they were to wipe the blood of that lamb on their door frame. That night, the Lord would go through the land killing the firstborn of every human and livestock. Any house that had the blood on its doorframe would be *passed over*, and no harm would come to them. This was the first Passover and a foreshadowing of Jesus! Just as the body and blood of this perfect lamb saved God's people from death at this time, Jesus would be the ultimate Passover Lamb Who saves all of God's people for all of time through His body and blood. The doorframe represents our spiritual condition. Those who had the blood of the lamb on their doorframe were exempt from God's wrath. Likewise, those who are trusting in the saving blood of Jesus are not under God's wrath, but under God's grace. When judgment comes, God will see Jesus in our place and will *pass over* condemning us for our sins.

God told the people that they were to remember this and celebrate the Passover every year. This was a way for future generations of God's people in the Old Testament to understand and glorify God for what He had done for them and help them to remain faithful to Him. It was also a way for future generations of God's people in the New Testament to understand Who Jesus is and what He did when He was crucified. Passover transitions into communion for Christians. While the main story of Passover is found in Exodus, the Passover feast is also mentioned in Leviticus, Numbers, and Deuteronomy.

Pharaoh, whose own son was killed the night of this plague, finally agreed to let the people go. Moses and *"about six hundred thousand men on foot, besides women and children"* **(Exod. 12:37b)** left Egypt. Right after they left, pharaoh changed his mind and gathered his army to go after them. God went ahead of the Israelites, leading them in a pillar of cloud during the day and a pillar of fire at night.

When the people realized that the Egyptians were coming after them, they grew terrified. They turned on Moses and said he should have just left them in Egypt. With the help of God, Moses convinced the people to keep going. When they arrived at the edge of the Red Sea, God instructed Moses to stretch out his staff. When he did, the waters parted. The Israelites walked across the Red Sea between two walls of water. When the Egyptian army crossed in pursuit of the Israelites, Moses again held out his staff, and the walls of water closed back down. The entire Egyptian army drowned. **Exodus 14:30-31** says, *"Thus the LORD saved Israel that day from the hand of the Egyptians, and Israel saw the Egyptians dead on the seashore. Israel saw the great power that the LORD used against the Egyptians, so the people feared the LORD, and they believed in the LORD and in his servant Moses."* They even sang a song of the wondrous events so they would not forget what God had done.

The high from their miraculous deliverance did not last long, though. After a few days with no water, the Israelites began to complain. God made a covenant with them. He told them that if they listened carefully to His voice, did what was right in His eyes, paid attention to His commands, and kept all of His decrees, He would not bring upon them any of the diseases which He brought upon the Egyptians. After, He led them to springs of water.

Shortly after God made this covenant with the Israelites, they began to grumble again because of lack of food. Having a flare for the dramatic, they whined that God should have just killed them in Egypt instead of bringing them out of the land to die. They romanticized about Egypt saying they had pots of meat and life was good. Apparently, they forgot what it was like in Egypt when they had to not only slave to make bricks, but they had to find their own straw to do it! God, ever merciful and gracious, gave them manna and quail to eat. Manna was a thin, wafer-like bread. God had it rain down from the sky so that it was lying on the grass every morning for six days each week. For five of the days, the Israelites were told to gather all they needed just for that day and not to save any overnight. On the sixth day, however, they were to gather twice as much so they would have it for the seventh day, which was the Sabbath. There would be no gathering of food on the Sabbath. The quail was sent in the evenings, and it was the same deal with them as it was with the manna. Despite the instructions given, some saved the manna and quail overnight during the five days, and it became covered in maggots. Others did not collect double on the sixth day and had none for the Sabbath. Manna was a foreshadowing of the ultimate Bread of Life God would send from Heaven to feed His people for all time! Jesus is the essential, permanent, and perfect Bread. When we partake of Him as our Lord and Savior, we will never be hungry again because our souls will be satisfied, and we will have eternal life. **John 6:35** says, *"Jesus said to them, 'I am the bread of life; whoever comes to me shall not hunger.'"*

While traveling in the desert, the Israelites were attacked by a pagan tribe called the Amalekites. This was a totally unprovoked attack. Because of it, God said to Moses in **Exodus 17:14**, *"Write this as a memorial in a book and recite it in the ears of Joshua, that I will utterly blot out the memory of Amalek from under heaven.'"* (Remember this, as it comes up again later in the Old Testament.)

MOUNT SINAI

After three months of traveling, the Israelites reached the base of Mount Sinai. Moses climbed to the top of the mountain and met with God, Who reminded Moses of His covenant with the Israelites. **Exodus 19:4-5** says, *"'You yourselves have seen what I did to the Egyptians, and how I bore you on eagles' wings and brought you to myself. Now therefore, if you will indeed obey my voice and keep my covenant, you shall be my treasured possession among all peoples, for all the earth is mine; and you shall be to me a kingdom of priests and a holy nation.'"* Moses brought this message to the people, and they pledged to do everything the Lord had asked.

The Lord came down from Mount Sinai in the form of smoke, thunder, and lightning to meet with the Israelites and give them the Ten Commandments **(Exod. 20:2-17)**. But the people were so afraid of God, they told Moses to talk to God by himself and then relay back to them what the Lord said. Moses went back up Mount Sinai, where God gave him two tablets of stone each with all Ten Commandments that God Himself wrote with His finger.

Over the course of the next nine months, Moses frequently traveled up Mount Sinai to meet with God. The Lord gave Moses other laws that the Israelites were to follow. In total, there were 613 laws that God gave the Israelites.[9] These laws were recorded throughout the books of Exodus, Leviticus, Numbers, and Deuteronomy. There were two types of laws given: direct commands (e.g. you shall not . . . or you have to . . .) and situational examples (e.g. if this occurs . . . then you shall . . .). For example, one situational law said to rest your ox and donkey on the Sabbath. This law served as an example that the people were to give a day of rest to all their animals that labored for them. God was teaching the Israelites to treat their animals kindly.

All of the 613 laws had a dual purpose. First, they were to show the Israelites (and us!) that we could never keep God's Law. Like God, the Law is perfect and impossible for sinful human beings to ever adhere to completely.

---

9   Douglas Stuart, Ph.D., "Lecture 6: The Law: Covenant Structure," BiblicalTraining. org, accessed January 29, 2019, www.biblicaltraining.org/law-covenant-structure/old-testament-survey.

Thus, it shows us that we need another way to be reconciled with God. We need a Savior Who can keep God's Law perfectly and can, therefore, be our Substitute before God. (More on that when we get to the New Testament!) Secondly, the Law separates God's people from the rest of the world. It shows that God's people are to be holy and righteous.

The Lord also gave strong warnings to Moses that the Israelites must guard against idolatry. This proved to be a warning Israel should have listened and adhered to. Because of their idolatry, God used pagan nations to oppress the Israelites throughout the Old Testament.

Laws and warnings aren't the only things God discussed with Moses on Mount Sinai. The Lord also instructed the Israelites on proper worship, including establishing a priesthood and a central place of worship. The first responsibility for all believers is to worship the One Who made salvation possible. God showed Moses how this was to be done. He instructed him to build a sanctuary where the Lord would dwell among His people. This sanctuary, also called the Tabernacle or the Tent of Meeting, was a large and elaborate tent with a courtyard. Don't be fooled by the word *tent*. I guarantee you have never camped in anything like this! The Tabernacle had fine, linen curtains of blue, purple, and scarlet hand-embroidered and hung with solid gold hooks. The altar was made of bronze, and items made out of gold, silver, and bronze were placed throughout.

Inside the Tabernacle, they built and placed the Ark of the Covenant. The Ark was a chest of acacia wood overlaid with pure gold both inside and out, with a seat on top, called the mercy seat. Two angels made by hammering solid gold adorned each side of the mercy seat. Within the Ark of the Covenant, Moses was to place the Ark of the Testimony (two copies of the Ten Commandments), which God gave them to remember His Law. They were also to place a jar of manna (which God made not to rot) to remember how the Lord provided for His people and Aaron's rod that God made sprout to show that Aaron was His chosen high priest. You can read about Aaron's sprouting staff in Numbers 17.

The Ark of the Covenant not only had specific instructions on how it was to be made, but also in the way in which it was to be carried.

The Israelites were also to make a table on which they were to regularly put fresh bread, called the Bread of the Presence or Show Bread. This bread was to be consecrated and only for the priests to eat. Finally, there was to be a lampstand resembling a menorah with the center resembling a tree trunk and three branches on either side. The top of each branch was to be open like an almond flower. This lampstand was both symbolic (pointing to Jesus) and practical (giving light).

The very detailed instructions on how all the elements of the sanctuary were to be constructed are found in both Exodus and Deuteronomy. The Tabernacle that the Israelites built would later give way to the temple built under King Solomon. Ultimately, both structures point to Jesus, Who is not just the place where God dwells among His people, but God, Himself, dwelling among His people!

As we said, God also gave instructions about establishing a priesthood. Moses' brother, Aaron, was to be the first high priest. He and his sons were consecrated and given special garments to wear. These garments were not drab, black robes with white collars! Their attire included a breast plate of judgement made out of gold, blue, purple, and scarlet yarn and fine linen. It had twelve precious stones on it, including emeralds, sapphires, diamonds, and amethysts. It also had an ephod, or overlay, that was made from the same materials as the breastplate but had two engraved onyx stones on the shoulders. The robe under the ephod was made out of blue linen, which is hand-embroidered with blue, purple, and scarlet pomegranates. Gold bells were also put around the hem. These bells were used when the high priest went into the Holy of Holies to make atonement for the people's sins. Before doing this, the priest had to make atonement for his own sins. If he failed to do this or did it ceremonially incorrectly, he would drop dead. As nobody but the high priest was allowed in this most sacred room, people would stand outside listening as the priest made the sacrifice. If they stopped hearing the bells or heard them thump on the ground, they would pull the dead priest out by the rope around his waist! These articles, and others, that the priests were to wear had very specific instructions found in Exodus 28.

In Leviticus and Numbers, God makes it clear that only those Levites who were descendants of Aaron were to be priests. The other Levites were to serve in the Tabernacle and later the temple, but not perform priestly duties.

How could a band of vagrants possibly accomplish all of this? Remember, when God had the Israelites' Egyptian neighbors give them their valuables? That and anything of value they brought of their own are what they used for materials. God then filled some of the Israelites with the Holy Spirit, Who gave them the skill and ability to do what God had asked. Amazing, isn't it?!

The plans for all of the above are given in Exodus; the work and progress on them is mentioned in Leviticus; and the dedication of the Tabernacle occurs in the book of Numbers.

During one of Moses' excursions to the top of Mount Sinai, the Israelites sinned grievously against God and soon learned that the Lord meant what He said when He told them there would be punishment for worshipping any god but Yahweh. In Exodus 32, the Israelites began to get worried because Moses was up on the mountain for so long. They lost faith in God and Moses, demanding to Aaron in **Exodus 32:1**, "'*Up, make us gods who shall go before us. As for this Moses, the man who brought us up out of the land of Egypt, we do not know what has become of him.*'" Aaron, giving into the mob mentality, instructed the Israelites to take off the gold earrings they were wearing. He melted them down and molded them into a golden calf, presenting it to them as a god for them to worship. God, knowing what they were doing down in the desert, burned with anger against the Israelites. After an exchange between Moses and Him, Moses went down the mountain with the copies of the Ten Commandments that God wrote with His very hand. When Moses saw the Israelites dancing and worshiping the golden calf, he threw the tablets, and they broke.

Aaron blamed his actions on the pressure from the people. Moses called the Levites, who had remained faithful to God and had not worshipped the golden calf together, and told them in **Exodus 32:27**, "*'Thus says the LORD God of Israel, Put your sword on your side each of you, and go to and fro from gate to gate throughout the camp, and each of you kill his brother and his companion and his neighbor.'*" Three thousand men died that day.

Moses then went back up the mountain to make atonement for the people's sin. The Lord sent a plague on the people who worshipped the calf and after told Moses it was time for them to move on in their journey toward the Promised Land. He instructed Moses to carve out two new stone tablets, and the Lord, again, wrote the Ten Commandments on each. The Lord told Moses He would drive out the current pagan inhabitants of the Promised Land and warned Moses that the people must take care so they would not become ensnared by the pagan ways of the foreign tribes. God told Moses the people must tear down all of the altars to the false gods and be sure not to make any covenants with these pagans and not to intermarry with any of them

It was during this that Moses requested to see the face of God. Knowing that seeing the glory of God would kill him, God hid Moses behind a rock and allowed him to see His back while He passed by. Moses' face turned a bronze color with radiance from the experience; so much so, Moses wore a veil over his face while talking to the Israelites. Exodus ends with the Tabernacle being erected and the glory of the Lord filling it. After this, God gets down to the business of teaching His people to be different from the rest of the world.

LEVITICUS

The book of Leviticus, which means "of the Levites,"[10] emphasizes how God's people were to be set apart, holy, and righteous in all areas of life.

---

10   *Merriam-Webster*, s.v. "Leviticus," accessed January 26, 2019, https://www.merriam-webster.com/dictionary/Leviticus.

Leviticus gives us a longing for cleanliness before the Lord that can, and will, only come through Jesus Christ.

Since Jesus had not yet come, it was up to the people to try to be holy and set apart. God helped them by instructing Moses on various kinds of offerings for different types of worship and on sacrifices that were to be made by the people for sin.

The offerings are described throughout the book of Leviticus. The "burnt offering" is probably the most familiar one. This was the burning of an entire animal sacrificed to God to atone for sin. Some of the other offerings, when put together, represent an entire meal! There was the grain offering (usually bread made from olive oil, flour, and salt), the drink offering (wine), and peace offering (meat). After a portion of these offerings were dedicated to God, the priest and the worshipers would sit together and eat the rest!

There were also offerings for guilt where you made reparations to the people you had wronged and for unintentional sin or purification. This offering was to cover any sin you may have made but weren't aware of and for purifying yourself because of that sin. Again, God gave very detailed instructions on how all were to be done.

Many of the sacrifices required an animal that was without defect. **Leviticus 17:11** tells us why: *"For the life of the flesh is in the blood, and I have given it for you on the altar to make atonement for your souls, for it is the blood that makes atonement by the life."* What this verse is saying is that a person or animal's life is in their blood. God was taking the blood (life) of an animal as a substitute for the life of His people as payment for their sin. **Hebrews 9:22** confirms this truth: *"Indeed, under the law almost everything is purified with blood, and without the shedding of blood there is no forgiveness of sins."* The blood sacrifices in the Old Testament were imperfect and, therefore, only sufficed for a limited amount of time before having to be repeated. God was showing His people (and us!) that our sin is so offensive to God that nothing we do on our own could ever be good enough to reconcile us permanently with Him.

These inadequate, temporary sacrifices helped the Israelites look forward to a coming time when God would provide the perfect blood sacrifice that would be good for His people for all time.

Along with offerings and sacrifices for the people to observe, the Lord gave Moses instructions about consecrating Aaron and his sons as the first priests. A priest stood as the intercessor between God and the people. He sacrificed animals, gave offerings, and made atonement to God on behalf of the Israelites. We mentioned that animals were often the offering or sacrifice given. The priests were the ones who slaughtered and cooked the animal. Besides being priests, they were butchers and chefs! (Talk about multi-tasking!) This position was so sacred, and it was so important to follow the duties exactly as prescribed by God, that when Aaron's sons, Nadab and Abihu, took it upon themselves to offer incense lit with fire to the Lord without the Lord commanding it, the fire came out and consumed them. The Lord, through Moses, told Aaron, *"I will be sanctified, and before all the people I will be glorified"* **(Lev. 10:3)**.

After this, God continued giving Moses more of the 613 laws and regulations. Some gave instructions on how to eat, how to clean oneself, how to deal with bodily functions, how to handle diseases, and even how to clean the house. Again, the goal was to be a holy nation, achieving holiness and purity in all areas of life. Some of the regulations found in these books may seem silly or over the top to us; but when you look at them in light of the times, God was showing the Israelites that the holiest way to live was also the healthiest!

All of the laws given can be categorized into two main purposes. These purposes are reiterated by Jesus when He gives the two great commandments in Luke 10:27. For one, they showed the Israelites how to be a holy nation devoted to God. In other words, "love the Lord your God with all of your heart . . . soul . . . strength . . . and mind. For another thing, they showed the Israelites how to be a righteous nation looking out for each other and respecting each other. In other words, "love your neighbor as yourself." These two great commandments, along with the Ten Commandments (which also fit under the two great commandments), are the only ones of the 613 laws from the Old Covenant that transfer to the New Covenant.

Leviticus continues with the Lord again reminding Moses of the covenant He made with the Israelites. If they followed His decrees, there would be blessings. But if they disobeyed, there would be curses brought on them by God. This was important because it would come up over and over, especially in the Books of the Prophets.

You would think nine months on top of Mount Sinai talking to God is a tremendous amount of time, but God had a tremendous amount of information to give to Moses! Not all of it was rules, regulations, and instructions, though! While God wants His people to obey Him and to be set apart from the world, God also wants them to enjoy life and enjoy fellowshipping together! In the book of Leviticus, God gave Moses seven festivals that the people were to celebrate. Three required that they travel to a place of God's choosing—the Passover, the Feast of Weeks, and the Feast of Booths—while the others could be celebrated where they were.

The festivals were meant as a time to honor and remember God for His mercy and grace, but also as a time of fellowship and fun. Some of the festivals foreshadowed Jesus and/or transitioned into the New Covenant. The most important of these festivals was the Day of Atonement. On this day, Aaron would sacrifice as a sin offering a bull for himself and his family and a goat for the people. The blood of both animals was to be sprinkled on the Ark of the Covenant. Aaron would then bring a second goat and lay his hands on its head. Over it, he would confess Israel's sin and wickedness and send it out with an appointed man who released it into the wilderness. This is where we get the term "scapegoat." By transferring the sins on the goat's head, the goat was being "blamed" for Israel's sins.

The Israelites were not able to use a scapegoat for all their sins and paid a hefty price for their disobedience, as we will see in the next chapter.

Chapter 5

WANDERING IN THE WILDERNESS

NUMBERS

We've seen that Exodus is the story of how God delivered the Israelites out of Egypt, and Leviticus' focus is on the holiness of God's people. The book of Numbers, which gets its name from the two censuses of the tribes of the Israelites that are taken before the first and second attempt to enter the Promised Land, shows God's constant leadership and care for His people. The first twelve chapters tell of the Israelites getting ready to enter the Promised Land for the first time.

Chapter thirteen has them on the brink of entry. God told Moses to send a man from each tribe to spy out the land. All twelve came back and told the others that the land was awesome but strongly held. All twelve agreed that conquering it wouldn't be easy. However, Joshua, from the tribe of Ephraim, and Caleb, from the tribe of Judah, told the people in **Numbers 14:8-9**, "*If the Lord delights in us, he will bring us into this land and give it to us, a land that flows with milk and honey. Only do not rebel against the LORD. And do not fear the people of the land, for they are bread for us. Their protection is removed from them, and the LORD is with us; do not fear them.*" The Israelites' reaction to Caleb and Joshua's encouragement? They wanted to stone them! It is only because of God's interference that they didn't.

God's anger burned against the Israelites, and He told them their punishment for their unbelief was to not only be barred from entering the Promised Land, but also they would wander in the desert for forty years. One year for each day the spies were scouting in the Promised Land. During that time, everyone twenty years and older would die. Only Caleb and Joshua would live and be permitted to enter the Promised Land at the end of the thirty-nine years. In **Numbers 14:30-33**, God told the people, *"Not one shall come into the land where I swore that I would make you dwell, except Caleb, son of Jephunneh, and Joshua the son of Nun. But your little ones, who you said would become a prey, I will bring in, and they shall know the land that you have rejected. But as for you, your dead bodies shall fall in this wilderness."* In a nutshell, God was sending the adult Israelites out into the desert to die. Regretting their decision to not listen to Caleb and Joshua, the Israelites tried to make amends by saying they would go into the Promised Land and fight the inhabitants. They weren't afraid anymore. Moses warned them that God was no longer with them and that they couldn't win. They didn't listen and were defeated and chased by the Amalekites (remember them?) and the Canaanites.

During their exile in the desert, the Lord continued to speak to Moses, giving him more laws, precepts, and pertinent information for the new generation of Israelites who would be allowed to enter the Promised Land.

You may wonder why Moses and Aaron weren't included in the people who would be permitted to enter the Promised Land after the exile. It wasn't for the same reason as the others. They did not rebel and refuse to enter the Promised Land the first time. The reason they weren't permitted to enter is recorded in Numbers 20. Close to the end of their years of exile in the desert, the people were grumbling again that there was no water. While Moses and Aaron were praying to God about this, the Lord told Moses to pick up a staff and command a rock to bring forth water before all the Israelites. Moses did this, but he and Aaron took the glory for this miracle away from God by adding drama to the miracle and reprimanding the Israelites (something God did not tell them to do.) Aaron died shortly after in the desert.

Another significant event recorded in the book of Numbers is the incident involving the bronze serpent, which also occurred toward the end of the thirty-nine years of exile. In Numbers 21, while the Israelites were going around the land of Edom because Edom's king refused to let them pass through the land, the people became impatient and spoke against God and Moses. The Lord sent fiery serpents among the people to bite them. Anyone who got bit died. The people cried out to God, repenting of their sin. The Lord said to Moses in **Numbers 21:8**, *"'Make a fiery serpent and set it on a pole, and everyone who is bitten, when he sees it, shall live."* Why is this narrative so important? Because it is another foreshadowing of Jesus! We see this in **John 3:14-15**: *"And as Moses lifted up the serpent in the wilderness, so must the Son of Man be lifted up, that whoever believes in him may have eternal life."*

The last part of the book of Numbers is the new generation of Israelites preparing to enter the Promised Land around 1407 B.C. Another census was taken, and Joshua was chosen to succeed Moses as leader of the Israelites. In the latter chapters of the book, God gave Moses the boundaries of the Promised Land and named the tribal chiefs for each of the twelve tribes. Because all of those who would have been old enough to understand all that went on during the original journey to the Promised Land were dead, Moses recounted their journey, beginning with the exodus out of Egypt. Moses did his best to prepare this new generation for entering the Promised Land as we will see in Deuteronomy.

DEUTERONOMY

The name Deuteronomy means "Second Law."[11] It is named for the retelling of the Law by Moses right before the second entry attempt into

---

11   M. G. Easton, M.A. D.D, "Deuteronomy Definition and Meaning-Bible Dictionary," Bible Study Tools.com, accessed January 26, 2019, www.biblestudytools.com/dictionary/deuteronomy.

the Promised Land. In Deuteronomy, Moses preached to a new generation of Israelites as they wandered in the desert preparing to enter the Promised Land. These were the Israelites, who were either younger than twenty years old at the first entry attempt or who were born during the forty years in the wilderness. Perhaps the most important theme of Deuteronomy is that it, along with all of Scripture, is the story of God's covenantal love for His people. It is the most important book of the Law books for understanding the overview and big picture of the Bible. Because Moses was preaching to a new generation, much of what was said in the previous books is repeated. Moses wanted to be sure this new generation did not forget what God had done for them nor the covenant God made with them. Again, they were reminded of the blessings they would receive for obeying God and the curses they would receive for disobedience. Reiterating the warning made to the former generations, Moses strongly warned of the dangers of idolatry and mixing with the pagan inhabitants of the Promised Land.

At the end of their time in the desert, Moses was 120 years old. He preached one last time to the Israelites. He told them not to be afraid to enter the Promised Land because God would be with them and would never leave nor forsake them. He summoned Joshua before the entire group to tell Joshua he would now lead the Israelites. God went before him, assuring his victory. They gained the land, and Joshua divided it up among the tribes as their inheritance. Moses read the law to them one last time and prophesied that the Israelites would rebel against God and would be cursed because of it. He recited a song about Israel's redemption, God's goodness, and a warning against idolatry. It was during this time that Moses composed Psalm 90. Finally, he blessed the tribes.

Aaron died in the desert without ever seeing the Promised Land. Even though Moses, too, was not allowed to enter it, God permitted him to see it before he died. God led Moses up Mount Nebo, where he could see the Promised Land laid out before him. God said to Moses, *"This is the land of which I swore to Abraham, to Isaac, and to Jacob,* I will give it to your offspring. *I have let you see it with your eyes, but you shall not go over there'"* **(Deut. 34:4)**. Deuteronomy closes with the death of Moses and the new generation of Israelites on the brink of entering the Promised Land.

Chapter 6

INHABITING THE PROMISED LAND

In this chapter, we see God's plan for giving His people a land of their own unfold in the book of Joshua, the consequences of the people trying to be their own god in the book of Judges, and a bright spark of hope in an otherwise dark period in Israel's history in the book of Ruth.

JOSHUA

As we said earlier, the book of Joshua is not one of the Books of the Law. It, along with the books of Judges and Ruth, falls under the genre of "historical books" of the Bible. Certainly, every book in the Bible is actual history, but there are some books, like these, that just don't fit into the other genres (e.g. The Law, Poetry, Prophecy, Epistles, etc.), so they are put into their own category. We aren't sure who the author of Joshua is. While it is likely that Joshua wrote it, someone else would have had to write the end of the book, since it is about Joshua's death and burial.

The book of Joshua takes place right after the end of Deuteronomy, around 1406 B.C. It is in this book that God's promise of giving Israel a land of their own comes to fulfillment. While Leviticus talks of the importance of God's people being set apart, the book of Joshua shows God physically setting His people apart as a holy nation. The book has two main parts. The first eleven chapters tell of the conquest of the Promised Land (a.k.a. Canaan) through holy war (we will get to that in a minute!), while the last thirteen chapters concentrate on the divvying up of the Promised Land between each of the twelve tribes of Israel.

After Moses' death, God appointed Joshua as the new leader of the Israelites. God commanded Joshua to lead the new generation across the Jordan River and into the Promised Land. God told Joshua in **Joshua 1:6**, *"Be strong and courageous, for you shall cause this people to inherit the land that I swore to their fathers to give them."* "Be strong and courageous" is a recurring theme throughout this book. God instructed Joshua not to let the Law depart from his mouth and to meditate on it day and night so that he would do everything written in it. If he did this, he would be prosperous and successful. God also gave Joshua a very detailed plan on how the fighting campaigns to conquer the Promised Land would occur. The Israelites were told to launch three major campaigns against the inhabitants of the Promised Land: a Central Campaign (chapters 1-8), a Southern Campaign (chapters 9–10), and a Northern Campaign (chapter 11). The end goal was to clear out the Promised Land so that the Israelites might take it over.

It can be difficult to read that God is intentionally sending His people into war with instructions to completely annihilate entire populations of people groups. There is something in us that screams, "That's not fair! Those people were there first!" Our finite minds struggle to comprehend our infinite God. As we talked about in Genesis, God is the Almighty Creator, and His plan before the creation of the world was to create and bring a people unto Himself. Everything He does, He does for His glory and for the good of His elect. Since everyone and everything has been created and is sustained by God, He is free to do as He pleases. (Remember how God put Job in his place when he questioned God?) Therefore, God is completely justified in sending His people in to clear out the land because, ultimately, holy war is a war of God's judgement, not human judgement. The fact that God was the One doing the real fighting and the One Who gave the Israelites success in these campaigns is to His glory. The fact that pagan civilizations, who could ensnare the Israelites into practicing idolatry, were destroyed is for the good of God's people. One final note, since God is completely sovereign over salvation, it is possible that some of those within the pagan groups who were killed—including children—were saved. We don't know this for sure, of course, but the fact that God is the One Who chooses who will be saved always leaves that door of hope open in every situation!

What makes the battles in the book of Joshua righteous—unlike wars started by man—is that they fall under the definition of holy war (not to be confused with the Islam term "Holy War"). Biblical holy war, or Divine war, has very specific characteristics. It has no standing army—no one is forced to fight; all of the soldiers are volunteers, and therefore, receive no pay. No spoil or plunder is ever to be taken by God's people. Everything is to be destroyed, with valuables like gold, silver, and jewels being taken only to be put into the treasury of the Lord. Holy war is for the express purpose of the conquest or defense of the Promised Land and is only initiated at God's call, which is given through a prophet. Something really extraordinary about holy war is that God does the real fighting! The situation is such that the people couldn't possibly win on their own. It is always a religious undertaking, which involves fasting, self-denial, and/or celibacy. The enemy is to be completely annihilated. Also, anyone, even an Israelite, who violates the rules of holy war becomes the enemy. Deuteronomy 20, where the rules of holy war can be found, tells us that God may make exceptions to holy war.

Islam, and others, have claimed holy war when they initiated a war on other nations, claiming they are fighting for God. But true, biblical holy war is the exact opposite. God's people do not fight for God, as if He needs them to! Instead, God fights for His people.

Holy war becomes "spiritual warfare" in the New Testament. (Much more on that when we get to the New Testament!)

THE CAMPAIGNS

The first campaign, also called the Entry Campaign or Central Campaign, has eight chapters devoted to it. It begins in a city you have probably heard of—Jericho. Before the Israelites crossed the Jordan River to conquer Jericho, Joshua sent two spies there to case out the land and its defenses. Jericho's main defense was that it was surrounded by a wall. While in Jericho, the spies met a prostitute named Rahab. She invited them to stay with her. When the king of Jericho heard about the spies, he commanded Rahab to bring him the men. Instead, she hid them and, later that night, helped them escape via a rope out of her window in the wall. In return, they promised to spare her and her family when they destroyed Jericho. Note that Rahab went on to marry Salmon and became the mother of Boaz (from the book of Ruth) and part of the lineage of Jesus.

After the spies returned, the Israelites set out for Jericho. Getting there required that they cross the Jordan River, which was at flood stage at that time. The priests went ahead of the people, carrying the Ark of the Covenant. Reminiscent of the Red Sea parting during the exodus, when the priests reached the edge of the Jordan River, the waters parted, and the nation of Israel walked across dry land. Once all were safely on the other side, the waters came together again. Upon reaching the other side of the Jordan, twelve stones—one for each tribe—were taken from the Jordan River and set up as a memorial to remember what the Lord did that day. Joshua made flint knives out of sharpened stone and circumcised all of the males who had not been circumcised during the forty-year wilderness period. Lastly, the people celebrated the Passover together.

As we said, Jericho was a city with a wall built around it. This was a common way to fortify a city against potential enemies. No one went in, and no one went out (unless you were let out a window by a rope!) The commander of God's army, an angel, appeared to Joshua and told him that God commanded the Israelite army to march around the city of Jericho once a day for six days. Then on the seventh day, they were to march around the city seven times. At the conclusion of the seventh time, seven priests were to blow seven trumpets. When the people heard the trumpets, they were to shout. At this, the walls of Jericho would collapse and enable the Israelite army to enter Jericho and burn the city to the ground. They were to kill everyone but Rahab and her family.

The fall of Jericho is an excellent illustration of holy war in effect. God initiated the war with Jericho, which was part of the Promised Land. God did the real fighting. The Israelites just had to march and shout. Once the defenses of Jericho crumbled, the city was delivered to Israel for them to burn everyone and everything in it. They took no plunder for themselves, only taking silver and gold to add to the treasury of the Lord. Or at least that's what everyone thought!

Right after the tremendous success at Jericho, the Israelites battled Ai, a much smaller town. Even Joshua's spies reported that they would not need all of their men to defeat Ai. The men of Ai ended up not only chasing Israel's army away and defeating them, but also killing thirty-six Israelite men. Joshua fell before the Lord, asking why God had turned against them. God answered Joshua in **Joshua 7:10**, *"Get up! Why have you fallen on your face? Israel has sinned; they have transgressed my covenant that I commanded them; they have taken some of the devoted things; they have stolen and lied and put them among their own belongings."* To put it another way, someone in the Israelite army took some plunder for themselves. They violated the rules of holy war. The only way for Israel to get back into God's good graces was to find the perpetrator and kill him.

Joshua gathered the people together and the Lord, by lots, eventually singling out Achan, from the tribe of Judah, as the offender. Achan admitted to taking a cloak, five pounds of silver, and a gold bar and hiding them inside his tent to keep for himself. Remember, under the rules of holy war, the violator becomes the enemy, and the enemy and all of their belongings are to be annihilated. Therefore, Achan, his entire family, his livestock, and all of his belongings were stoned and burned. After, the Israelites once again battle Ai, but this time, with God now doing the fighting for them, they completely destroy the town, killing all twelve thousand inhabitants and leaving Ai in a burning heap of ruins.

The Southern and Northern Campaigns are similar to the Central Campaign, except for a miraculous event that occurred during the Southern Campaign in Joshua 10. The king of Jerusalem heard about how the Israelites were conquering the land of Canaan and how the powerful nation of Gibeon had made peace with the Israelites. He became scared and asked four other kings to ban together with him and fight against Gibeon. The men of Gibeon sent word to Joshua and begged him to send his army to save them. The Lord told Joshua that He would deliver these enemies into Israel's hands. While Joshua and his army were making their way to Gibeon, God threw the army of the five kings into a panic. Israel was able to launch a strike, killing some of the men and forcing them to retreat. As they were fleeing, the Lord threw down large stones from Heaven on them! Many more of the kings' men died from the gigantic hailstones God rained down than died by the swords of the Israelites (because God does the real fighting). As the Israelites were giving the enemy chase, Joshua commanded the sun to stand still. While that may sound crazy, it's even more amazing that God does it! The sun stopped! This was so the Israelites could finish off killing the kings' armies in the daylight without the enemy being able to hide under the cover of darkness. This was a one-time only event, as **Joshua 10:14** tells us, *"There has been no day like it before or since, when the LORD heeded the voice of a man, for the LORD fought for Israel."*

In the later chapters of the book of Joshua, we see how the Promised Land was divided up and allotted to each of the twelve tribes, with the very last two chapters being a farewell address from Joshua. At the end of Joshua's life, the Lord gave the Israelites rest from their enemies. Joshua called the Israelites together and reminded them of all that God had done for them and how God had fought for the nation of Israel to give them a land of their own. Joshua told them in **Joshua 23:6-8**:

> *Therefore, be very strong to keep and to do all that is written in the Book of the Law of Moses, turning aside from it neither to the right hand nor to the left, that you may not mix with these nations remaining among you or make mention of the names of their gods or swear by them or serve them or bow down to them, but you shall cling to the LORD your God just as you have done to this day.*

Like Moses, Joshua was warning them not to fall into idolatry. He told them to choose whom they would serve—the pagan gods or Yahweh. He declared in the very familiar verse of **Joshua 24:15b**, *"As for me and my house, we will serve the LORD."* The Israelites emphatically pledged that they would serve and obey the Lord only, and Joshua renewed the covenant between them and God. We will see in the very next book of Judges how quickly the Israelites forgot all that Joshua told them.

The book of Joshua ends with Joshua's death. He was a good, strong leader who feared and obeyed God. When they no longer had his leadership, the Israelites went downhill quickly.

JUDGES

The book of Judges opens right after Joshua's death in 1375 B.C. As we said earlier, it falls under the genre of "historical books" of the Bible. The book spans a total of approximately 275 to three hundred years. We aren't sure who the author is, but the prophet Samuel is a possibility. The book depicts one of the darkest periods in Israel's history. It is the story of the military, spiritual, doctrinal, and moral decline of the Israelites, due in large part to their failure to obey God's command to rid the Promised Land of the pagan inhabitants who lead them into idolatry and syncretism. Throughout the book, there is a desperate struggle to hold onto the Promised Land as God sends enemy after enemy to oppress His disobedient and unfaithful people. The theme of the book is the apostasy of God's people and their need for a righteous king, as is repeated throughout the book in the phrase, *"There was no king in Israel. Everyone did what was right in their own eyes."* Apostasy can best be described as declaring your faith in and love for God and then abandoning it.

You may wonder who these biblical judges were and what their functions were. They were not what we think of judges today. They were God-appointed spiritual and/or military leaders. They were a deliverer, a type of savior. In fact, only one judge, Deborah, performed any type of "judicial duties" that we equate with a judge.

Throughout the book, we see a circular pattern being repeated over and over called the "Deuteronomic Cycle," named for the covenant God made with His people in the book of Deuteronomy. If you remember, Israel agreed that Yahweh would be their only God and that they would remain faithful and keep His commands. In return, God would bless the nation. If, though, the Israelites were not faithful, curses would befall them. This is the pattern that undergirds chapters three through sixteen. God's people rebel; God gets angry; God sends one of Israelites' enemies to oppress them; the people cry out in repentance; they are saved by a chosen leader (a judge); there's peace for a while; the judge dies; the cycle starts all over again. The graph below depicts this cycle.

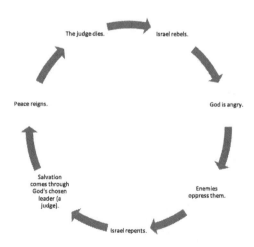

God's sovereignty can be seen in everything that happens throughout the entire book. The enemies of God's people had no power to oppress the Israelites unless God allowed it; and once the Lord decided to deliver His people through a judge from said enemy, they had no power to stop it.

Something to keep in mind when reading the book of Judges is that the chapters are not in chronological order. For example, chapters seventeen through twenty-one actually occurred at the beginning of the time of the judges, not at the end. We see this several times throughout Scripture. The writers' main focus is conveying a theme or relaying a point to the readers, not keeping events in the order that they occur. However, for our purposes and to keep things less confusing, we will go through the book in numerical chapter order.

Chapter one opens with the tribes of Israel asking the Lord which of the current pagan inhabitants in the Promised Land they should go up against. As in the book of Joshua, the Lord gave them detailed instructions, and the Israelites, once again, embarked on holy war. Things seemed to be going well. The men went into battle with God handing the enemy into their hands. But things are not always as they seem, as we see at the end of chapter one. You would think that knowing the Lord was doing the real fighting for you and was working things out for your good, you would carry out His commands exactly as ordered. But as Joshua's farewell speech (Josh. 23:6-8) tells us, such was not the case. The Israelites failed to completely eradicate some groups and to completely drive out others, as they were instructed to do. This was blatant disobedience. This disobedience caused consequences for Israel almost immediately. Judges 1:27-36 is a sort of "Hall of Shame," telling of the tribes' failure to complete the conquest of the Promised Land.

Because of their failure, instead of being the only inhabitants of Canaan, they were living amongst the pagan people. God told them of the consequence of their disobedience. In **Judges 2:1b-5,** God said to them,

"I brought you up from Egypt and brought you into this land that I swore to give to your fathers. I said, 'I will never break my covenant with you, and you shall make no covenant with the inhabitants of this land; you shall break down their altars.' But you have not obeyed my voice. What is this you have done? So now I say, I will not drive them out before you, but they shall become thorns in your sides, and their gods shall be a snare to you."

With so many other cultural and religious practices around them, God's people were faced daily with the choice between believing and obeying God only or following the pagan ways of the other nations with whom they shared the Promised Land. Instead of keeping themselves separate and holy, they used compromise and tolerance to try to live in peace with the other people groups. Interfaith relationships and even marriages began happening, which led to syncretism. Syncretism is the taking of two or more religious systems and, in an attempt to reconcile them, molding them into something with parts of both or all. This was what the Israelites were mostly guilty of. It's not that they didn't believe in Yahweh and worship Him, but they added worship of the pagan gods along with it.

Chapters three through sixteen tell us about the twelve judges of Israel. Six are considered major judges, and six are considered minor. The only difference between a major and minor judge is the amount of text that is written about him or her. Here are the judges, and a brief summary about each, listed in the order they served:

1. **Othniel** – The people of Israel began worshipping the pagan gods. God sold them into the hands of the king of Mesopotamia. After they were enslaved by him for eight years, they cried out to God, so God raised up Othniel to deliver them. Othniel was a strong leader, who was faithful to God. After he defeated the king of Mesopotamia and saved Israel, the nation had peace for forty years until Othniel's death.

2. **Ehud** – Again, Israel did evil in the eyes of the Lord by worshipping pagan gods. Again, God raised up an enemy to oppress them. This time, it was the king of Moab. Israel served Moab for eighteen years until they once again cried out to the Lord for deliverance. God raised up Ehud. Through some bizarre (and gross) events that occurred because Ehud is left-handed, he was able to kill the very fat king of Moab. **Judges 3:21-22** tells of the assassination, *"And Ehud reached with his left hand, took the sword from his right thigh, and thrust it into his belly. And the hilt also went in after the blade, and the fat closed over the blade, for he did not pull the sword out of his belly; and the dung came out."* Ehud delivered the Israelites, and the land was at rest for eighty years until Ehud died.

3. **Shamgar** – The first of the minor judges, Shamgar gets only one verse of Scripture. We can infer, though, that the cycle was the same as it is with the other judges. This time, the enemy was Philistia. Shamgar killed six hundred Philistines with an ox goad (a wooden tool with an iron tip) and saved Israel.

4. **Deborah** – She was the only female judge and the only judge who actually "judged." While Deborah held court, deciding cases amongst the Israelites, again, they did evil in the eyes of the Lord. The enemy of choice this time was Canaan, who conquered and oppressed the Israelites for twenty years. Deborah accompanied Barak, a commander in the army, as God sent him out to fight against the Canaanites. But it is Jael, whose husband was a relative of Moses' wife, who got the win when she drove a tent peg through the skull of the general of Canaan's army! Israel was again delivered from their slavery. There was peace in the land for forty years.

5. **Gideon** – No surprise, after Deborah's death, the Israelites were at it again! And, again, God was angry, this time empowering the

Midianites to oppress Israel for seven years. After the Israelites cried out to God, he raised up Gideon to save His people. Gideon was best known for doubting God and "putting out a fleece" to have God prove He was with him. Although Gideon's actions were sinful, God was gracious and did as he asked. Once Gideon was on board, God wanted to show Gideon, the Israelites, and Israel's enemy that it was the Lord Who would deliver His people. He had Gideon whittle his army of thirty-two thousand men down to three hundred men who drink from the river like a dog! These men went to the Midian camp to blow trumpets and break jars as God had instructed. The men in the Midian army started killing each other! Gideon defeated the army; Israel was saved; and there was peace for forty years until the death of Gideon. After Gideon's death, his son, Abimelech, staged a coup and tried to make himself king over Israel, but he was killed when a woman dropped a millstone on his head, crushing his skull, and his armor-bearer ran him through with his sword.

6. **Tola** – Tola is another minor judge who does not get a lot of press. We aren't sure which enemy God sent to punish Israel during Tola's reign. We only know that he saved Israel, and there was peace for twenty-three years.

7. **Jair** – Jair is also a minor judge. He reigned as judge for twenty-two years. Scripture tells us he had thirty sons who rode thirty donkeys, and they had thirty cities. This is an indication Jair was very wealthy.

8. **Jephthah** – Jephthah is perhaps best known for making a rash and costly vow. After the Israelites once again did evil in the eyes of the Lord, God sold them into the hands of the Philistines and the Ammonites. For eighteen years, the people were crushed by these enemies. The people cried out to God, repenting of their sin. God lifted up Jephthah to rescue His people. While fighting, Jephthah

made a vow to the Lord, saying, *"If you will give the Ammonites into my hand, then whatever comes out from the doors of my house to meet me when I return in peace from the Ammonites shall be the LORD's and I will offer it up for a burnt offering"* **(Judges 11:30-31)**. Sadly, when he returned, it was his only child, his daughter, who came out to greet him. As he vowed, he sacrificed his daughter as an offering to the Lord.

9. **Ibzan** – The fourth of the minor judges, Ibzan judged Israel for seven years. All we are told about him is that he had thirty sons and thirty daughters who all married outside of their clan.

10. **Elon** – Elon gets the distinction of having the least amount of information of all of the judges. He judged Israel ten years and then died.

11. **Abdon** – The last of the minor judges, Abdon served Israel for eight years. He had forty sons and thirty grandsons, who all rode seventy donkeys.

12. **Samson** – God has a habit of doing things the opposite way the world would expect. Here, with Samson, God turned an old cliché on its head as He saved the worst for last! Despite being the most famous of the judges and the subject of countless movies and stories, had it not been for the sovereignty of God, Samson's twenty-year reign as judge would have been a total disaster, which is ironic because Samson is the only judge whose birth was foretold and prophesied. Samson grew to become an arrogant, selfish, immature, violent sex addict, yet God used him to fulfill His will. During Samson's reign as judge, God once again raised up the Philistines to punish unfaithful Israel. Samson fought the Philistines, but not to deliver Israel. He fought them for his own revenge for what they did to him personally. God, though, worked through Samson's continual sin for His purpose, which was to deliver the Israelites out of the hands of

the Philistines. Samson killed many Philistines throughout his life, but none more than at the end. After Samson was captured by the Philistines (because of his own stupidity), blinded, and weakened, he was chained to the pillars of the temple of the Philistine pagan god, Dagan. The Philistines mocked Samson. Samson prayed to God for one more bit of strength so that he may be avenged. God gave it to him. Samson pushed down the pillars he was chained to, killing over three thousand Philistine men and women.

The last five chapters of the book of Judges are, perhaps, the most disturbing. They tell of the severe spiritual and moral decline of many of the Israelites, but most especially the Levites, who were chosen by God to be the spiritual leaders of Israel. The Israelites had gone from fighting their enemies together to fighting each other!

Micah, a man from the Israeli tribe of Ephraim, made an idol out of silver that he initially stole from his mom. Micah also made a shrine to put the silver statue in and images of other pagan gods. He then hired a Levite who was passing by to become his personal priest (something forbidden under Levitical Law) and reside over his shrine and pagan gods. In a classic example of syncretism, Micah thought God would prosper him, despite the fact that he was worshipping idols, because he had a Levite performing all the priestly duties.

Micah wasn't the only one whose thinking was twisted. Six hundred men from the Israeli tribe of Dan were on a quest to secure land for their tribe. Because they hadn't completely eradicated the Amorites during the conquests in Joshua, they weren't able to live in the land intended for them and needed somewhere to dwell. They stole Micah's shrine, silver idol, pagan gods, and the Levite priest for themselves as sort of "good luck charms" against their enemies. They attacked the city of Laish, burned it to the ground, and rebuilt it, naming it Dan. They set up Micah's carved images, as well as some of their own, with the Levite priest presiding over their syncretism and idolatry.

Chapter nineteen tells of another Levite who was passing through the Israeli territory belonging to the tribe of Ephraim. This Levite had a concubine from the fellow Israelite tribe of Benjamin. His concubine was unfaithful to him, but it appears he forgave her, and they reconciled. They traveled to Gibeah, which was within the land of Ephraim but inhabited by Benjaminites. An old man spotted them sitting in the town square and took them in for the night. While there, some of the Benjaminites beat on the door of the house, demanding that the Levite come out so they could have sex with him. The old man instead offered his virgin daughter and the Levite's concubine to the men, telling the men they may do what they wish to the two women, but they could not hurt the Levite man under his protection. (Sound familiar?) The men wouldn't listen, so the Levite sent his concubine out to the men. Unlike the story of Sodom, though, there were no angels to protect the woman, and she was raped and abused all night long.

When the Levite discovered his concubine was dead, he cut her up in twelve pieces and sent a piece of her to each of the twelve tribes of Israel as a call for the tribes to rally against the men of Benjamin. All of the tribes met together to deal with the situation. The Levite told the tribal chiefs that he and his concubine were surrounded by the Benjaminites and that they violated and killed her. (He conveniently leaves out his deplorable behavior that contributed to her abuse and death!) Since the leaders of the tribe of Benjamin had not dealt with the men who violated and killed the concubine, the remaining eleven tribes demanded that they hand the men over to be put to death. The Benjaminite leaders refused, and the other tribes went to war with them. After three days of war, the whole city of Gibeah and all of the Benjaminites were slaughtered, except for six hundred men who escaped into the desert. Since no Benjaminite women survived and the other tribes had made a vow not to let their daughters marry a Benjaminite, effectively, one whole tribe would be wiped out.

Feeling pity for the soon-to-be-extinct tribe, the other tribal leaders met to figure out a way to help the Benjaminite men without breaking the vow made. They came up with a couple of twisted plans. The men from one of the towns within the tribe of Manasseh did not show up to fight against the Benjaminites. As punishment, the other Israelite tribes sent twelve thousand men to kill everyone in this faction of Manasseh, except for the virgin women, which totaled four hundred. They then took the four hundred captured women and gave them to the six hundred surviving Benjaminite men. Still needing another two hundred women and not wanting to break their vow by *giving* their daughters to the Benjaminites, they had two hundred Benjaminite men wait in the bushes during a festival, so they could kidnap single women from the other tribes while they were dancing!

Fittingly, the book of Judges ends with, *"In those days there was no king in Israel. Everyone did what was right in his eyes"* **(Judges 21:25)**. The sad truth is that Israel had declined so far spiritually, doctrinally, militarily, and morally that they could be likened to Sodom and Gomorrah. The message of the book of Judges is the need of God's people for a righteous King and Savior. As with everything in the Old Testament, this points to Jesus, the only righteous King and perfect Savior!

RUTH

Although the book of Ruth comes after the book of Judges, the events in it take place during the time of the Judges (approximately 1140 B.C.). Like the book of Judges, we don't know who the author is, but the Prophet Samuel is, again, a likely candidate.

As part of God's judgement on Israel's apostasy, there was famine in Bethlehem, Judah. Because of this, a man named Elimelech took his wife, Naomi, and their two sons away from the land God had given to them and into the pagan land of Moab. While in Moab, Elimelech died, and his sons took Moabite wives, Orpah and Ruth. When the sons died as well, Naomi decided to return to Bethlehem and urged her daughters-in-law to return to their own people. Orpah did, but Ruth insisted on staying with Naomi, telling her in **Ruth 1:16b**, *"For where you go I will go, and where you lodge I will lodge. Your people shall be my people, and your God my God."* This gives us a glimpse into the character of Ruth. She was not only loyal to her mother-in-law but was willingly forsaking her pagan Moab gods and becoming a devoted follower of Yahweh.

When they arrived back in Bethlehem, Ruth, in order to provide food for her and Naomi, went out to a wheat field to pick up the stalks that get dropped or left behind during harvesting. Although Ruth thought she had randomly just picked a field to glean in, God providentially had her go to a field belonging to a relative of Naomi, named Boaz. Boaz showed himself to be a godly man and immediately put Ruth under his protection. He made sure his men did not take advantage of her and that they left plenty of wheat on the ground for her to gather.

Naomi came up with a plan to get Boaz to marry Ruth. He did, and they had a son, Obed, who became the father of Jesse, who became the father of King David, putting Ruth and Boaz in the lineage of Jesus.

There are two themes that run throughout this book. One is the Hebrew word *hesed*, which basically means "absolute love and loyalty."[12] It includes so many things: love, grace, mercy, kindness, faithfulness—all of the positive displays of affection that flow out of a covenantal relationship. Acts that go beyond duty and obligation. While the term *hesed* is used to describe the actions of Ruth and Boaz, it ultimately points us to the only One Who could ever show perfect *hesed*—Jesus!

The other theme is the "kinsmen-redeemer." A kinsman-redeemer is defined in Mosaic Law as a male relative who was the family representative and

---

12   *Theopedia*, s.v. "hesed," Theopedia.com, accessed February 05, 2019, https://www.theopedia.com/hesed.

had the responsibility to act on behalf of a relative who was in trouble, danger, or need. The term designates one who delivers or rescues. In the Book of Ruth, Boaz was the kinsmen-redeemer. While Boaz was a real man, he was also a prophetic symbol looking forward to Jesus as the ultimate Kinsman-redeemer.

The book of Ruth is a beautiful story of integrity and faithfulness and is a bright spot in an otherwise dark time in Israel's history. It is an encouragement that not all of the Israelites were falling into syncretism and idolatry during the time of the judges. The book provides a bridge between the judges of Israel and the monarchy of Israel. It shows us that Gentiles were always part of God's plan of redemption, as Ruth—like Rahab from the book of Joshua—is a Gentile who was grafted into the lineage of Jesus!

PART 3

THE KINGS

1 SAMUEL THROUGH 2 CHRONICLES, PSALMS, PROVERBS, ECCLESIASTES, AND THE SONG OF SOLOMON

As we move forward in the historical timeline, God's people, Israel, were still in need of a godly leader. The book of Judges leaves no doubt of that. Despite God's gracious rescue of them time after time, through judge after judge, the Israelites returned to their sin as a dog returns to its vomit. They needed a godly king. They needed someone righteous to lead them; and as we will see, they asked for a king, but not exactly for the right reasons.

The books about the kings of Israel are found in 1 and 2 Samuel, 1 and 2 Kings, and 1 and 2 Chronicles. While our English Bible has these as six books, they were originally only three (Samuel, Kings, and Chronicles). These books give us the history of Israel's monarchy, both united and divided. There is an important theme that runs through all of them: God's people needed a godly king who would come through the line of David, who is from the tribe of Judah.

This fits the narrative of the whole Old Testament, which is constantly pointing us to King Jesus! In addition to 1 and 2 Samuel, 1 and 2 Kings, and 1 and 2 Chronicles, we will be covering the books of Psalms, Proverbs, Ecclesiastes, and The Song of Solomon in this chapter. Since these books were in large part written by the kings, they fit perfectly into this chapter.

The story of Israel's move toward a monarchial society starts in the books of 1 and 2 Samuel, which covers God's peoples' history from the last judge, Samuel, through the reign of the first king, Saul, and continues through King David's reign. The book of 1 Samuel introduces Israel's first two kings of the monarchy, Saul and David. However, it starts out with a man named Samuel, who functioned as both a prophet and a priest for Israel.

Chapter 7

THE UNITED MONARCHY

1 SAMUEL

The book actually begins before Samuel's birth, where we're introduced to his father, Elkanah, and his two wives—his beloved Hannah, who was barren, and her fertile rival Peninnah, who relentlessly provoked Hannah because she was childless. As you may have guessed already by the way God has worked in the lives of barren women up to this point, Samuel was the son of the barren woman.

Right from the beginning of 1 Samuel, we're also introduced to the family of priests that were serving the Lord in the Tabernacle at Shiloh at this time—Eli the priest and his two sons, Hophni and Phinehas, who were also priests. As it was with many priests in the time of Judges, Hophni and Phinehas were wicked. Just as Boaz and Ruth were pictures of godly people living within that corrupt society, Samuel's family was also a picture of a family living righteously, despite the wickedness of their religious leaders at that time.

Elkanah was a Levite, who was living within the tribe of Ephraim. At one of the yearly sacrifices and feasts in Shiloh, Elkanah took his wives to worship and sacrifice to the Lord, according to the Law. As God's people gathered together to have their sins atoned for and to make offerings to the Lord, they feasted and rejoiced as the chosen people of God. But for Hannah, the fact that God had left her childless left her feeling sad and distressed.

At this particular feast, Hannah was praying in such a fervent manner that Eli the priest didn't recognize that she's actually praying, but instead thought she was drunk! When he confronted her about the situation, she explained that she was not and told him about her predicament. Eli said to her, *"'Go in peace, and the God of Israel grant your petition that you have made to him'"* **(1 Sam. 1:17)**.

Hannah's prayer was no ordinary prayer or petition to the Lord. She made a vow to the Lord that if He gave her a son, she would raise him according to the Nazirite Law, which was a vow of separating yourself for service to the Lord. When a man or a woman made the vow of a Nazirite, they didn't drink wine or other alcohol or use any vinegar made from either. They didn't drink any grape juice or eat grapes or anything produced by the grapevine, not even the seeds or the skins. They did not cut their hair nor go near a dead body, even if it was his or her father or mother. Hannah vowed that if she was given a child, she would give him to the Lord for all of his life. Sometime later, the Lord answered Hannah's prayer, and she gave birth to a son, whom they named Samuel, in 1100 B.C.

Hannah wasn't kidding when she vowed to give the Lord her son. She kept the child at home with her until he was weaned, and then she took him to the Tabernacle to be in service to the Lord under the tutelage of Eli. It was very likely that Samuel was about three years old at the time. Each year, Hannah made her son a new tunic and brought it to him when they came to the feast. While we can't understand what this would be like for a mother, Hannah was devoted to the Lord and was thankful that He took away her reproach from being barren.

As Hannah headed for home after leaving Samuel, she sang a song to the Lord that's recorded for us in **1 Samuel 2:1-11**. In verse five, she sings, *"The barren has borne seven."* This verse may seem like a miscalculation when having only one child, but the number seven is often used in the Bible as a number of "completeness." Even though she only had one son,

Hannah was acknowledging the complete goodness of God. The Lord opened Hannah's womb again, and in the end, she was blessed with three sons and two daughters.

After this the focus is switched to the wicked priesthood of Eli and his family, namely his two sons, Hophni and Phinehas, who *"did not know the LORD"* **(1 Sam. 2:12)**. They slept with women who were prostituting themselves in front of the temple. Also, they shirked God's regulations for how the priests were to handle the offering, namely, what portions they took for themselves and how they went about getting those portions. They even went so far as to take parts of the fat portions that were to be burned for the Lord. Although their father pleaded with them not to act so wickedly, Hophni and Phinehas refused to listen to their father because *"it was the will of the LORD to put them to death"* **(1 Sam. 2:25b)**, which He eventually did. Samuel ministered before the Lord under Eli's instruction, and the Lord was with him as he grew up. Eventually, Samuel became known as a prophet in all of Israel.

In 1070 B.C., there was still war going on for acquisition and defense of the Promised Land. After another loss to the Philistine army, who was battling them from the west, the defeated Israelites returned bewildered and wondering amongst themselves, *"Why has the LORD defeated us today before the Philistines?"* **(1 Sam. 4:3)**. God allowed war for the purposes of acquiring or defending the Promised Land, but He had specific rules and instructions for how it was done. When holy war is done God's way, He always goes out in victory before His people. Knowing this, they should have examined their behavior and sought the will of the Lord about what to do next.

Unfortunately, they didn't do either of those. Instead, they made a grave decision to take the Ark of the Covenant from the Holy of Holies in the Tabernacle at Shiloh and bring it with them to the battlefield. In essence, they took the place where God's Presence met with the high priest, and they treated it as if it was nothing more than a good luck charm. Acting according to their true natures, Eli's sons, Hophni and Phinehas, did nothing to stop them. In fact, the two of them went back to the army camp, along with the Ark.

When the Philistines hear about the Ark being in the Israelite camp, they believed that the Israelites had a "god" in their camp with them. Effectually, that's what the Israelites believed, too, but they were proven wrong the next day when thirty thousand of their men were killed in the battle and the Ark was captured by the Philistines. Neither side had any idea that having the Ark with them didn't guarantee that God Almighty was with them. In fact, the presence of the Ark had nothing to do with it! Eli's sons were among those who died that day, fulfilling the Word of the Lord. When their father heard that the Ark had been captured, he fell off of his chair and broke his neck. God put Eli and his sons to death, ending their wickedness and their roles in the priesthood.

The Philistines were not blessed by having the Ark with them. According to pagan custom, they believed there were all kinds of "gods," and this was just one more they could add to their side. As would have been the custom in that day, they took the Ark of the Covenant and put it in the temple of their god, Dagon. For the next two mornings, they awakened to find the statue of Dagon face-down on the ground, the second morning with his hands broken off! This wasn't their only problem. Everyone in the vicinity of the town was being plagued by tumors, which also happened to the next town that they moved the Ark to. The third city cried out when they tried to move the Ark there, so the Philistines gathered their priests and diviners and asked, "*What shall we do with the ark of the LORD? Tell us with what we shall send it to its place*" **(1 Sam. 6:2b)**. Their answer was to send it back to the Israelites, but not empty. Instead, they sent it with a guilt offering of five golden tumors and five golden mice, the number of the lords of the Philistines, hoping that they would be healed if they did this. However, not being totally sure that the God of Israel had brought these calamities on them or whether it was just a coincidence, they came up with a very creative way to send the Ark back to Israel so they would know for sure. You can read about it in 1 Samuel 6.

When the Ark was returned to the Israelites, the men of the town worshiped the Lord for returning it. However, after worshiping, they failed to follow the laws governing the Ark, and seventy of them died because they opened it to look into it. To make matters worse, the Israelites didn't return it to the Tabernacle either. Instead, they took it to someone's house and left it there for several years.

Meanwhile, Samuel had been serving Israel in several different capacities. Not only was he a prophet, but he was the last judge, in addition to being a priest and serving as Israel's military leader. During this time, the people *"lamented after the LORD"* **(1 Sam. 7:2)**, but were not wholeheartedly worshiping Him. They continued worshiping the foreign gods of Baal and Asherah, too, until Samuel called them to repentance, and they put their false gods away and served the Lord exclusively for a while.

Twenty years after the incident with the Ark, Israel assembled for worship and repentance at a place called Mizpah under Samuel's godly leadership. When the Philistines heard that Israel was gathered there, they decided it would be a good time to attack. When the Israelites got wind that the Philistines were coming, they asked for Samuel to plead to the Lord on their behalf. Just as Samuel was sacrificing the burnt offering, the Lord thundered from Heaven so loudly that it threw the Philistines into a panic, and Israel slaughtered a large number of them as they fled back to their homes. The thing to be learned is that the Lord fights the battles for His people when they obey and have faith in Him. When Israel put away their idols, repented of their sin, and worshiped, the Lord fought for them.

Samuel continued to judge Israel, and the Lord subdued the Philistines all throughout his lifetime. When Samuel grew old, he appointed his sons, Joel and Abijah, as judges for Israel, but they perverted justice by taking bribes and were being dishonest for their own benefit. So, Israel's leaders came up with a "better" idea; they asked for a king to rule over them. They made the decision based on their own desires. They didn't ask God for direction; they didn't ask for His help; they just did what seemed right in their own eyes. Their reason for wanting a king stemmed from a desire to "be like the other nations." But God's chosen people weren't to be like the other nations. They were to be separate. Distinct. Living *in* the world, but not being *like* the rest of the world.

Because of the peoples' desire for a king, Samuel felt rejected, so he prayed. In **1 Samuel 8:7**, the Bible says, *"And the LORD said to Samuel, 'Obey the voice of the people in all that they say to you, for they have not rejected you, but they have rejected me from being king over them.'"* Doing as the Lord directed him, Samuel anointed a young man named Saul as king. In **1 Samuel 9:2**, we're told he was the son of a wealthy Benjaminite, who was a *"handsome young man. There was not a man among the people of Israel more handsome than he. From his shoulders upward he was taller than any of the people."* Sounds good, right? But regardless of his outward qualifications, he was from the line of Benjamin, and the people were going to need a godly king who came from the godly line of Judah.

SAUL'S REIGN

In 1042 B.C., about a year after being made king, Saul's first kingly "war duty" came about when the Ammonites attacked and laid siege to the people living in Jabesh-Gilead. The men of the town pled with the Ammonites:

> *"Make a treaty with us, and we will serve you." But Nahash the Ammonite said to them, "On this condition I will make a treaty with you, that I gouge out all your right eyes, and thus bring disgrace on all Israel." The elders of Jabesh said to him, "Give us seven days' respite that we may send messengers through all the territory of Israel. Then, if there is no one to save us, we will give ourselves up to you." When the messengers came to Gibeah of Saul, they reported the matter in the ears of the people, and all the people wept aloud"* **(1 Sam. 11:1-4).**

And the Ammonites did what made virtually no sense in a time of war—they gave their enemy, Israel, seven days to consider their proposal and to see if anyone would come to their rescue!

When the report of what was happening reached King Saul's ears, the Holy Spirit came upon him, and he burned with anger. He cut two oxen to pieces and sent them throughout Israel in order to gather everyone for battle. The point was, if they didn't come, they'd be like the oxen. Saul and Samuel led Israel into war with the Ammonites, saving the eyes of the men of Jabesh-Gilead. This was Saul's first victory as king, and he gave all the glory to the Lord. He fully acknowledged that this was the Lord's battle. At Samuel's suggestion, the people reaffirmed Saul as their king in the presence of the Lord, and they worshiped together and had a great celebration.

By this time, Samuel was old and gray. He'd been Israel's leader from the time he was a youth until Saul became king. It was time for him to make his farewell speech, and Samuel took this opportunity to remind the people of their history. He reminded them that the Lord brought their ancestors out of bondage in Egypt, that He fought for them as they moved to the Promised Land, and that He gave them judges who rescued them out of the hands of their oppressors. But then, he also reminded them that, at every stage, their ancestors turned away from the Lord and His commands. And now, they themselves had forsaken the Lord as their King and asked for an earthly king, a request that the Lord granted. Then Samuel told them:

> "If you will fear the LORD and serve him and obey his voice and not rebel against the commandment of the LORD, and if both you and the king who reigns over you will follow the LORD your God, it will be well. But if you will not obey the voice of the LORD, but rebel against the commandment of the LORD, then the hand of the LORD will be against you and your king" **(1 Sam. 12:14-15)**.

Samuel gave this speech on the first day of the wheat harvest; and to make sure they understood just how evil it was for them to have rejected God as their king, Samuel called upon the Lord to send thunder and rain. When the rain started falling, the people realized their sin and asked for Samuel to intercede so that their crops wouldn't be ruined by the weather. Samuel interceded for them and continued with his warnings to be obedient. Finally, the farewell speech was ended, but Samuel's time on Earth was not quite finished yet. It didn't take long before his warnings to the Israelites went unheeded.

A year after victory with the Ammonites, King Saul and his son Jonathan found themselves fighting the Philistines on two different fronts. When Jonathan won his battle in Gibeah, it roused the Philistine army to bring out thirty thousand chariots and six thousand horsemen against Israel. Because one of Philistia's borders was the Mediterranean Sea, their only alternative for more land to live on was the Promised Land.

King Saul gathered the terrified Israelites to fight. The Israelites didn't have chariots or horses, and they were faced with an enemy who had thousands and thousands of both. If they had only believed and had faith that the Lord doesn't need people, or horses, or chariots to win a battle, regardless of its size, things might have been different. If King Saul had believed this, things might have been different. The Lord didn't *need* anything to win the battle, but He did have *requirements* from His people in order to battle for them. Those requirements were trust and obedience, from both the people and their king.

Because a holy war was a religious undertaking, before they went into battle, the priest sacrificed and made burnt offerings to the Lord. Samuel told Saul that he would come to the battlefront within seven days to do that. So, King Saul and his terrified army waited. On the seventh day, with no word from Samuel, the people were afraid. Many of them started to desert and go home rather than wait for what they believed was sure death from the Philistines. To keep his army from fleeing, Saul took matters into his own hands and sacrificed the burnt offering himself, trying to gain the Lord's favor. This was not something the king should have done; it was a priestly duty. If Saul had been patient a little longer, Samuel would have been there to do it. Because King Saul did not heed the word of the Lord, God told him his kingdom would not continue, and He was going to appoint someone else to be king over His people. It didn't happen right away. Saul remained king for many more years but never learned to obey the Lord during his reign.

One specific instance of his disobedience, and maybe the most blatant one, had some consequences both for Israel's next king, David, and also for the Jews in the time of Esther. Through the word of the Lord, Samuel was told that King Saul should go out to fight with King Amalek of the Amalekites. If you remember back in Exodus 17:14, the Lord had declared that there would be total destruction of the Amalekite people because they had unjustly attacked Israel without any provocation when they were headed toward the Promised Land. King Saul and his army were going to be the Lord's instrument of justice used to do this. Samuel told Saul, *"Now go and strike Amalek and devote to destruction all that they have. Do not spare them, but kill both man and woman, child and infant, ox and sheep, camel and donkey"* **(1 Sam. 15:3)**.

King Saul and his army went to war with the Amalekites; but instead of destroying everything and everyone, they brought back King Agag and the best of the livestock. It became apparent later in the Bible that they left some other Amalekites alive, too. When Samuel confronted Saul about his disobedience, Saul made an excuse that they brought the spoil back to use for making sacrifices to God. Instead of obeying the command, King Saul decided to try to please God in his own way—by bringing animals back with him for sacrifice. What he should have done was treated everything as "the ban"—spoil and plunder devoted to God in a holy war, usually burned up on site. *"And Samuel said, 'Has the Lord as great delight in burnt offerings and sacrifices, as in obeying the voice of the LORD? Behold, to obey is better than sacrifice, and to listen than the fat of rams"* **(1 Sam. 15:22)**.

The Lord desires our obedience over our offerings, an important lesson for all of us and one that Saul never learned. Saul's disobedience grieved

Samuel, but the Lord had a new king for him to anoint. So, He sent Samuel to the town of Bethlehem in Judah to anoint the man of His choosing. You might be asking, "Didn't God send Samuel to anoint Saul? Why didn't He choose someone from the tribe of Judah right from the beginning?" God anointed Saul as king to give the people the kind of king they wanted. He gave them a king who fit the world's standards. Soon, He would give them a better king—one who was from Judah, the godly line, and with a heart that was devoted to Him.

Following God's command, Samuel traveled to Bethlehem in Judah to the family of Jesse, one of whose sons would be the Lord's choice for a king. As Samuel had Jesse bring out his first son, Samuel was convinced that he would be the one! Just like Saul, this son had a fine appearance and was tall. *"But the Lord said to Samuel, 'Do not look on his appearance or on the height of his stature, because I have rejected him. For the LORD sees not as man sees: man looks on the outward appearance, but the LORD looks on the heart"* **(1 Sam. 16:7)**.

Seven sons passed in front of Samuel without the Lord telling him to anoint any of them. So, Samuel inquired of Jesse if he had any more sons. And Jesse did have another son—the youngest, who was a shepherd named David. When David arrived at the house, the Lord told Samuel to anoint him; and when he did, David was filled with the Holy Spirit. Just a few verses later, we find out that the Holy Spirit had left King Saul. In fact, **1 Samuel 16:14** says, *"Now the Spirit of the LORD departed from Saul, and a harmful spirit from the LORD tormented him."* We don't know exactly what that means. It could have been either a demon or an angel, since both are totally under God's control.

The fact that David had been anointed king didn't mean that he sat on the throne right away. Saul was still king of Israel, and at this point, David's anointing was known only to Samuel, David's family, and the prominent men of their town of Bethlehem, Judah. Finally, there's evidence that Israel would have a king from the right tribe! But for now, Saul was still reigning.

Because Saul was tormented so badly by the harmful spirit, someone came up with the idea that harp music might help give him relief. God works in the normal, every-day things to bring about His plans. As we've said already, there are no coincidences. Nothing happens by chance. In this case, someone in the king's court knew David and his family and knew that David played the harp! So, they sent for David; and he entered the service of King Saul, and Saul loved him greatly. Whenever David played the harp, the harmful spirit departed from Saul. David was going to get a firsthand look at what the life of a king was like. He now had a front-row seat to witness the kind of decisions a king makes and all that ruling entails.

Whether you're a Christian or not, it's likely that you've heard the story of David and Goliath. The story is often portrayed as one in which a weak, small person can do great things, even such great things as kill a giant to win the battle! Because David's father sent him with provisions to his brothers who were in the army, many people assume that David was still just a shepherd boy living in his father's house. However, by this time, David was already King Saul's armorbearer, and his living quarters were somewhere near the king's. Also, we know he's anything but a small child at this point because before David had even been assigned to play music for the king, the king's servant referred to David as *"a man of valor, a man of war, prudent in speech, and a man of good presence, and the LORD is with him"* **(1 Sam. 16:18)**.

Regardless of his size, David killed the giant when no one else would even try! And as you can imagine, everyone found out about it. This became a problem for David when they returned home. The women from the towns of Israel came out to meet the men coming home from war, and this time they weren't singing about King Saul. Instead, they were singing, *"'Saul has struck down his thousands, and David his ten thousands'"* **(1 Sam. 18:7)**. This was a blow to the king's ego and caused him to become very jealous of David.

Saul's daughter, Michal, fell in love with David. Saul used this to try to get David killed by setting the bride price at one hundred Philistine foreskins.

(Yes, that means what you think it does!) Not only did David not get killed, he ended up killing two hundred Philistines, and now Saul had two hundred foreskins! Although Saul loved David at first, now he saw him as a threat. King Saul wanted him dead, despite the fact that his daughter was married to him and he was his son Jonathan's best friend. After another attempt on his life, David was warned by Jonathan to leave, so he departed to the land of the Philistines. When they recognized him, he acted like he was a madman so they would let him go. Many other things happened along the way, but there are too many to go into here.

David began to gather men around him, including his brothers and other downtrodden people of the land. King Saul was constantly in pursuit of the bunch. **First Samuel 23:14** says, *"And Saul sought him every day, but God did not give him into his hand."* The only time David got a break from being hunted down was when the Philistines made a raid on the land and Saul took a break from hunting David to fight for control of the land. But the story between these two wasn't finished yet. After fighting off the Philistines, the chase resumed. This time, David and his men were hiding out in a cave, unbeknownst to King Saul, who went into the cave to relieve himself. David's men believed it was the time for victory. They expected David to strike Saul dead and take over as king. And David could have done it. In fact, he approached the king and cut off the corner of the king's robe, but he did not kill him. When Saul finished relieving himself, David took the corner of the robe and followed the king outside the cave. David entrusted his own life, as well as that of his troops, to the Lord. He showed King Saul the proof of his opportunity to kill him and said, *"May the LORD therefore be judge and give sentence between me and you, and see to it and plead my cause and deliver me from your hand"* **(1 Sam. 24:15)**.

> *"As soon as David had finished speaking these words to Saul, Saul said . . . to David, "You are more righteous than I, for you have repaid me good, whereas I have repaid you evil . . . So may the LORD reward you with good for what you have done to me this day. And now, behold, I know*

that you shall surely be king, and that the kingdom of Israel shall be established in your hand" **(1 Sam. 24:16-17, 19b-20)**.

David wrote some of his Psalms while he was on the run from Saul, including Psalms 57 and 142.

King Saul asked David for one thing—that when David became king, he would not cut off Saul's offspring, thereby not destroying his name. And David agreed. Then Saul returned home, and David and his men continued to live in a stronghold for a while.

In 1011 B.C., the prophet Samuel died. David and his men were not idle during this time. They'd been in the wilderness of Paran; and while they were there, they helped guard the three thousand sheep and other property of a man named Nabal, whose name means "fool." And Nabal was a fool, as he proves by refusing provisions to David and his men after all of the help they'd given him. Now, Nabal most likely knew that it was David and was probably unsure how King Saul might react if he gave them provisions. But nonetheless, it was foolish to refuse the request for supplies that David and his men needed.

When you're a foolish man, it's good to have an intelligent wife, and Nabal did! Her name was Abigail; and not only was she appreciative of all that David and his men had done in protecting their livestock, but she also recognized the danger of Nabal's refusal to reward them. Wisely, she gathered supplies and took them to David and his men without Nabal knowing it. When Abigail returned home, he was feasting and drinking wine, so she waited till morning to tell him what she'd done; and when she told him, he *"became as a stone"* **(1 Sam. 25:37)**. Ten days later, the Lord killed him, and Abigail became David's second wife.

Saul still could not let the idea of killing David go, so he hunted him again. This time, just like the last, David had an opportunity to kill Saul, but didn't. Again seeing the proof, King Saul repented and returned home. Many more things happened in Saul and David's lives, including Saul meeting with a witch at Endore to try to talk with Samuel from the grave. Saul eventually died in a battle with the Philistine army. He was wounded by Philistine archers, but died by his own sword in order not to be killed by uncircumcised men. His son Jonathan died in the battle that day, too.

2 SAMUEL

When David heard about the death of Saul and Jonathan, he mourned the two men and afterward inquired of the Lord if he should go back to Judah. God affirmed that he should, and David was anointed king of Judah in 1010 B.C. However, Abner, the commander of Saul's army, took Saul's son Ishbosheth and made him king over the other eleven tribes. His reign lasted two years. This was the first time that God's people were split and ruled by two different kings. It wouldn't be the last. David was king over the house of Judah for seven years and six months.

There was a long war between the house of Saul and the house of David. **Second Samuel 3:1** says, *"And David grew stronger and stronger, while the house of Saul became weaker and weaker."* By this time, David had six wives, in addition to his first wife, Michal, who had been taken from David by her father, Saul, and given to another man for marriage. Although God allowed many of the men in the Old Testament to have multiple wives, it does not mean that polygamy is not sinful in God's eyes. Marriage was meant to be between one man and one woman only. It was always to be that way. God did not condone it back in Old Testament times any more than He does today. Sin is sin. God does not change. But despite David's sin of polygamy, God blessed him. David's wives gave birth to six sons during this period.

In the process of getting David on the throne over all of Israel, there were secret deals, lots of intrigue, several power plays, revenge killings for the deaths of family members, and some skirmishes between Judah and the other tribes. There is too much detail to go into here, but it is like reading a spy thriller! Even men who knew that the Lord had anointed David to be their king didn't act according to what they knew. They liked the power they had and didn't want to hand it over, not even when they knew it was what God wanted!

Through it all, David was heart-wrenched at the idea of honorable men dying from either side. David wouldn't kill Saul, "the Lord's anointed," so that his own time as king would begin. He trusted God to take care of putting him into leadership in His own timing. Likewise, David was not pleased with men who tried to make it happen on their own either. When the two men killed Ishbosheth in his bed and brought David the "good news," David had them killed! His answer to their news was this:

> "As the LORD lives, who has redeemed my life out of every adversity, when one told me, 'Behold, Saul is dead,' and thought he was bringing good news, I seized him and killed him at Ziklag, which was the reward I gave him for his news. How much more, when wicked men have a killed a righteous man in his own house on his bed, shall I not now require his blood at your hand and destroy you from the earth?" **(2 Sam. 4:9-11)**.

So, David had his men kill the messengers, cut off their hands and feet, and hang the bodies beside the pool at Heshbon.

DAVID'S REIGN

In 1003 B.C., the eleven tribes who previously fought David came before him at Hebron and made him king over all of Israel. David was thirty years old when he began his seven-year reign over Judah and reigned for an additional thirty-three years over all of Israel. King David didn't continue to reign from Hebron. Instead, he took over the city of Jerusalem, making it the capital city for Israel. Jerusalem was also referred to as Zion or the City of David. With the taking of Jerusalem, David also took more wives and concubines. His large family and his failure to be a strong father figure to so many children would be a problem for him down the road.

Now that Jerusalem was the new capital city, it was time for the Ark of the Covenant to be brought to the Tabernacle so that proper worship could be restored to Israel. David gathered thirty thousand men and went to the place where the Ark had been left ever since it was returned by the Philistines.

Instead of Levites carrying the Ark by poles made for that purpose, as commanded by God in Exodus 37, David and his men decided to carry the Ark to Jerusalem on a new cart pulled by oxen. On the journey back to Jerusalem, the oxen stumbled, and Uzzah, one of the sons whose house the cart had resided in, put out his hand to steady the Ark so that it wouldn't fall off the cart. There were consequences, and **2 Samuel 6:7** tells us his fate: *"And the anger of the LORD was kindled against Uzzah, and God struck him down there because of his error, and he died there beside the ark of God."* It seems unreasonable to most of us that God would strike someone down for touching the Ark when Uzzah was trying to do something good. But God was very specific when He gave instructions for the temple worship and transportation of the holy things. It is not our idea of what is good and bad that matters. God, as the Creator of the whole universe, has the right to make all of those decisions.

We aren't the only ones who thought this seemed unreasonable. David was angry because of what God did to Uzzah, and he was afraid, too. So afraid that he would not take the Ark to Jerusalem that day. Instead, he left it outside the city in the house of Obed Edom for three months before bringing it into the Tabernacle, which was now set up at Jerusalem. Obed Edom's house was blessed during that time! When David heard this, he decided to bring the Ark to Jerusalem, and he did it the right way this time—on poles, carried by Levites. On the way into the city, David was dancing before the Lord. Some say the text implies that David was naked. But David probably wasn't totally naked; most likely, he just took off his royal garments, meaning only his outer clothing. His wife Michal despised him for his dancing in front of everyone. David scolded her, and she spent the rest of her life barren and died childless.

During the time between Saul's death and David becoming king, the Philistines started encroaching on more of the Promised Land. Had it not been land God promised for His people, the Philistines would have won the battles. They were far superior—both culturally and militarily—to the Israelites. The Philistines had paved floors in their homes, made pottery, had iron, and were able to sharpen their weapons—all things the Israelites were lacking. Nevertheless, God fought the battles for His people. *"And David inquired of the LORD, 'Shall I go up against the Philistines? Will you give them into my hand?' And the LORD said to David, 'Go up, for I will certainly give the Philistines into your hand'"* **(2 Sam. 5:19)**. After winning that battle, the Philistines encroached again and were defeated a second time. It was now 998 B.C., and this victory prompted David to write several Psalms, including Psalms 24, 105, and 106.

As David continued further along in his reign, he was bothered by the fact that he lived in a palace, while the Ark of the Covenant, the actual place God met with the High Priest, resided in a tent. To rectify the situation, he decided that he wanted to build God a temple for worship. David discussed his idea with Nathan the prophet, who at first thought it was a good idea but then changed his mind when God came to Nathan in a dream that night. What He said is recorded in **1 Chronicles 22:8**: *"'You have shed much blood and have waged great wars. You shall not build a house to my name, because you have shed so much blood before me on the earth.'"* David's son was the one who would build the temple.

David accepted God's Word and did his best to get the ball rolling in preparation. He planned for acquiring materials and amassed much of what would be needed for such a large, beautiful building. Part of this was done while strengthening the kingdom by subduing more lands, thus extracting more tax money from the pagan nations. David dedicated all the spoils of war to the Lord, and the Lord gave him victory wherever he went.

One day as David was reminiscing about his close friendship with Jonathan, he asked, *"'Is there still anyone left of the house of Saul, that I may show him kindness for Jonathan's sake?'"* **(2 Sam. 9:1)**. And there was one descendant, a son of Jonathan, who was still alive but lame in both feet. His name was Mephibosheth. King David brought him to the palace and declared that Mephibosheth would always eat at his table, making him like one of the king's sons. Not only did King David do this, but he gave Mephibosheth all that had belonged to Saul.

Mephibosheth did nothing to earn this special favor from the king. He didn't seek the king out. King David initiated contact with Mephibosheth, provided for all of his needs, and, for all intents and purposes, made him like his own son. This is a picture of what God does for His people. He chooses a remnant of helpless people who have no regard for Him and are not looking for Him and brings them to Himself, making them His sons and daughters through Jesus' work on the cross. He does it solely for His own reasons and His own pleasure.

In the year 993 B.C., ten years after David first became king over the whole nation, we see a change start to happen in him—one that's not for the better. **Second Samuel 11:1** says, *"In the spring of the year, the time when kings go out to battle, David sent Joab, and his servants with him, and all Israel. And they ravaged the Ammonites and besieged Rabbah. But David remained at Jerusalem."* David sent his army out to war, while he stayed in the comforts of home. This does not sound like the *"man of valor, a man of war"* that David was described as when he first came into the service of King Saul!

While he was home in the comfort of the palace, he decided to take a walk on the roof. While he was walking, he saw a woman bathing, and she was very beautiful. Through some inquiry, he found out that her name was Bathsheba, and she was the wife of Uriah the Hittite, one of David's fighting men who was out battling the Ammonites. David summoned her to the palace, and he slept with her, resulting in a pregnancy. As if adultery wasn't bad enough, David piled sin upon sin. He had her husband return from the battle under the guise of getting information about how the battle was going, in hopes that Uriah would sleep with his wife while he's home and no one would know that the baby was King David's. When Uriah showed up, David sent him home, but Uriah didn't go. When David asked him why he didn't go home, Uriah's answer was, *"The ark and Israel and Judah dwell in booths, and my lord Joab and the servants of my lord are camping in the open field. Shall I then go to my house, to eat and to drink and to lie with my wife? As you live, and as your soul lives, I will not do this thing"* **(2 Sam. 11:11)**. Uriah was a righteous man, the kind of man the king was supposed to be! Just like Uriah, David knew that God's rules for a holy war included fasting and abstaining from sex. He even acknowledged that earlier in 1 Samuel. When these rules weren't followed by the men in battle, God did not go ahead of them in the fight! David was at home, but he should have been in the battle; and even if he had been home with good reason, he should have abstained from sex while his men were fighting.

As if all of this was not enough, King David had Uriah stay one more night in the city so that he could get him drunk, thinking that Uriah would surely go to his house and sleep with his wife then! But Uriah didn't go that night either. David had one more idea after this. The horrible plan was laid out in **2 Samuel 11:14-15**, where it says, *"In the morning David wrote a letter to Joab and sent it by the hand of Uriah. In the letter he wrote, 'Set Uriah in the forefront of the hardest fighting, and then draw back from him, that he may be struck down, and die."* David was having an innocent man killed because of his own adultery and the resulting pregnancy! Uriah did die, and Bathsheba became another of David's wives. The Lord moved the prophet Nathan to confront David about his sin through the use of a parable. When David heard the words God spoke to him through Nathan, he was convicted of his sin and repented. While the Lord forgave him, He still sent consequences to David because of his sin.

> *"Now therefore the sword shall never depart from your house, because you have despised me and have taken the wife of Uriah the Hittite to be your wife." Thus says the LORD, 'Behold, I will raise up evil against you*

out of your own house. And I will take your wives before your eyes and give them to your neighbor, and he shall lie with your wives in the sight of this sun" . . . *"You shall not die. Nevertheless, because by this deed you have utterly scorned the LORD, the child who is born to you shall die"* **(2 Sam. 12:10-11, 13b-14)**.

Despite David's pleading, the child did die. David and Bathsheba had another child some time later. His name was Solomon, and he would become the third king of Israel.

How can someone who sins so egregiously be God's chosen man to lead His people? How can God consider King David to be *"A man after my heart, who will do my will,"* as is said about him in **Acts 13:22**? Like all of humanity, David was born a sinner. He needed a Savior just like we all do. But what made David a man after God's own heart was that he never worshipped anyone but Yahweh. David did not practice syncretism like the other kings of Israel. Yes, he sinned. But when he did, he repented, and he never worshipped the gods of the other nations or of his own making. David only worshiped the one true God. King David is in the line of Jesus. Therefore, that is why God had told him that he would have a descendant on the throne forever. Jesus is the godly King to Whom the whole Old Testament is pointing.

Like we said earlier, David had many consequences. He had family strife. He was cursed by someone from Saul's family. His beloved son Absalom tried to steal the throne from him. David found himself back at war with his enemies, the Philistines. During this time, he committed another grievous sin. He counted the number of troops he had. This was forbidden by God for a few reasons. Because of this sin, the Lord punished David and his people. The Lord allowed David to choose his punishment out of three options: three years of famine in all the land, three months of running from his enemies, or three days of pestilence throughout his kingdom. David picked the three days of pestilence throughout the land because, as he says in **2 Samuel 24:14b**, *"Let us fall into the hands of the LORD for his mercy is great; but let me not fall* *into the hand of man.'"* Even though the Lord mercifully cut the three days short, seventy thousand men of Israel died. Much more about David's life is explained in detail in the last thirteen chapters of 2 Samuel, but they are too detailed to include here. David was old, but his life was not over yet. His story continued for a bit in the book of 1 Kings.

1 KINGS

The book of 1 Kings was finished sometime during the latter part of the southern kingdom of Judah's eventual exile in Babylon. It was written and/or put together by a chronicler under Divine inspiration in order to continue documenting the nation's history through the period of the kings. It was also to show the people (who were in exile by that time) that their exile was justified to give them continuing hope in the House of David and to help call them to repentance.

The Book of 1 Kings opens with, *"Now King David was old and advanced in years. And although they covered him with clothes, he could not get warm"* **(1 Kings 1:1)**. Even at his advanced age, David was still having family issues. A son from his wife Haggith, named Adonijah, was trying to put himself on the throne. He decided to be king! But he was not God's choice for the next king; Solomon was. Nathan the prophet told Bathsheba what Adonijah was planning, and together, they brought the matter to David's attention and reminded him that he swore on oath to God that Solomon would be the next king. So, David crowned Solomon king, having him anointed before the people so that no one could have any doubt who was king in Israel. And the people rejoiced that Solomon was ruler over them, everyone except Adonijah and his crew, that is! When they heard about it, they were afraid.

When David was about to die, he gave Solomon these instructions:

> *"I am about to go the way of all the earth. Be strong, and show yourself a man, and keep the charge of the LORD your God, walking in his*

ways and keeping his statutes, his commandments, his rules, and his testimonies, as it is written in the Law of Moses, that you may prosper in all that you do and wherever you turn, that the LORD may establish his word that he spoke concerning me, saying, 'If your sons pay close attention to their way, to walk before me in faithfulness with all their heart and with all their soul, you shall not lack a man on the throne of Israel'" **(1 Kings 2:2-4)**.

In the year 970 B.C., David died.

SOLOMON'S REIGN

The Lord affirmed Solomon as king by getting rid of Adonijah and his supporters. Solomon loved the Lord and followed his father's instructions about the Lord's commandments, except that he made offerings and sacrifices in places other than the tabernacle. Nevertheless, one night after sacrificing at one of these places, the Lord came to him in a dream and said in **1 Kings 3:5b**, *"Ask what I shall give you."* And Solomon responded in **1 Kings 3:7-9**:

> *"And now, O LORD my God, you have made your servant king in place of David my father, although I am but a little child. I do not know how to go out or come in. And your servant is in the midst of your people whom you have chosen, a great people, too many to be numbered or counted for multitude. Give your servant therefore an understanding mind to govern your people, that I may discern between good and evil, for who is able to govern this your great people?"*

It pleased the Lord that Solomon asked for wisdom and not for earthly goods and resources; and because of that, God promised him that He would make him wiser than anyone before or after him. In addition, God promised him riches and honor that would be without comparison.

Solomon's wisdom proved to be true when two prostitutes, who were roommates and who both had recently given birth, stood before Solomon for judgement. The problem was that one baby had died, and both women were claiming to be the mother of the living child. The wisdom God had given Solomon gave him the ability to come up with the perfect solution! *"And the king said, 'Bring me a sword.' So a sword was brought before the king. And the king said, 'Divide the living child in two, and give half to the one and half to the other'"* **(1 Kings 3:25)**. Solomon knew that the real mother of the child would rather give him up than see him sawn in two. The real mother did exactly that!

Under the reign of King Solomon, the nation flourished. Solomon came the closest of any of the kings to subduing all of the land that God had promised His people. He had a vast kingdom, with other countries paying tribute taxes to it. He was wise beyond measure, and his fame spread to all the surrounding nations. He spoke three thousand proverbs, and he wrote over a thousand songs. He had knowledge about all kinds of nature, and kings and people from other nations came to hear his wisdom. For a time, Solomon's kingdom fulfilled the mission of God's people: to show His glory to the nations, so that they come to Him!

When Solomon had been on the throne for about three years, he decided it was time to build the temple. He made arrangements for cedar and cypress to be sent from a land called Tyre, and he drafted forced labor of about thirty thousand men out of all of Israel to go and help cut the trees. He didn't send them all at once but worked out a plan where they would work one month and then have off two. They also quarried stone for the foundation of the temple, and all of the stonework was finished at the quarry so that the sound of the iron tools was not heard in the house while it was being built.

The inside of the temple was lined with carved cedar, and some of it was overlaid with gold. It was 480 years since God had led the people out of Egypt before the temple was started. The Bible says that Solomon spent seven years building the temple but took thirteen years building his own house. We can see by this detail that the chronicler is giving us a hint to show us something about Solomon's priorities.

When the temple was made ready, Solomon offered up prayers and petitions before the Lord, in front of all the people, acknowledging all that the Lord had done for Israel and asking Him to hear their petitions and cries for forgiveness *when they sinned.*

When you read this chapter, don't miss this. Israel continued to sin; we all do. King Solomon was acknowledging that fact here. But the next part of his prayer tells us Solomon understood the reason why God would hear their (and our) prayers, despite their sin: *"For you separated them from among all the peoples of the earth to be your heritage, as you declared through Moses your servant, when you brought our fathers out of Egypt, O LORD God"* **(1 Kings 8:53)**. Solomon was saying something that's central to the theme of the whole Bible. The Israelites were not better people than any of the other nations, and they certainly did not choose God themselves. God chose them out of all of the other nations of the world to be His people. They had no merit of their own on which to stand. It was only because they were God's elect that the Lord heard them and rescued them. The same is true of all believers for all time.

On the day the temple was dedicated, Solomon offered peace offerings of twenty-two thousand oxen and 120,000 sheep, along with fat offerings and grain offerings. All of Israel feasted that day and throughout the rest of the week. On the eighth day, everyone headed for home full of joy because of all that the Lord had done for the House of David and all of Israel.

The Lord appeared to Solomon when he was finished building and said:

> *"And as for you, if you will walk before me, as David your father walked, with integrity of heart and uprightness, doing according to all that I have commanded you, and keeping my statues and my rules, then I will establish your royal throne over Israel forever, as I promised David your father, saying 'You shall not lack a man on the throne of Israel.' But if you turn aside from following me, you or your children, and do not keep my commandments and my statues that I have set before you, but go and serve other gods and worship them, then I will cut off Israel from the land that I have given them, and the house that I have consecrated*

*for my name I will cast out of my sight, and Israel will become a proverb
and a byword among all the peoples. And this house will become a heap
of ruins"* **(1 Kings 9:4-8)**.

This may seem like a stern warning for a king who had just overseen
the building of such a gloriously beautiful and large temple and for a people
who had just worshiped and sacrificed over 140,000 animals. But God knows
His creatures. He knows the fickleness of our hearts, and our tendency to
wander. And it wasn't long before it started to happen. If you read the story
of Solomon carefully, you start to see the cracks. The people reading 1 Kings
originally would have known something went terribly wrong with Solomon
in order for the nation's people to be in the predicament they were in at the
time, which was exile. As they read or heard these words, they would have
seen his failures start to show, particularly in three areas which the Lord
had warned Israel about in **Deuteronomy 17:16-17** about the king they would
have ruling over them: *"Only he must not acquire many horses for himself or cause
the people to return to Egypt in order to acquire many horses, since the LORD has
said to you, 'You shall never return that way again.' And he shall not acquire many
wives for himself, lest his heart turn away, nor shall he acquire for himself excessive
silver and gold."*

King Solomon did all of these things and more. He built a fleet of ships
that carried back incredible amounts of gold from foreign lands; he imported
horses from Egypt; and he took one thousand wives! He built store cities,
cities for his chariots, cities for his horsemen, and anything else he desired.
King Solomon acquired so much gold that silver was considered worthless.
Virtually everything from shields to drinking glasses was made of gold. Even
his throne of ivory was overlaid with gold.

In order to strengthen the kingdom, Solomon made an alliance with
pharaoh, the king of Egypt, which included marriage to pharaoh's daughter.
Since Solomon's son Rehoboam was born in his first year of reigning over
Israel, it's evident this Egyptian woman was not Solomon's first wife. Not

only was he living a life of polygamy, but he was also marrying someone outside the covenant people. This is not a problem if the person converts and worships the Lord, just as Ruth did in the time of the Judges. But this Egyptian never did that, nor did the other foreign women King Solomon eventually married.

As we continue with his story, it's obvious that King Solomon excelled over all the kings of the whole Earth. All of them wanted to meet with him; and when they did, they brought him even more gold, horses, garments, mules, and spices. At the height of Solomon's power, word of everything he'd done in the land, as well as word of his wisdom and knowledge, spread far and wide. In the year 946 B.C., the Queen of Sheba heard of his fame and came to him, bringing a large caravan of gold, precious stones, and spices— more spices than had ever been brought to the land or ever would be again. She asked him all kinds of questions, and there was nothing she asked that he couldn't answer. *"And she said to the king, 'The report was true that I heard in my own land of your words and of your wisdom, but I did not believe the reports until I came and my own eyes had seen it. And behold, the half was not told me. Your wisdom and prosperity surpass the report that I heard'"* **(1 Kings 10:6-7)**. And King Solomon gave her everything she desired and asked for before going back to her own land. But before she left, she said, *"Blessed be the LORD your God, who has delighted in you and set you on the throne of Israel! Because the Lord loved Israel forever, he has made you king, that you may execute justice and righteousness"* **(1 Kings 10:9)**. King Solomon should have listened carefully to these words from the mouth of the pagan queen. If he had, he might have been reminded of his true kingly duties and turned from his sin. But he did not.

King Solomon's massive amount of wealth and the treaties he made came with a price. In **1 Kings 11:3**, we learn that in addition to acquiring wealth, *"He had 700 wives, who were princesses, and 300 concubines."* He should have been content with his first wife and not taken wives from foreign countries, not even for the sake of making treaties. These wives ended up turning his heart away from the Lord and toward worshiping idols. Unlike his father, King Solomon began to practice syncretism, worshiping both the Lord and idols. Not only did he worship these false gods, but he also built places of worship for them throughout the land—even for the abominable gods of Moab and Ammon, Chemosh and Molech, whose worship included child sacrifice.

Less than ten years from the height of King Solomon's fame and the visit from the Queen of Sheba, the Lord began to raise up adversaries against him because of his sin, one of which was his own servant, Jeroboam.

God promised to Jeroboam through the prophet Ahijah, *"Behold, I am about to tear the kingdom from the hand of Solomon and will give you ten tribes"* **(1 Kings 11:31)**. And then He further promised Jeroboam that if he was obedient to the Lord, he would rule over all that he desired, that he would have his own dynasty, and also that the Lord would be with him in his endeavors. Solomon tried to kill him over this, but he escaped.

Solomon reigned a total of forty years over Israel. He accomplished many things, including writing many proverbs, and he gained control over most of the land the Lord had originally promised Israel. But he forsook the Lord and worshiped idols. In the year 931 B.C., Solomon died and was buried in Jerusalem.

THE DIVIDED KINGDOM

Although we know that King Solomon had made the Israelites laborers when building the temple, it was only when Solomon's son, Rehoboam, came to power that we learn that King Solomon had "put a heavy yoke" on his fellow Israelites and had put them to "harsh labor." Because of that, the people asked King Rehoboam for reprieve, but he foolishly refused and promised them even harsher circumstances. In response, Israel revolted, and in fulfillment of God's Word through the prophet Ahijah, the ten Northern tribes called Jeroboam to be their king.

God's people were once again a divided nation in a civil war that was never resolved. The split nation that had united under King David would never be one nation again. Rehoboam would rule over what is now referred to as "Judah," "the Southern Kingdom," or "Jerusalem," which consisted of the tribes of Judah and Benjamin. The tribe of Simeon, who originally had land within the Southern tribe of Judah, was now included within the tribes of the North because at some point many of them moved north and settled among the Northern tribes. A large number of them returned to the South later, but for now, they were counted as a Northern tribe.

As God promised, Jeroboam ruled over the ten Northern tribes. The Northern tribes were referred to now as "Israel" or sometimes "Ephraim" (since Ephraim was the strongest tribe in the North), and they can also be referred to as Samaria because its capital city was located in the northern part of the region.

In the Bible, the rest of the books of the Kings are written in a way that goes back and forth between the kings of Judah and the kings of Israel, using the reigning year of one nation's king to introduce the start of the next king in the other nation. As an example, **1 Kings 15:9-10** says, *"In the twentieth year of Jeroboam king of Israel, Asa began to reign over Judah, and he reigned forty-one years in Jerusalem."* And then **1 Kings 15:25** tells us, *"Nadab the son of Jeroboam began to reign over Israel in the second year of Asa king of Judah, and he reigned over Israel two years."* This going back and forth can be a bit confusing, so, for the sake of understanding, we are going to list all of the Northern kings together and tell about each of their reigns, and then do the same for all the Southern kings.

One thing to note when you read this section in the Bible is you will come across what seem like contradictions within the text, as well as problems with synchronization with dates and lengths of reigns. The Bible is without error and contradiction. Dating of the kings is a complex issue that takes many things into account, including differences in how a king's reign was dated and co-regencies.13 So, when you read *"Nadab the son of Jeroboam began to reign over Israel in the second year of Asa king of Judah, and he reigned over Israel two years,"* in **1 Kings 15:25**, and then read, *"So Baasha killed him [Nadab] in the third year of Asa king of Judah and reigned in his place,"* in **1 Kings 15:28**, be assured, not only does it not change the overarching theme, but there are explanations!

Although horrendous and terrible things are mentioned about some of the kings, the main focus is on the things pertaining to idol worship. Even in the descriptions of Judah's few relatively good kings, the fact that they didn't take down the high places where idol worship occurred is always stated. This is the major problem. As you'll see when you read about these kings in the Bible, the one thing that is mentioned over and over again are the things pertaining to idol worship.

---

13   Edwin R. Thiele, "Chapter Two: The Fundamental Principles of Hebrew Chronology," in *The Mysterious Numbers of the Hebrew Kings New Revised Edition* (Grand Rapids: The Zondervan Corporation, 1983).

Chapter 8

KINGS OF THE NORTHERN NATION OF ISRAEL

As we said in the last chapter, for the sake of understanding, we're listing the Northern kings and the Southern kings separately. To begin with the Northern, we'll start where we left off with Jeroboam, who had just been called to be king of the Northern nation of Israel.

- **Jeroboam:** Despite the promises the Lord made to prosper him, to be with him, and to give him a dynasty if he was faithful and obeyed, Jeroboam's insecurity caused his downfall and started a major spiritual decline of the tribes he was ruling over. Jeroboam feared that the people would not stay with him if they went to the Southern kingdom of Judah, where the temple was located, to give God proper worship. His lack of faith in the Lord's promises led him to forsake God's commands and set up idol worship in two places within the Northern borders—a golden calf in Dan and another in the town of Bethel—leading the people into syncretism. Jeroboam reigned over the Northern kingdom twenty-two years.

Insecurity led to idolatry. When we're not trusting in God's security and promises to us, we always trust in something lesser, some idol of a lesser nature. This is not what God desires for His people. When we have faith and trust in God, He fights our battles for us. He is always faithful to keep His promises. We need to believe that and rest in the assurance of it. Jeroboam didn't, and the Lord eventually wiped out his entire household, all of whose dead bodies were eaten by dogs or birds, except for one of his children, a son, about whom the Bible tells us, *"All Israel shall mourn for him and bury him, for he only of Jeroboam shall come to the grave, because in him there is found something pleasing to the LORD, the God of Israel, in the house of Jeroboam"* **(1 Kings 14:13)**. This is not the only instance in the Bible where the wicked are eaten by dogs or birds instead of being buried.

- **Nadab:** Nadab was next on Israel's throne. He ruled for just two years before being killed by one of his military commanders, whose name was Baasha.

- **Baasha:** Baasha became ruler in 908 B.C. and ruled for twenty-four years during which he continued Israel's idolatry and waged war with Judah. The Arameans from Damascus in Syria attacked the Northern cities during his reign. The prophet Jehu predicted the downfall of his family.

- **Elah:** Baasha's son Elah came to the throne in 886 B.C. He only lived two years before one of his chariot officers, Zimri, killed him while Elah was drunk.

- **Zimri:** Zimri took over the throne in Israel next, but only lasted for seven days before he set the palace on fire and committed suicide because the people found out he murdered the king.

- **Omri:** The people decided to make Omri their king next but only after being divided for four years because half of the people supported a man named Tibni, instead of Omri, for king. **First Kings 16:22** tells us, *"But the people who followed Omri overcame the people who followed Tibni the son of Ginath. So Tibni died, and Omri became king."* King Omri's reign lasted twelve years, with a starting date of 885 B.C. His reign was the beginning of a new dynasty in Israel. It was also the most wicked dynasty of all. While he was king, he built a fortified city and named it Samaria. King Omri kept the title of "most wicked" only until his son Ahab came to power.

- **Ahab:** Ahab came to power in 874 B.C. Ahab married a woman named Jezebel, who was a Baal worshiper, which prompted the king to institute Baal worship throughout the Northern kingdom, in addition to the already ongoing worship of the golden calves. The prophet Elijah was very active during this time, and he was prophesying greatly against Baal. Jezebel was very angry about it and threatened his life. He wasn't the only one who feared for his life because of her. A godly man who worked in the palace had already hidden one hundred prophets in a cave to keep Jezebel from killing them. There is a lot more to Ahab's story, including details of his palace inlaid with ivory, the type of which archaeologists have found in this region of Samaria. During Ahab's time, pressure was starting to be felt from outside the Promised Land, namely from the area of Damascus in Syria, also called Aram. Eventually, God did judge King Ahab and Queen Jezebel, a judgment which is partially fulfilled at Ahab's bloody death in his chariot, after which the Bible tells us, *"And they washed the chariot by the pool of Samaria, and the dogs licked up his blood, and the prostitutes washed themselves in it, according to the word of the LORD that he had spoken"* **(1 Kings 22:38-39)**.

- **Ahaziah:** Ahab's son, Ahaziah, began to rule in 853 B.C. He was hurt when he fell through the upstairs lattice and sent someone to inquire of Baal whether or not he was going to die. On the way, they met up with the prophet Elijah, who said Ahaziah will die. Ahaziah sent out a group of fifty men to seize Elijah, and the Lord consumed all fifty men with fire from Heaven. The same thing happened a second time. Elijah met with him after the third group of fifty men (whom Elijah doesn't have consumed) came, and he told Ahaziah that he would, indeed, die for inquiring of Baal. Ahaziah's reign lasted less than two years.

2 KINGS

The book of 2 Kings is a continuation of the history of the kings of Israel and Judah.

- **Joram:** Joram, another son of Ahab, ruled next. He did evil in the eyes of the Lord, but he got rid of the sacred stone of Baal that his father had made. However, he didn't rid the land of the golden calves. His story begins in the book of 2 Kings. By the year 852 B.C., the king of Moab and his people were subject to Israel and being taxed. With King Ahab dead, they decided to rebel. Joram decided to ask Jehoshaphat, king of Judah, to go with him to fight the Moabites. Although Israel and Judah are enemies, sometimes they did come together to fight a common enemy. So, they set out—along with the king of Edom, who was subject to Judah—and they set off to war together against the Moabites but ran out of water on the way. Because the Lord had regard for the king of Judah, He gave word through the prophet Elisha, *"You shall not see wind or rain, but that streambed shall be filled with water, so that you shall drink, you, your livestock, and your animals.' This is a light thing in the sight of the LORD. He will also give the Moabites into your hand"* **(2 Kings 3:17-18)**. And that's exactly what happened. Before they went home, the three kings fulfilled the word of the Lord by stopping up every spring of water, ruining every good piece of the land with stones, overthrowing the cities, and taking down all of the good trees in the land of Moab. King Joram reigned in Israel for twelve years, and then he was killed by his military officer, Jehu, who was the next king.

- **Jehu:** King Jehu was anointed by Elisha to destroy every male offspring of Ahab, and he also prophesied, *"And the dogs shall eat Jezebel in the territory of Jezreel, and none shall bury her"* **(2 Kings 9:10)**. This prophecy was fulfilled when Jehu had her thrown out her window by two or three eunuchs, splattering her blood on the wall. The horses on the street below trampled her underfoot. When they went out to get her body for burial, they found nothing except her skull, her feet, and her hands. The wicked dynasty that started with Omri was not totally over, though, because one of the kings of Judah married Ahab's daughter, who was at least as bad as her mother, Jezebel. Jehu reigned for twenty-eight years after killing not only Joram, but also Ahaziah, king of Judah. He eliminated Baal worship and carried out the prophecy against the house of Ahab, but he still allowed the people to worship the golden calves.

- **Jehoahaz:** Jehu's son, Jehoahaz, reigned after him, and he didn't remove the golden calf idols from the area either, so Israel continued to sin against the Lord by worshiping them. This caused the Lord's anger to burn against Israel, so he kept their struggle against the king of Syria going, until Jehoahaz sought the Lord's favor and the Lord rescued them from the severe oppression they'd been put under. Even after their rescue, Israel still didn't turn away from their sin, and they still continued to worship the goddess Asherah. Then Jehoahaz rested with his ancestors, and they buried him in Samaria.

- **Jehoash:** Jehoahaz's son, Jehoash, started his reign in 798 B.C. He and all of Israel continued in the same sin as their forefathers. When the king of Syria died, Jehoash took back all the land his father had lost to them. During his reign, he went to war with the South against

Amaziah, king of Judah, and plundered the city of Jerusalem, also known as the City of David. He reigned for sixteen years. His son, Jeroboam II, became a co-regent with him in 793 B.C., something that was common for kings in those days, and the two ruled together for eleven of Jehoash's sixteen years.

- **Jeroboam II:** Jeroboam II went on to reign another thirty years, and in that time, he rescued Israel from oppression by Syria and expanded Israel's boundaries to the North, something that had been prophesied by Jonah.

With the next king, Zechariah, came the beginning of a long power struggle that lasted thirteen years and involved revolutions and counter-revolutions. During this time, five kings, starting with Zechariah, came to power. There was a lot of instability in the land.

- **Zechariah:** Jeroboam II's son, Zechariah, took the throne in 753 B.C. He was publicly assassinated six months later by a conspirator named Shallum, who reigned after him.

- **Shallum:** Shallum reigned for only one month before he was assassinated by a man named Menahem, who succeeded him.

- **Menahem:** Menahem was a wicked king; and like much of the warfare at that time in history, he was brutal. As he was on his way to attack King Shallum to take over the kingdom, he attacked the city of Tiphsah and everyone in its vicinity because they would not open the gates to him. Because of this, he *"sacked it, and he ripped open all the women in it who were pregnant"* (**2 Kings 15:16b**). Menahem reigned for ten years, doing the same evil his predecessors did. When the land was invaded by Assyria, who was the up-and-coming superpower in the region, Menahem paid them a thousand talents of silver to gain their support and strengthen his own hold on the kingdom.

Menahem extracted the silver from his own people, Israel. Then the king of Assyria withdrew from the land.

- **Pekahiah:** Menahem's son, Pekahiah, succeeded his father. He reigned for two years. Pekahiah did evil in the eyes of the Lord because just like the others, he did not turn away from the sins of idol worship at the golden calves. Pekahiah was assassinated by one of his chief officers, Pekah, and fifty men from Gilead.

- **Pekah:** Chief Officer Pekah reigned in his place. Pekah was king of Israel for twenty years. He was evil in the eyes of the Lord because he continued the idol worship instituted by Jeroboam, just like the others did. It was during his reign that the devastation of the Northern tribes began.

THE CONQUERING OF THE NORTHERN NATION OF ISRAEL

During Pekah's reign, Assyria attacked and conquered all of the Northern kingdom of Israel. They took most of the people from their lands and deported them to Assyria, a common way of assimilating a conquered people to your own culture, thus lessening the likelihood of a future fight for the land you've taken and now occupy.

Then a man named Hoshea attacked Pekah and took over as king of Israel.

- **Hoshea:** Hoshea took over in 732 B.C. and reigned for nine years. He was the final king in Israel. While he was king, Hoshea became a vassal to the king of Assyria, to whom he paid tribute year after year until he made the dire decision to stop. Secretly, he decided to send an envoy to the king of Egypt for help. When the king of Assyria found out, he attacked him, put him in jail, and took over the rest of the Northern kingdom of Israel after three years of laying siege to Samaria.

As you can see, there was more political instability during the times of the split kingdom, especially in the North, where they weren't always allied amongst themselves! You can see this political upheaval in the short lengths of reign many of these kings had. The kings in the South generally reigned for longer periods of time.

Why did all of this happen to ten of the twelve tribes of Israel? Because this was God's judgement on them for the sin of breaking the covenant God made with them through Moses and renewed again through Joshua.

And the Assyrians weren't done. To strengthen their hold on Israel's land, they brought people from Babylon and placed them in the cities of Samaria instead of the people of Israel. Pagan strangers now possessed the cities in the land God had promised His people, a land flowing with milk and honey.

What happened to the pagans who were occupying the land? They didn't know the Lord, nor did they fear Him. So, He sent lions among them to kill them. When the king of Assyria heard what was happening, he ordered that one of the priests of Israel be returned to the land to teach the people about the Lord and His Law. One of the priests was returned to live in Bethel, and he taught the people how they should fear the Lord. **Proverbs 9:10** says, *"The fear of the LORD is the beginning of wisdom, and the knowledge of the Holy One is insight."*

How did these new people fare after learning about the Lord? No better than the ones who dwelt there before them. These nations feared the Lord and also served their carved images. Their children did likewise, and their children's children as their fathers did.

This is the story of the kings of the Northern kingdom and the pagans who settled in their land after Israel was exiled to Assyria. Do the kings ruling God's people in the South do any better? As you keep reading, you'll find out.

Chapter 9

KINGS OF THE SOUTHERN KINGDOM OF JUDAH

As we said before, the precipitator of the split nation was Solomon's son, Rehoboam, who wanted to put the people to even harsher labor and burden than his father had, thus causing the ten nations in the North to split off from the other two.

- **Rehoboam:** Rehoboam, king of the Southern nation of Judah, didn't take the split lightly. He assembled 180,000 men at Jerusalem to fight against the North and restore the kingdom. However, the Word of God came to the prophet Shemaiah, who was told:

"Say to Rehoboam the son of Solomon, king of Judah, and to all the house of Judah and Benjamin, and to the rest of the people, 'Thus says the LORD, You shall not go up or fight against your relatives the people of Israel. Every man return to his home, for this thing is from me.' So they listened to the word of the LORD and went home again, according to the word of the LORD" **(1 Kings 12:23-24).**

Although they go home that time, **1 Kings 14:30** tells us, *"There was war between Rehoboam and Jeroboam continually."* In Rehoboam's fifth year of reign, the king of Egypt came against him in Jerusalem and took away the treasures from both the Lord's house and also the king's house. The gold Solomon had hoarded was gone. The splendor of his father's kingdom was not going to be his. Rehoboam began his reign in 930 B.C. and reigned for seventeen years. Rehoboam's rule was followed by his son Abijam's.

- **Abijam:** In the year 913 B.C., Abijam began his reign. He walked in all the sins his father did. Abijam also made war with Jeroboam. He reigned for three years, and then his son, Asa, took the throne.

- **Asa:** King Asa reigned for the next forty-one years over Judah. Asa was a good king, who *"did what was right in the eyes of the LORD, as David his father had done"* **(1 Kings 15:11)**. Asa got rid of the male cult prostitutes and the idols his father had made. His mother was an Asherah worshiper, so Asa cut down her Asherah pole, burned it, and removed her from being the Queen Mother. During his reign, there was war with Israel's king, Baasha, who built up the city of Ramah located just north of Jerusalem. Baasha did this to limit access to Judah, and it was effective. In order to stop Israel from attacking and encroaching on Judah, King Asa took the silver and gold that were left in the temple treasury and the palace and made a treaty with the king of Syria to get him to break his covenant with Israel and attack their Northern cities. And that's exactly what happened. Asa's next move was to conscript Judean laborers to remove the stone and timber from Ramah and use it to fortify their own territory. He left no one exempt from the labor. Then Asa died and was buried in the City of David.

- **Jehoshaphat:** After a few years of co-reigning with his father, Asa's son, Jehoshaphat, ascended to the throne in 872 B.C. Like his father, he, too, was a godly king. He walked in the ways of the Lord and removed the rest of the male prostitutes and idols from the land. Judah was at peace with Israel during his reign. King Jehoshaphat made an alliance with Israel's wicked king Ahaziah, and together, they built a fleet of trading ships to bring gold from Ophir. But they never set sail; they were wrecked at the maritime base where they were located. Jehoshaphat was a good king, who traveled from Beersheba in Judah all the way to the hill country of Ephraim in the North to bring people back to the Lord. As Christians, we could take a lesson from him on that. He appointed righteous judges and charged them to do their work *"in the fear of the LORD, in faithfulness, and with your whole heart"* **(2 Chron. 19:9)**. Jehoshaphat reigned for twenty-five years, co-reigning with his son, Jehoram, for the last five.

- **Jehoram:** By the year 848 B.C., Jehoram had established himself fully on the throne of Judah. Jehoram was thirty–two years old when he became king. From the first few lines of the text regarding Jehoram, we can see that he did not follow in his father's and grandfather's footsteps. If you don't read the text carefully, you might miss the fact that although it's an account of a king from Judah, it's very different from the others. The text about him says, *"And he walked in the way of the kings of Israel"* **(2 Kings 8:18)**. Why does the account of a king from Judah say he walked in the ways of Israel? The next half of the sentence tells us, *"for the daughter of Ahab was his wife."* Jehoram's wife, Athaliah, led him astray because she was the daughter of Ahab and Jezebel, the Baal worshiper. As we said earlier, the wicked Omri dynasty wasn't finished yet. Now one of them was in Judah. If there's one thing all of God's people should know, it's that you don't intermarry with an idol worshipper and that idol-worshipping women had led the men astray many times already throughout Israel's history. Jehoram led Judah for seven years before dying from a terrible intestinal disease. He was followed by his son, Ahazia,

- **Ahazia:** Ahazia reigned for one year. During Ahazia's short reign, he did evil in the sight of the Lord just like his maternal grandfather and grandmother, Ahab and Jezebel. While Ahazia was in the North visiting his wounded uncle, Joram, king of Israel, there was an attempted coupe, and Ahazia, king of Judah, was killed, as well as his uncle.

- **Athaliah:** Ahazia's mother, Athaliah, was wicked and a Baal worshiper, just like her parents were. When she found out that her son was dead, she killed all of the rest of the royal family—her own sons, daughters, and grandchildren—except for Ahazia's son, Joash, also known as Jehoash, who was secretly stolen away and hidden with his nurse by his aunt. He remained hidden in the house of the Lord for six years while Athaliah reigned over Judah. When he was seven years old, Joash's uncle, who was Judah's High Priest, brought him out of hiding surrounded by guards and crowned him king. He sent guards to Athaliah, and they put her to death by the sword.

- **Joash:** Joash was a good king, who served God as long as his uncle was alive. While he was king, he gave instructions to the priests to use money donated to the temple for repairs. The building repair employed carpenters, craftsman, stone cutters, and many others—all trustworthy employees, who *"did not ask for an accounting from the men into whose hand they delivered the money to pay out to the workmen, for they dealt honestly"* **(2 Kings 12:15)**. However, the people were still worshiping in the high places at that time because he didn't remove them; and like many of the other kings before him, instead of trusting the Lord to fight his battles, he paid off the king of Syria to keep Syria from attacking Jerusalem. Joash was assassinated in his bed as revenge for killing his uncle's son, Zechariah. Joash came to power in 835 B.C., and he reigned in Judah for forty years.

- **Amaziah:** Amaziah, son of Joash, came to power in 796 B.C. He was twenty-five years old when he took the throne, and he reigned for twenty-nine years, with his son Azariah as co-regent for all but the first four. Amaziah was a good king, but once again, we see the same words written about him as all the rest of the kings who were good: *"And he did what was right in the eyes of the LORD, yet not like David his father. He did in all things as Joash his father had done. But the high places were not removed; the people still sacrificed and made offerings on the high places"* **(2 Kings 14:3-4)**. After he came to power, he put to death all of the officials who had murdered his father but followed the Law by not putting the children to death; only the ones who had committed the crime died. During his reign, Israel's King Jehoash invaded Jerusalem in Judah and took all of the gold from the temple and the palace. Amaziah went to war against the Edomites and won, but he was ensnared by idolatry after bringing back their idols.

- **Azariah/Uzziah:** Azariah helped his father reign in the South starting in 792 B.C. when he was sixteen, but now had sole reign over Judah. He went by two names, the other being Uzziah. He reigned for fifty-two years and followed God, just as his father had, but didn't remove the high places either. He rebuilt many cities and went to war with the Philistines. He became so powerful that his name was known all the way to Egypt. Although he was a good king and followed the Lord, his pride got the best of him when he tried to make an offering to the Lord on the altar of incense, something that was a priestly duty. He became angry when he was confronted by the priests; and before leaving the temple, the Lord struck him with leprosy, which he had until the day he died. Because of the leprosy, Uzziah lived the rest of his life in a house by himself and was excluded from the temple, dying a lonely man because of his sin. His son, Jotham, took over his duties and co-reigned with him for the last ten years. Then he ascended to the throne in the year 740 B.C.

- **Jotham:** King Jotham reigned a total of sixteen years. He followed God, just as his father and grandfather did, but didn't remove the high places. It was in his day that the Lord sent the king of Syria and Pekah, king of Israel, against him in order to try to force Judah into an alliance against the Assyrians. King Jotham built cities, forts, and towers, as well as strengthened the gates of the temple. **Second Chronicles 27:6** says, *"So Jotham became mighty, because he ordered his ways before the LORD his God."* Then he rested with his fathers and was followed by his son, Ahaz.

- **Ahaz**: Ahaz was twenty years old when he became king of Judah, serving with his father for just a short time. He did not do what was right in the Lord's eyes. *"But he walked in the way of the kings of Israel. He even burned his son as an offering, according to the despicable practices of the nations whom the LORD drove out before the people of Israel. And he sacrificed and made offerings on the high places and on the hills and under every green tree"* **(2 Kings 16:3-4)**. Because of all of this, the Lord sent Pekah, the king of Israel, and the king of Syria against Ahaz, whom they attempt to dethrone because they wanted to put someone from Syria on the throne of Judah to gain strength against Assyria. Their attempt to push Ahaz from the throne failed, but Judah suffered huge losses. We're told in **2 Chronicles 28:8**, *"The men of Israel took captive 200,000 of their relatives, women, sons, and daughters. They also took much spoil from them and brought the spoil to Samaria."* But a prophet of the Lord, whose name was Oded, went out to meet the army and told them to send the captives back to Judah. Heeding Oded's warning, certain chiefs in Israel stood up for their captive brothers and sisters from Judah. They clothed the ones who were naked and gave them sandals, food, and drink. They anointed their wounds, carried the feeble on donkeys, and returned them to the land of Judah. King Ahaz wanted an ally to keep Israel and Syria from attacking again and to help the Philistines, who were taking land away from him on another front. Once again, the silver and gold from the temple and the royal palace were given to a pagan king—this time the king of Assyria—making Judah subject to him. Ahaz did this, despite the fact that Isaiah had prophesied to him that he could rely on the Lord's help against Israel and Syria. Instead of trusting the Lord for total deliverance, he trusted in man! His alliance with the king of Assyria accomplished what he wanted in the short term. They attacked Syria, killed their king, and deported their people, taking Syria out of the fight with Judah just like Ahaz wanted. King Ahaz journeyed to visit the Assyrian king; and while he was there, he saw an impressive altar. He made sketches and plans and sent them back to Uriah the priest in Judah, with instructions to have it built. When he returned, the massive altar was finished, and Ahaz presented offerings on it. Uriah the priest followed the commands of King Ahaz. After that, the king removed many more things from the temple, probably using the bronze to pay more tribute to Assyria.

Not only was Syria out of the picture now, but it's around this time that the Northern kingdom of Israel stopped paying tribute to Assyria. This was the beginning of the destruction of the ten Northern tribes of Israel (as we talked about earlier). Assyria laid siege to Israel, taking most of the people captive and occupying the land of the ten Northern tribes. Both of Judah's enemies to the North were gone, so they thought. For the time being, Judah was still intact, but now Assyria was right on their own doorstep.

- **Hezekiah:** Hezekiah, son of Ahaz, became king of Judah in 716 B.C., co-reigning with his father for some time before. We see something totally different in his description than we've seen with any of the other kings. In **2 Kings 18:3**, it says:

  "And he did what was right in the eyes of the LORD, according to all that David his father had done. He removed the high places and broke the pillars and cut down the Asherah. And he broke in pieces the bronze

serpent that Moses had made, for until those days the people of Israel had made offerings to it (it was called Nehushtan). He trusted in the LORD, the God of Israel, so that there was none like him among all the kings of Judah after him, nor among those who were before him. For he held fast to the Lord. He did not depart from following him, but kept the commandments that the LORD commanded Moses."

Because of his devotion to the Lord, the Lord was with Hezekiah and gave him success in his endeavors. He refused to serve the king of Assyria, and he struck down the Philistines again, taking back land. In the first year of his reign, he repaired the doors of the temple, purified it, and restored proper worship to the Lord. *"And Hezekiah and all the people rejoiced because God had provided for the people, for the thing came about suddenly"* **(2 Chronicles 29:36).** King Hezekiah also instituted the celebration of Passover again. In the book of 2 Chronicles, we're told he even invited the Israelites who were still residing in the North, who were probably left there by Assyria to take care of the lands and herds. It was a great celebration, and a large number of people were there. Hezekiah contributed offerings from his own possessions and encouraged the people to give of theirs, too, which they do! However, in the fourteenth year of his reign, Assyria attacked and captured all of the fortified cities in Judah, prompting King Hezekiah to pay for the withdrawal of their troops. Hezekiah stripped off all the gold of the doors and doorposts that he had just restored to help pay for this. But the king of Assyria wasn't satisfied with the towns he had already conquered and decided to take Jerusalem. Chapters eighteen and nineteen of 2 Kings tell the full story of what took place—the war preparations Hezekiah made, the taunts the enemy used to put fear into the people of Jerusalem, and Hezekiah's encouraging words to them. But what matters most is that King Hezekiah prayed to the Lord for rescue. And the Lord answered him by telling him:

"And this shall be the sign for you: this year eat what grows of itself, and in the second year what springs of the same. Then in the third year sow and reap and plant vineyards, and eat their fruit. And the surviving remnant of the house of Judah shall again take root downward and

bear fruit upward. For out of Jerusalem shall go a remnant, and out of Mount Zion a band of survivors. The zeal of the LORD will do this" **(2 Kings 19:29-31)**.

This is the theme of the whole Bible: God is going to save a remnant, and He's going to do it by His own hand. King Hezekiah was a good king in Judah, but his pride got the best of him. He developed an illness and almost died. He prayed to the Lord for healing and was given a promise and the sign of a "shadow moving backward ten steps" that he would be healed. He was promised fifteen more years of life, something that not much good comes out of. For all the good that there had been so far about Hezekiah, he was about to make a big mistake. At this time in history, Babylon was under Assyrian rule, which they wanted to throw off. When envoys from Babylon showed up on Hezekiah's doorstep, he ended up making an alliance with them against the Assyrians. He did not continue to rely on the Lord for rescue, but instead was counting on help from pagan countries. Isaiah the prophet told him the result of his decision:

"Hear the word of the LORD, 'Behold, the days are coming, when all that is in your house, and that which your fathers have stored up till this day, shall be carried to Babylon. Nothing shall be left, says the LORD. And some of your own sons, who will come from you, whom you will father, shall be taken away, and they shall be eunuchs in the palace of the king of Babylon" **(2 Kings 20:16-18)**.

- **Manasseh:** Hezekiah's son, Manasseh, was twelve years old when he began to reign alongside his father, and he reigned for a total of fifty-five years. However, he was a very wicked king, who followed the evil practices of the nations the Israelites removed from the land. He was considered the most evil of all of Judah's kings. He desecrated the temple with an Asherah pole, erected altars to Baal, shed a huge amount of blood, and led the people astray further by worshiping the sun, the moon, and the stars and practicing divination. He practiced sorcery and witchcraft, consulted mediums and spiritists, and burned his sons as offerings in the fire. And this is what the prophets spoke about him in **2 Kings 21:11-12**:

> *"Because Manasseh king of Judah has committed these abominations and has done things more evil than all that the Amorites did, who were before him, and has made Judah also to sin with his idols, therefore thus says the LORD, the God of Israel: Behold, I am bringing upon Jerusalem and Judah such disaster that the ears of everyone who hears of it will tingle."*

- When it comes to Manasseh, don't miss the fact that as king, he was the peoples' representative. As Robert Rothwell of Ligonier Ministries states: "The king represents the people before God, and thus his fate is shared by his subjects. Manasseh's reign as recorded in Chronicles links the destiny of the king with the destiny of his people. As one of Judah's last kings, Manasseh's wickedness brings the curse of exile even upon David's line. While he is carried into Babylon before the rest of Judah, he is restored to the throne upon his repentance **(2 Chron. 33:1–20)**. God's people will later face the same punishment for their sins, but they will also receive the same restoration."[14]

The Assyrians came, and they captured Manasseh and led him to Babylon in bronze shackles and with a hook in his nose. In his distress, Manasseh prayed to the Lord, and the Lord rescued him and brought him back to Jerusalem. Manasseh's true change of heart is evidenced by the fact that he removed the foreign gods and all the altars he had built from the temple. He restored the proper altars and instituted proper worship, imploring all of Judah to worship the Lord properly like he now did. But the people only half-heartedly listened. They sacrificed to the Lord exclusively, but they still did it at the high places instead of at the temple.

Because the book of the Kings would have been put together for God's people who were in exile over a hundred years later than Manasseh's time, in

---

14 Robert Rothwell, "The Everlasting Kingdom," Ligonier Ministries, accessed April 7, 2019, https://www.ligonier.org/learn/articles/everlasting-kingdom.

the time of its writing, the chronicler was using Manasseh's repentance as a picture for the people who were in exile, telling them that if they repented, they would be saved by the Lord! Manasseh was the most wicked king in Judah, but his sin was no match for God's electing love. Israel's sin wasn't either, and neither is yours. No matter how wickedly we've sinned in our past, if we ask God for forgiveness and turn from our sin, He will forgive us!

- **Amon:** Manasseh's son, Amon, reigned after him. Amon was twenty-two years old when he came to the throne, and he reigned for two years. He did evil in the eyes of the Lord, but unlike his father, he never humbled himself and worshiped God. He was assassinated by his officials in the palace. Then the people of the land killed all who had plotted against him, and they made his son, Josiah, king in his place.

- **Josiah:** Josiah was only eight years old when he came to the throne in 640 B.C. In the eighteenth year of his reign, the High Priest found the Book of the Law and delivered it to the king, who then had it read in his presence. When King Josiah heard the Word of the Lord, he was so distraught that the stipulations of the Law were not being observed that he tore his robes. He had men inquire of the Lord through the prophetess Huldah about Judah's unfaithfulness and the curses promised in the Book of the Law for disobedience. She told them that judgment was coming. King Josiah read the Book of the Law to all the people and made a covenant with the Lord to keep His commandments with all his heart. He ordered the priests to clean the temple of all the idols and destroy them; he took down the high places; he got rid of the mediums and necromancers who tried to speak with the dead; he killed the priests of the high places; he did whatever else was needed to institute proper worship of the Lord; and he rid the land of idol worship and evil. Then the king commanded the people to observe the Passover, calling them to renew their covenant with the Lord.

Nevertheless, the Lord did not turn away from his anger at Judah because of all that Manasseh had done to provoke Him. Judgement was still going to come. **Second Kings 23:26-27** says:

> *Still the LORD did not turn from the burning of his great wrath, by which his anger was kindled against Judah, because of all the provocations with which Manasseh had provoked him. And the LORD said, "I will remove Judah also out of my sight, as I have removed Israel, and I will cast off this city that I have chosen, Jerusalem, and the house of which I said, My name shall be there."*

At this time, Assyria was losing its power in the region. There was a new nation on the rise, and its name was Babylon. While Josiah was king, the king of Egypt went to help Assyria against Babylon. King Josiah marched out to meet him in battle, and the Egyptian king killed Josiah. Then, his son, Jehoahaz, was made king in Judah.

- **Jehoahaz:** Jehoahaz was made king when he was twenty-three years old, and he reigned for three months. He did evil in the eyes of the Lord, and he was taken captive and carried to Egypt, where he died.

- **Eliakim/Jehoiakim:** In 609 B.C., the king of Egypt placed Eliakim, son of Josiah, on the throne and changed his name to Jehoiakim. He reigned in Jerusalem for eleven years and did evil in the eyes of the Lord.

During that time, King Nebuchadnezzar of Babylon defeated the Egyptian king; and in 605 B.C., he invaded Judah for the first of three times, this time making King Jehoiakim his vassal and taking the first captives to exile. The king of Egypt placed a tribute tax on Judah, which King Jehoiakim paid. Things went on this way for three years until Jehoiakim rebelled in 601 B.C. Then the Lord sent Babylonian, Aramean, Moabite, and Ammonite raiders against Judah to destroy it, just as the prophets had told them because of the sins of Manasseh.

- **Jehoiachin:** Jehoiachin, son of Johoiakim, was eighteen when he came to the throne in 598 B.C., and he reigned three months. He did evil in the eyes of the Lord, just like his father.

- In 597 B.C., Nebuchadnezzar, king of Babylon, advanced on Jerusalem and laid siege to it, and the king of Judah and all his officials surrendered to him. King Nebuchadnezzar took all of the treasures from the temple of the Lord as well as from the palace. He took the people of Judah and carried ten thousand of them into exile, leaving only the poorest people in the land to work the fields and vineyards. He took seven thousand fighting men—all the craftsmen and artisans, all of the brightest and best—and exiled them to Babylon. This was the second exile from the Southern tribes. Then King Nebuchadnezzar placed Jehoiachin's uncle, Mattaniah, on the throne of Judah and changed his name to Zedekiah.

- **Mattaniah/Zedekiah:** He reigned in Jerusalem eleven years and did what was evil in the eyes of the Lord. In his ninth year of reign, in 588 B.C., Zedekiah rebelled against the king of Babylon. So, Babylon marched against Jerusalem, surrounded it, and besieged it for two years until the famine in the city became so severe, there was no food for the people to eat. King Zedekiah and his sons escaped, only to be captured by the Babylonian troops, who killed his sons while he watched and then put his eyes out and took him to Babylon.

- Nebuchadnezzar destroyed Jerusalem. He burned the temple, the palace, the houses, and every important building in the city. He carried into exile any who were remaining in the city and took all of the bronze from the temple and carried it away, too. Then he appointed a well-known native named Gedaliah as governor over the area. In his seventh month as governor, a man of royal blood came with ten men and assassinated Gedaliah.

By 586 B.C. the monarchy was over; Jerusalem was destroyed; most of the people of Judah were exiled in Babylon; and the rest were either working the land for the Babylonians or hiding in Egypt, the land of their ancestors' exile, also under the control of Babylon. Judgment had come to the rest of God's people. Many of the exiles never saw their homeland again. The remnant wouldn't come back to the land for seventy years—a lifetime or more in that day and age.

In **2 Samuel 22:2-4**, King David wrote these words in a song, *"The LORD is my rock and my fortress and my deliverer, my God, my rock, in whom I take refuge, my shield, and the horn of my salvation, my stronghold and my refuge, my savior; you save me from violence. I call upon the LORD, who is worthy to be praised, and I am saved from my enemies."* David knew God's saving love, despite how sinful he was. He knew that his own righteousness was not what saved him. He knew no outsider and no other god could save him. He knew it was faith in God alone that had saving power.

As we saw in the lives of the idolatrous kings, God wants our whole-hearted devotion to Him. He wants to be more precious to us than anything else in our lives, more precious than our families, our money, or our health. He wants to be the sole Receiver of our worship! He wants to be the main focus, and He should be. After all, if we're His, He's saved us from all our enemies!

1 AND 2 CHRONICLES

The books of 1 and 2 Chronicles were written to the post-exilic community; and like the books of Samuel and Kings, it is looking at the past, pre-exile times but with an emphasis on some specific things. At this point in history, the writer was trying to encourage the people *coming back from exile*. The focus of the chronicler was on the Southern tribes of Judah and Benjamin as well as the tribe of Levi. This was because the Righteous King they (and we all) needed was King Jesus, Who came from the line of Judah through David. There was also a focus on the temple and worship of the Lord because this was the time after exile when the remnant was coming back to Jerusalem to re-build the temple.

Likewise, the tribe of the Levites is emphasized in the book because they were in charge of worship. There are lots of parallels with the books of Samuel and Kings, and there are lots of details given in Chronicles that are not seen before. If you ever want to study any of Judah's kings, you should make sure to look for their history in Chronicles, too, not just the other books!

The writer starts out with a genealogy, making sure that those who had come back from exile saw that they were part of God's divinely-ordained past—all the way back to the creation of the world. Next, he moves on to point out the failings of King Saul, namely that he took his own life, and goes on to say, *"So Saul died for his breach of faith. He broke faith with the LORD in that he did not keep the command of the LORD, and also consulted a medium, seeking guidance"* **(1 Chron. 10:13)**, ending this way to show King Saul's failings in order to introduce the greatness of King David by way of contrast.[15]

The next several chapters give accounts of the life of King David, including God's promise to David that he would always have a descendant on the throne; it gives some of his victories, a Psalm of thanksgiving that he wrote, as well as his preparations for building the temple.

Then the focus switched to the Levites and the division of their duties in the temple, followed by David's plans for the temple, more of his prayers to God, and the crowning of Solomon as King. The book of 1 Chronicles ends with David's death.

---

15   Gordon D. Fee and Douglas K. Stuart, *How to Read the Bible Book by Book a Guided Tour* (Grand Rapids: Zondervan, 2002).

After a few chapters about Solomon, his reign, the dedication of the temple, and his death, the focus is on the remaining kings of Judah's monarchy, with sections on each king of Judah's reign. The people are reminded that there is blessing when the king does what is right in the eyes of the Lord and cursing when the king does not follow the Lord's ways. The chronicler points out that it was the Lord who split the monarchy, but that the Northern tribes should come and worship in Jerusalem, with emphasis that proper worship is done only at the temple in Jerusalem. Like we said, the temple rebuilding is of utmost importance!

The last chapter contains the story of the fall of Jerusalem and ends with the decree of King Cyrus of Persia to have the people return from exile and rebuild the temple.

Chapter 10

THE POETRY BOOKS

PSALMS

We end this section with the poetry books, beginning with the book of Psalms. The book of Psalms has many authors. They were Moses, David, Solomon, the sons of Korah, the sons of Asaph, Ethan the Ezrahite, and several unknown authors. They were written to be sung. The Psalms are an excellent springboard for our prayer life.

There are 150 psalms, of which about seventy are laments. A lament is a type of psalm that's a prayer to God in times of trial. They were asking the Lord for relief, rescue, or help of some nature, confident that the Lord would provide deliverance according to His will. Psalms 5, 64, and 102 are examples of lament Psalms.

There are psalms of thanksgiving. They begin with an invitation to start praising, then an explanation of why they're praising (because they've been delivered out of misery), followed by a description of the misery and details of the rescue. Similar, but not the same, are the psalms that fall into the category of hymns. They also have a call to praise. Psalms 95, 100, and 147 fit into this category.

There are several other types of psalms, such as wisdom psalms, trust psalms, and Messianic psalms, which are psalms that are talking about Jesus, such as this psalm written by David: *"The LORD says to my LORD: 'Sit at my right hand, until I make your enemies your footstool'"* **(Psalm 110:1)**.

The Psalms are a collection of songs that were, and still are, sung by God's people, giving the Lord the praise He deserves and giving the people reminders of God's faithfulness, love, and constant care.

PROVERBS

The book of Proverbs is full of all kinds of every-day wisdom for living. They were written by Solomon, Hezekiah, Agur, Lemuel, and some other anonymous authors. Although they are suited for every age, their purpose was to provide a resource for teaching wisdom to the young men from the families of Israel. It is still a great resource for teaching to youth today!

The proverbs were compiled over 150 years between Solomon and Hezekiah, and some of them are from two Arab kings, Lemuel and Agur, whose proverbs Solomon most likely added to his own collection. No matter who wrote them, the collection was put together under Divine inspiration! The collection includes warnings, advice on choosing a spouse, sexual purity, and useful, every-day advice of many kinds. They're written in an easy-to-memorize format.

The proverbs are like puzzles; they are not intended to be simple. The meaning of them is not always evident right away. However, most adults can figure out what they mean without much problem! One example is **Proverbs 22:3**, *"The prudent sees danger and hides himself, but the simple go on and suffer for it."* This proverb is talking about the prudent man, one who is careful about his behavior, so he stays away from sin. He hides from it, avoiding places where sin is tempting. But the simple man goes headlong into everything and anything he pleases. In the end, he will suffer, possibly both in this life and for eternity.

Although they may sound like it, the proverbs are not a collection of absolute promises saying, "If you do this, then the result will be that." In fact, the whole book is centered around the fact that to gain the wisdom of the proverbs, you must begin with having a "fear of the Lord." What does it mean to fear God? It means to know Him by being one of His people.

As we've said before, the whole Old Testament points us to Jesus, and the book of Proverbs does also. Jesus is the perfect Wise Son of Proverbs, and the book ends with a description of the ideal bride for a king. Many believe these last verses of Proverbs are a picture of what the perfected, sanctified Church—the Bride of Christ—will look like some day.

ECCLESIASTES

The book of Ecclesiastes was most likely written by Solomon. It was written from the point of view of an existentialist. In other words, from someone who had the view that there is no God and that this life is all that there is. Its purpose is to demonstrate that life viewed from merely a humanistic view can only result in pessimism. Without God, life is meaningless. Without God, nothing matters after death; therefore, nothing good or evil that you do will matter.

Ecclesiastes is a philosophical approach to the condition of all humanity. Like Job, it deals with the difficulty that comes when we can't understand what God is doing and what our response should be in all circumstances, which is always "fear God and obey His commandments," trusting Him in all situations. At the end of the day, after examining all of these different aspects of life, the writer comes to this conclusion: *"The end of the matter; all has been heard. Fear God and keep his commandments, for this is the whole duty of man. For God will bring every deed into judgment, with every secret thing, whether good or evil"* **(Eccl. 12:13-14)**.

THE SONG OF SOLOMON

Traditionally, Solomon has been credited with writing the book of The Song of Solomon. However, we're not sure of this, but it's possible he did. The purpose of the book is to celebrate romantic, exclusive love between husbands and wives! The love story is told using mainly three "voices": the male shepherd, the Shulamite girl, and her friends. It is written in the form of poetry and includes a lot of imagery. **The Song of Solomon 7:1-9** will give you a taste of what the book is like:

> *How beautiful are your feet in sandals, O noble daughter! Your rounded thighs are like jewels, the work of a master hand. Your navel is a rounded bowl that never lacks mixed wine. Your belly is a heap of wheat, encircled with lilies. Your two breasts are like two fawns, twins of a gazelle. Your neck is like an ivory tower. Your eyes are pools in Heshbon, by the gate of Bath-rabbim. Your nose is like a tower of Lebanon, which looks toward Damascus. Your head crowns you like Carmel, and your flowing locks are like purple; a king is held captive in the tresses. How beautiful and pleasant you are, O loved one, with all your delights! Your stature is like a palm tree, and your breasts are like its clusters. I say I will climb the palm tree and lay hold of its fruit. Oh may your breasts be like clusters of the vine, and the scent of your breath like apples, and your mouth like the best wine.*

Some people believe the Song of Solomon can be looked at as a picture of God and His covenant people or Christ and the Church, which He refers to as His "bride." However, it is not just an allegory for that. Using similar language to that of Proverbs, this book is clearly celebrating sexual love that God created and established to be enjoyed within the confines of marriage between one man and one woman.

PART 4

THE PROPHETS

EZRA, NEHEMIAH, ESTHER, ISAIAH THROUGH MALACHI, AND THE TIME BETWEEN THE TESTAMENTS

We hope all those kings didn't make your brain hurt! If they did, Part 4 will probably not help it any! In this section, we will cover all of the prophetic books as well as Ezra, Nehemiah, and Esther. These latter three books are not of the prophetic genre; they are historical. However, they take place during the time of the post-exilic prophets, so they fit in nicely. Rather than go through the books in the order they appear in the Bible, we will go through them in chronological order. This will give us a timeline of where they fall in history, under which kings they served, and which of the prophets were contemporaries.

The books of the prophets are probably the least read and least understood of all of the books in the Bible. Their puzzling language, mysterious visions, and complex symbolism can sometimes lead to erroneous interpretations, which can leave the reader baffled, terrified, or both! Our goal in this chapter is to present a foundation for each of the books, ignite a hunger for the prophetic genre, and give you confidence to read them fully for yourself to discover all the rich theology contained in them! We will address the main message and themes of each book and flesh out some of the more confusing language, visions, and symbols.

The Bible contains five major prophetic books—Isaiah, Jeremiah, Lamentations, Ezekiel, and Daniel—and twelve minor prophetic books—Hosea, Joel, Amos, Obadiah, Jonah, Micah, Nahum, Habakkuk, Zephaniah, Haggai, Zechariah, and Malachi. The only distinction between a major and minor prophet is in the length of the message they received.

Before we look at each individual prophet, it will help to get a general understanding of prophets and prophecy. The definition of a prophet is *"one who utters divinely inspired revelations."*[16] Also called seers, watchmen, men of God, messengers, or servants of the Lord, prophets were men, and sometimes women, who literally spoke *for* God. They were divinely chosen to relay God's messages to His people. These messages were sometimes reinforced by a vision given to them by God (e.g. Daniel and Ezekiel). True prophets never spoke on their own authority or gave their own opinions; they only gave the message given to them by God. Think of it as the prophets taking dictation from God and reading it back to the people. This is a unique distinction with the prophetic books. While all of the books of the Bible are divinely inspired, in most of them, the Holy Spirit has allowed the author's own writing style to come through. For example, Paul's epistles are letters written by Paul. The messages are God's messages, but the writing style and format is all Paul. The prophets, by contrast, wrote verbatim what was told to them by God.

Peter confirms this in **2 Peter 1:20b-21**: *"No prophecy of Scripture comes from someone's own interpretation. For no prophecy was ever produced by the will of man, but men spoke from God as they were carried along by the Holy Spirit."* Anything that was not a direct revelation from God was considered false prophecy and was punishable by death. Sadly, this did not stop false prophets

---

16   *Merriam-Webster*, s.v. "Prophet" accessed February 22, 2019, https://www.merriam-webster.com/dictionary/prophet.

from pedaling their untruthful messages. (We will take a deeper look at this when we get to Jeremiah).

Speaking only what they were told by God was crucial for the prophets because of the opposition they often faced. Frequently, their message was one of coming judgment and punishment and, therefore, was not welcomed by many. Because they only spoke exactly what God directed them to, they could stand strong in the face of persecution, knowing it was God's Words the people were angry at, not their own.

There are some that think the books of the prophets are full of new and mysterious revelation meant for us today. They try to fit current events into the prophets' visions and messages. We will go into this deeper in the last chapter when we look at the book of Revelation. But for now, while it is true that a small percentage of prophecy in the Bible is about still-future events, the vast majority of the messages in the books of the prophets in the Old Testament come directly from the Pentateuch (the first five books of the Bible). The prophets were saying things in a new way, but, for the most part, they were not saying anything new. God was just reinforcing through them what the Israelites had already been told through Moses. You will see the concepts of Mosaic Law throughout all of the prophetic books, even without direct quotes. Just to give you an example, none of the prophets quote the commandment, *"You shall have no other gods before me"* **(Exod. 20:3)**; however, you will see many of them telling the Israelites they have broken the covenant with God by prostituting themselves to false gods. The concept of the commandment is there, even without direct citation of it.

As we've said, there is a small percentage of biblical prophecy that does deal with still future events, and we will look at those; but for the most part, the prophets were "covenant enforcement mediators."[17] Even though they sometimes prophesied *about* Israel's and Judah's enemies—except for

---

17   Dr. Douglas Stuart, "Lecture 23: Prophetical Books," BiblicalTraining.org, accessed March 07, 2019, https://www.biblicaltraining.org/prophetical-books/old-testament-survey-0.

Jonah—they were always prophesying *to* Israel and/or Judah. Their message was that under the covenant God had made with them, there were blessings for obedience and curses for disobedience. They told God's people that although God is patient and merciful, He would not contend with their disobedience forever. The time was coming when He would enforce the curses for their continued unfaithfulness. To help reinforce this, the prophets often used what is called in Hebrew a "rib formula" (pronounced "reeve"), meaning "lawsuit" or "law case."[18] The prophet would narrate an imagined scenario in which God was a Prosecutor Who has put the defendant, Israel, on trial for the crime of breaking the covenant. God presents the evidence against Israel, thereby proving their guilt. One difference in this court case from ordinary court cases, though, is that God was not only the Prosecutor, but the Judge and Jury as well! In other words, the Israelites didn't stand a chance!

One last thing to look for as you read through the books of the prophets is to notice the way in which they are arranged. Overwhelmingly, God gave the prophets their messages in the format of "blessings, curses, blessings." The prophet first recounted the blessings that God's people once enjoyed, then told them of the coming judgment for their disobedience, and finally, ended with a message of hope, looking forward to a future time when God would not only restore His people but also bless them beyond anything they could imagine. These, of course, are the prophecies that point to Jesus.

We have twenty books to cover! Grab some caffeine, and let's dig in!

---

18   Ibid.

Chapter 11

PRE-EXILIC

In this chapter, we will cover the prophets whose ministry begins before the nations of Israel and Judah were overthrown by Assyrian and Babylon, respectively.

OBADIAH

The little book of Obadiah has no known date, and scholars are split on its date. We are using the earlier date of 853 B.C., which makes it chronologically first in our journey through the prophets. While many of the prophets have messages against foreign nations in their books, only Obadiah's—and as we will see later, Nahum's—*entire* message is a prophecy against a foreign nation. For Obadiah, that nation was Edom. While Israel and Judah were descendants of Jacob, the Edomites were descendants of Esau, Jacob's twin brother. You may remember the enmity between these two brothers from Genesis. That enmity was passed down through the generations. Although a tiny nation, Edom proved to be Israel's worst enemy. Obadiah gave the people of Judah and Israel hope that God had not forgotten all that Edom had done to His people. They would pay for their sins. God's plan for the Edomites can be summed up in **Obadiah 1:15b**: *"As you have done, it shall be done to you; your deeds shall return on your own head."* Looking back through secular history, the nation of Edom was oppressed by many enemies and was eventually decimated.

JOEL

Like the Book of Obadiah, there is disagreement on when Joel received his prophecy from the Lord. Some date Joel's book after Judah's exile to Babylon around 586 B.C., while others place it 250 years earlier, around 835 B.C. As with Obadiah, we will use the earlier date of 835 B.C., during the reigns of Jehu in Israel and Joash in Judah.

The book of Joel is best known for its depiction of a locust plague. Scholars are split on this as well. Some believe the locust plague is a metaphorical plague that symbolized the invasion of Judah by Babylon. Others believe the plague is an actual locust plague; and still others think the plague is both literal and metaphorical. Whether metaphorical, literal, or both, Joel gives a dark picture to the people, telling them that this locust plague would be unlike anything that had ever happened. Joel described the locusts coming in successive hordes and covering the land. The hordes arrived first—eating, then swarming, then hopping, and finally destroying everything in the entire land. Judah experienced famine, drought, and financial ruin because of these locusts. This plague was so extraordinary and so devastating that Joel told the people in **Joel 1:3**, *"Tell your children of it, and let your children tell their children, and their children to another generation."*

What could be worse than being told you are about to experience a catastrophic event like this? Being told that it is being sent to you by God as punishment for sin! Joel told the people they needed to put on sackcloth (a sign of grieving), repent, and cry out to the Lord because things were going to be as bad as they could possibly be.

Chapter two begins with the second major theme of the book—the Day of the Lord. "The day of the Lord" is a phrase that is used by several of the prophets. What does it mean? It is the day that the Lord will appear and fight the ultimate battle forever, defeating evil and sin. It is a foreshadowing of the Second Coming of Jesus. Although Jesus did completely defeat evil and sin on the cross, the final culmination of His victory will come at His Second

Coming. If you are a believer, this is a glorious day to look forward to. If, however, you are not one of God's elect, this will be the most dreadful of days because along with defeating evil, God will also eternally punish all of His enemies (i.e. anyone not belonging to Him). Joel told the people in **Joel 2:11b**, *"For the day of the LORD is great and very awesome; who can endure it?"* Joel then answered his own question in verse **2:32**, *"And it shall come to pass that everyone who calls on the name of the LORD shall be saved."* In other words, all who are following God will not only be able to endure it but will be saved. In light of this, Joel urged the people to repent of their sin and turn back to the Lord, so they did not find themselves on the wrong side of God. Besides being used by other prophets in the Old Testament, the "day of the Lord" is also used in the New Testament by Paul and John, sometimes referred to as "the day of wrath."

Joel is one of the prophets who uses the "blessings, curses, blessings" format. The day of the Lord is certainly a future blessing for God's people, but God gives them even more reason for hope. The Lord told the people that He would pour out His Spirit on them. He said in **2:28**, *"And it shall come to pass afterward, that I will pour out my Spirit on all flesh."* This is a foretelling of Pentecost when God sent the Holy Spirit to indwell believers. Peter even quoted the book of Joel in his sermon at Pentecost in Acts 2:16-21.

Another part of the future blessings is that the Lord will judge and punish the nations who have oppressed and persecuted the people of God. This recurs in many of the prophetic books, so let's look at this further now. Even though it was God Who raised up and strengthened certain pagan nations to overtake Israel and Judah as punishment for their unfaithfulness, that did not excuse the actions of those oppressing Israel and Judah. Those nations were still accountable to God for their sinful actions and would be judged for them. God gave Assyria, Babylon, and other nations the means to sin against Israel and Judah, but the nations acted on it, which made them responsible. It may make your head spin a little, but we need to remember that while God works through sin for His purposes, He never forces people to sin. He doesn't have to! Given an opportunity, humans, especially non-believers, will chose to sin on their own, which makes them responsible for that sin. For those who have not placed their faith and trust in Jesus and His saving work, sin brings judgment and eternal punishment.

AMOS

Fast forwarding roughly seventy years to 766 B.C., we come to Amos, a sheep breeder and fig cultivator in Judah. A contemporary of Jonah and Hosea, Amos' agricultural business sometimes took him across the border, north to the nation of Israel. God used this as an opportunity for Amos to prophesy to the Northern nation.

While most of the book contains many oracles and visions of curses on the nation of Israel, it doesn't start out that way. Amos began by telling Israel that God would bring judgement against the neighboring pagan nations. He started with a message against Damascus, representing the nation of Syria. **Amos 1:3** says, *"Thus says the Lord: 'For three transgressions of Damascus, and for four, I will not revoke the punishment.'"* This odd phrase preceded each of the judgements Amos pronounced. It sounds puzzling, but it is not meant to be taken literally. It does not mean that the nation mentioned committed three or four sins. Instead, it means that the nation had continued to commit sin after sin after sin. Because of that, God would punish the nation. Syria's multitude of sins included their cruel destruction and torture of the Israelites during the Syrian War. For this, they would be annihilated.

Next, Amos had messages regarding Gaza (representing the nation of Philistia), Phoenicia (represented by its capital Tyre), Edom, Ammon, and Moab. All of these nations would be paid back for sins they committed against God's people. Although the curse for each nation varied, all would be plagued with some form of destruction. In some cases, there would be total decimation of the entire nation just as it was with Syria.

You can imagine the Israelites were pretty pumped to hear what God had planned for their enemies. Things got even better for them when Amos turned his attention to the Southern nation of Judah. Using the same phrase, *"'For three transgressions of Judah, and for four, I will not revoke the punishment'"* **(Amos 2:4)**, Amos told the Israelites that Judah's stronghold of Jerusalem would be destroyed. This is a foreshadowing of the Babylonian conquest of the Southern nation. Jerusalem was the capital of Judah; and like with pagan nations, Amos used the capital to represent the whole nation.

God was going to punish Israel's enemies and Judah?! If you were from the Northern nation, did it get any better? You can almost picture the Israelites cheering and high-fiving each other. Maybe they shouldn't celebrate just yet. Amos pronounced the next message from God—a judgement on Israel. Again, Amos started with the now-familiar phrase from 1:3. This is significant because God used the same phrase for Judah and Israel as He did for the pagan nations. In other words, because they had broken the covenant, Judah and Israel were no better than the pagan nations. Like those other nations, Judah and Israel were enemies of God and deserving of God's wrath. To make matters worse for Israel, the judgement against them was the longest of all! Through Amos, God used oracles and visions of locusts, fire, a wall, a basket of fruit, and an altar to show Israel that they were doomed and would be conquered by the Assyrians. **Amos 9:9** sums up the punishment of Israel: *"For behold, I will command, and shake the house of Israel among all the nations as one shakes with a sieve, but no pebble shall fall to the earth."*

God, ever gracious and merciful, did not leave His people in condemnation. Amos finished his book with restoration promises. God told Israel that a day was coming when He would restore His people to the Promised Land and restore their fortunes to them. While God's people were allowed to return to and rebuild Jerusalem after their captivity ended, God had a much grander Promised Land in mind here. He was foreshadowing Heaven!

JONAH

Jonah is one of the most familiar books of the prophets. Many of us probably have Sunday School memories of flannel boards depicting a little, bald Jonah sitting in the belly of a whale. The book of Jonah is unique in that it is not about the messages received by a prophet; it is a narrative about a prophet, a retelling of a significant event in the life of that prophet. Jonah is a great story, but it is also filled with some amazing truths!

The year 760 B.C. was a peaceful and prosperous time in the Northern nation of Israel. In that year, God told Jonah to go and preach repentance to the people of Nineveh. Nineveh was the capital of Assyria. If that nation sounds familiar, it should! Assyria was the nation that conquered Israel in 722 B.C., destroying the land and sending many of the Israelites into exile. Even forty years prior in 760 B.C., though, Assyria was an enemy of Israel–a hated enemy! God wanted Jonah to go and evangelize to his enemies.

Jonah always gets a bad rap for refusing to show compassion on the Ninevites, but imagine if God came to you today and told you to go to Iraq and preach to Isis to repent of their sins! Not only would you be afraid for your life, but you may also hesitate because you don't want them to be saved. In light of all of the evil they have done and all of the people they have killed, part of you may not want God to give them a chance to repent and be forgiven! This was the predicament Jonah was in. This doesn't excuse Jonah (nor would it excuse us!) for being disobedient, but it does help us see it wasn't an easy thing he was being asked to do.

Jonah tried getting out of going to Nineveh by running away from God and hiding aboard a ship (like the Creator of the universe couldn't find him on a ship!). God sent a great wind to toss the ship about. The sailors, rightly surmising that the storm was a result of God being angry at someone, drew lots to see who it was. The lot fell to Jonah. Jonah instructed the sailors to throw him overboard so their troubles would cease. Upon entering the water, Jonah was swallowed by a great fish (not necessarily a whale).

During his three days in the fish's belly, Jonah prayed a Thanksgiving Psalm thanking God for not letting him die after he was thrown from the ship. God answered Jonah's prayer by making the fish vomit him out onto dry land.

Convicted, and probably covered in fish vomit, Jonah went to Nineveh and preached to the city that they would be overthrown unless the people repented of their sins against Yahweh. Every person in Nineveh, even the king, responded by fasting, putting on sackcloth, and repenting. The king even ordered that all of the animals be clothed in sackcloth and fast! Nineveh did not become devoted followers of the Lord, but they did recognize Yahweh as the most powerful of all gods. When God saw their response, He forgave Nineveh, and they were not overthrown.

Although Jonah did what God asked, he wasn't happy about it. He said to God in **Jonah 4:2b-3**, *"For I knew that you are a gracious God and merciful, slow to anger and abounding in steadfast love, and relenting from disaster. Therefore now, O LORD, please take my life from me, for it is better for me to die than to live."* Jonah would rather die than see the Ninevites repent and God be merciful to them. In an object lesson, God had a lush vine grow over Jonah to give him shade as Jonah waited to see what became of Nineveh. While Jonah was enjoying the cool shade, God sent a worm to eat it, leaving Jonah sitting in the scorching sun. When Jonah got angry about the disappearing vine, God said to him in **Jonah 4:10-11**, *"'You pity the plant, for which you did not labor, nor did you make it grow, which came into being in a night and perished in a night. And should not I pity Nineveh, that great city, in which there are more than 120,000 persons who do not know their right hand from their left?"*

There are several things going on in the book of Jonah. First, can anyone ever run away from God? Of course not! Jonah obviously thought he could. This shows his theology was seriously flawed. This, in turn, shows that God doesn't necessarily wait for us to get our theology right to use us. Sometimes, He gives us on-the-job training! Second, the book shows God's almighty power over all creation—the weather, animal life, and plant life. God used His control over all three of these to work out His plan for Jonah and for Nineveh. Lastly, while later on, God destroyed Nineveh, along with the entire nation of Assyria, at this particular time in history, it suited His purpose to have mercy on them and keep them from being overthrown. As **Exodus 33:19b** says, *"I will be gracious to whom I will be gracious and will show mercy on whom I will show mercy."* God is God! He has the right and prerogative to show mercy or not to show mercy at any given time. He was not granting the people of Nineveh salvation; He was showing them common grace. Common grace is the mercy and blessing God bestows on non-believers as He wishes.

HOSEA

From an object lesson to a metaphor. The book of Hosea is fascinating to read as it is one long metaphor. Hosea, who is both from Israel and prophesying to Israel, first received the Word of God around 753 B.C. Unlike Amos and Jonah, Hosea's time as a prophet extended over forty years, during which the Northern nation of Israel was taken captive by Assyria.

God's first words to Hosea are a little shocking. **Hosea 1:2** says, *"'Go, take to yourself a wife of whoredom and have children of whoredom, for the land commits great whoredom by forsaking the Lord.'"* Many have thought that God forced Hosea to marry a prostitute. This is not the case. God used Hosea's family situation as a backdrop for the situation in Israel. Hosea's wife may have been unfaithful to him, but it's also possible that she was unfaithful to God, like so many of the other Israelites. God used Hosea as a metaphor for Himself. The pattern of Hosea's relationship with his wife is marriage, unfaithfulness, divorce, and restoration. This, too, is the pattern of God's relationship with Israel.

When God chose Israel, she became His bride. There was a marriage, so to speak. Now, though, God had become the longsuffering husband whose bride has been unfaithful prostituting herself with false gods. Prostitution and other sexual sins are often used as a metaphor for idol worship. Just as Hosea's bride's unfaithfulness caused Hosea pain, so, too, God's bride's unfaithfulness caused Him pain. God used metaphorical names for Hosea's children, like No Mercy and Not My People, which reflected how God would deal with Israel.

Remember, prophets speak exactly what is told to them by God. God used some pretty graphic language in His message to Israel. We see just a sample of it in **Hosea 2:2-3**: *"'Plead with your mother, plead—for she is not my wife, and I am not her husband—that she put away her whoring from her face, and her adultery from between her breasts; lest I strip her naked and make her as in the day she was born, and make her like a wilderness, and make her like a parched land, and kill her with thirst.'"* The Northern nation of Israel is the mother, and the faithful of Israel were told to plead with the rest of the nation to repent because God was going to "divorce" Israel by withdrawing His presence and raising up an enemy to conquer her.

Intermixed within this metaphor, we see Hosea using the "rib formula." If you remember, that is when God used a court hearing as an illustration of accusation and guilt. Here, the nation of Judah was added as a co-defendant with the nation of Israel. The verdict for both was destruction.

God did not permanently "divorce" His bride. Just as Hosea was told to redeem his wife and restore their relationship, God, too, would restore His bride to Himself. God said in **Hosea 14:4**, *"I will heal their apostasy; I will love them freely, for my anger has turned from them."* The greater blessings God promised were the blessings that will come from Jesus—blessings that will last for all eternity! Israel as God's Bride transcends into the New Testament as the Church being Christ's Bride.

ISAIAH

We now come to the most complex book of all the prophets, the book of Isaiah. While part of Isaiah's complexity is just from the sheer amount of narrative the book contains, part of it is also due to apocalyptic language Isaiah used when telling of future events. Getting a foundation on apocalyptic literature will help relieve some of the complexity. *Apocalyptic* can be defined as "forecasting the ultimate destiny of the world" or "ultimately decisive."[19] Many have twisted apocalyptic language in the Bible to create books and movies with some far-fetched, ridiculous predictions about the future of the world. But that is science fiction, not reality. Apocalyptic literature was used in biblical times to give hope to those being oppressed.

Remember, God was the One giving exact messages to the prophets and divinely inspiring the other biblical authors. No one was making any predictions of their own. Instead, they were relaying God's plan for the world and for His people, which was decided on by the Trinity before Creation. Therefore, the "ultimate destiny of the earth" is certain and is clearly revealed in Scripture. Christ will come again and bring to completion the victory He won on the cross and at His resurrection. He will gather His people to Him, judge and damn those that aren't His, and put an end to Satan, sin, and death.

Isaiah 1:18b gives us a picture of what Jesus' victory looks like for believers: *"Though your sins are like scarlet, they shall be as 'white as snow.'"* But **Isaiah 1:28** shows us the destiny of unbelievers, *"But rebels and sinners shall be broken together, and those who forsake the LORD shall be consumed."* It helps when reading apocalyptic language in the Bible to know that this is what all prophecy that is still in the future is pointing to. And while it's true that some of the apocalyptic language in the prophetic books and Revelation is mysterious, the vast majority can be interpreted by doing thorough biblical exegesis (study of Scripture). When interpreted correctly, we see that many of the "future events" biblical authors speak of were in the future to the original listeners but are in the past for us. For the prophecies that are still future to us, we can rest in knowing we already know how it all ends, that the future

---

19　*Merrian-Webster*, s.v. "Apocalyptic," accessed March 30, 2019, www.merriam-webster.com/dictionary/apocalyptic.

is "ultimately decided" because the Creator and Master of the universe, Who is unchangeable, has said it is so!

It would take a lengthy, in-depth study to unpack all that is in the book of Isaiah. There is no way to do a book like this justice in just a summary. However, we will touch on some of the important parts, look at the events that *are* still future to us, and hopefully, whet your appetite enough to want to pursue an in-depth study!

We aren't sure how long Isaiah's ministry lasted, but we know that it began around 739 B.C. Containing prophesies for both Israel and Judah, the book has two overall overarching themes: God's sovereignty, holiness, righteousness, and majesty and God's redemptive love for His people. Isaiah is written in the bifid structure, meaning it has two parts. Chapters one through thirty-nine are about the Southern nation of Judah—first, during the threat of being conquered from the nation of Assyria (which God allowed Judah to escape) and then about being conquered by Babylon (which they did not escape). Chapters forty through sixty-six are prophecies about the future of both the nations of Israel and Judah. The prophecies range from the end of the Babylonian exile of Judah to events still future to us.

Parts of Isaiah are similar to other prophetic books. Isaiah confronted Israel and Judah with their wickedness and unfaithfulness to God; he spoke of "the day of the Lord"; he told the people God would not contend with their sin forever and that they would be punished by being conquered by Assyria and Babylon; he prophesied against foreign nations who had sinned against God's people; and he gave the people encouragement, telling of a future time when God would restore His people and give them greater blessings than ever before. Since these things are looked at in detail in some of the other books, we will only look at some of the passages that are unique to the book of Isaiah.

The first one we will take a look at is found in Isaiah 20. God sometimes had His prophets do some pretty bizarre things to drive His message home to the people. We've already seen this with Jonah and Hosea, and now we see it with Isaiah. As a way of illustrating the coming judgement on the nation of Egypt, God told Isaiah in **Isaiah 20:2b**, *"'Go, and loose the sackcloth from your waist and take off your sandals from your feet,' and he did so, walking naked and barefoot."* Before you are too horrified, we should point out that Isaiah was not completely naked. He walked around in what is comparable to underwear, but he did this for three years! The message God was trying to convey was the complete degradation and humiliation Egypt would experience at the hands of the Assyrians as retribution for how they treated God's people.

Using apocalyptic language, the next passage, found in chapters twenty-four through twenty-seven is one of the passages that speaks of still-future events for us. We encourage you to read it in its entirety, but here are a few verses from it:

> *Therefore a curse devours the earth, and its inhabitants suffer for their guilt; therefore the inhabitants of the earth are scorched, and few men are left . . . They lift up their voices, they sing for joy; over the majesty of the LORD, they shout from the west . . . The earth staggers like a drunken man; it sways like a hut; its transgression lies heavy upon it, and it falls, and will not rise again* **(Isa. 24:6, 14, 20)**.

These chapters have been called *the little apocalypse*. It may be hard to see from just these selected verses, but these chapters tell of God's final judgement against His enemies and His final judgement for His people. Both will occur simultaneously at Jesus' Second Coming. God's final judgment will be as much *for* His people as it is *against* sin, Satan, and death. The last part of 24:6—*"Few men are left"*—indicates that God's elect will be few compared to the non-elect. (Isaiah 10:22 and Romans 9:27 are two other passages that also confirm this.) God's people will lift their voices in joy seeing that the Lord is setting all things right. But for the enemies of God—including unbelievers, Satan, and his demonic minions—they will fall into eternal punishment, never to rise again. If this picture makes you shutter for the non-believing world, good! This passage, and so many like it, should be the catalyst for us witnessing and preaching the Gospel!

We could go on and on quoting many amazing passages, promises, and foreshadowing in this book! However, we have room for only a few more, so let's look at the ones that emphasize the themes in the book. The first underscores the theme of God's sovereignty, holiness, and majesty. Isaiah received a vision from God. Visions were given either through dreams or through vivid apparitions. It was like God was peeling back the curtain to give the prophet a glimpse of what was happening behind the scenes. Often, visions were an accompaniment to a verbal message the prophet had received as a way to reinforce and/or further explain the message. **Isaiah 6:1-3** records the vision:

> *In the year that King Uzziah died I saw the Lord sitting upon a throne, high and lifted up; and the train of his robe filled the temple. Above him stood the seraphim. Each had six wings: with two he covered his face, and with two he covered his feet, and with two he flew. And one called to another and said, "Holy, holy, holy is the LORD of hosts; the whole earth is full of glory!"*

Uzziah was the king of Judah. If you remember, Judah was the kingly line of David. God made a covenant with David that a descendant of Judah and David would always be on the throne. God was showing Isaiah the ultimate fulfillment of the Davidic covenant. The vision showed that while the human line of kings from Judah (represented by King Uzziah) would die off (and they did!), the true King of God's people would reign forever. God was showing Isaiah Jesus! Throughout the Old Testament, we see earthly kings that, even though they were chosen by God, fell short. This was to point them to the fact that there is only one King—King Jesus—who was qualified to reign over them.

Using some of the most beautiful imagery in all of Scripture, Isaiah underscored the second theme of his book—God's love for His people with prophesies of the future Messiah. Here is just a sampling of them:

Isaiah 9:2, 6—*"The people who walked in darkness have seen a great light; those who dwelt in a land of deep darkness, on them has light shone. For to us a child is born, to us a son is given; and the government shall be upon his shoulder, and his name shall be called Wonderful Counselor, Mighty God, Everlasting Father, Prince of Peace."* This verse is a staple at Christmastime, but for its original readers, it would have been a lifeline! God was sending Israel and Judah into captivity under horrible, oppressive regimes. Their life would indeed be dark, but the darkness wouldn't last forever. God would deliver them. But let's not miss the deeper metanarrative of this verse. Everyone who is not a believer in Jesus as Lord and Savior is dead—dead spiritually and dead in their sin. Dead people are blind; hence, they are walking in darkness. A world filled with dead people is about as dark a land as there can be. But for God's people, a Light has shone! This Baby to be born would change everything! This verse should bring us to our knees in gratitude that the Holy Spirit has regenerated our hearts and allowed us to see that Light and escape the darkness!

Isaiah 42:1—*"Behold my servant, whom I uphold, my chosen, in whom my soul delights; I have put my Spirit upon him; he will bring forth justice to the nations."* An outstanding reference to the Trinity and Their unique roles, Isaiah said Jesus, being sent by God the Father, and coming in the power of the Holy Spirit, would bring justice. "The nations" foreshadowed Gentiles being brought into the family of God.

Isaiah 52:10—*"The LORD has bared his holy arm before the eyes of all the nations, and **all the ends of the earth** shall see the salvation of our God."* This verse is referring to Jesus coming in the flesh. *All* would see the strength of God—baring his holy arm—in Jesus' physical presence on earth; and all would see how God would save His people—through the crucifixion and resurrection of Christ. When we read further to 52:15, we see that "all the ends of the earth" is a prophecy that God includes Gentiles as part of His elect.

Isaiah 53:2-3—*"For he grew up before him like a young plant, and like a root out of dry ground; he had no form or majesty that we should look at him, and no* *beauty that we should desire him. He was despised and reject by men, a man of sorrows and acquainted with grief, and as one from whom men hide their faces he was despised, and we esteemed him not."* This is probably a familiar verse, but it's an important one because this is one of the verses that the Pharisees and other Jewish people either missed or misunderstood. They were looking for a grand, powerful, conquering king to ride in and rescue them from Roman oppression, but God makes it clear that was not going to be the case. Having no beauty does not mean Jesus was ugly! It means that He was going to look like everyone else; He was going to be ordinary. There would be nothing about His physical appearance to tip anyone off that He was the sovereign King. Isaiah continued by saying that God knew that the Pharisees and some of the Jews would get this verse wrong. They would despise, reject, and betray Jesus.

As we said, there is no way in a summary format to do the book of Isaiah the justice it deserves, but we pray that we have given you a glimpse into its richness! Tradition has it that Isaiah was killed by being sawn in two under orders of King Manasseh of Judah.

MICAH

Now, onto a minor prophet who is our last pre-exilic prophet and who is much less overwhelming than Isaiah! Micah, of Judah, prophesied to both Judah and Israel beginning around 735 B.C. His book is one of the easier prophetic books to understand because of its trifid pattern. The book is broken up into three groups of "woe/weal." "Woe/weal" was a literary device employed by some of the prophets. The "woe" is the judgement and punishment part. The prophet used funeral language to describe it. He was, in essence, saying, *I am singing your death song.* Fun, huh?! It gets better, though, when he gets to the "weal" part. "Weal" is the future blessings. The prophet was saying, *God has a remedy for your death.*

The first woe/weal we see is in chapters one and two. Micah told the people of Samaria (representative of the nation of Israel) and Judah that they would be punished for their unfaithfulness to God. After, though, came the weal. God's people would be released from captivity and reunited under Yahweh.

The second woe/weal is seen in chapters three through five. Micah's woe was against the corrupt leaders of Israel, corrupt Jerusalem, and false prophets. His weal spoke of Zion (the mountain of God and representative of Heaven), the Messiah, and the future purification of God's people. We find one of the prophecies of the coming Messiah in **Micah 5:2**, *"But you, O Bethlehem Ephrathah, who are too little to be among the clans of Judah, from you shall come forth for me one who is to be ruler in Israel, whose coming forth is from of old, from ancient days."* Joseph and Mary were living in Nazareth when Mary conceived Jesus, but because of the census Caesar Augustus ordered be taken so he could collect more taxes, every person had to register in their birth town. From this event, it was brought to light that Joseph was actually not from Nazareth, but from the small town of Bethlehem. They were in Bethlehem at the exact time Mary went into labor, and she gave birth, thus fulfilling this prophecy. Seven hundred thirty years before the event, God showed Micah that He was sovereign over everything and could orchestrate events in history to fulfill His purpose!

The third and final woe/weal is found in Micah chapters six and seven. Micah implemented the "rib formula" for this last woe, using trial language to indict Judah. The weal told of God's love and compassion toward His elect. Micah ended his book by glorifying God for His goodness. **Micah 7:18** says, *"Who is a God like you, pardoning iniquity and passing over transgression for the remnant of his inheritance? He does not retain his anger forever, because he delights in steadfast love."* Why doesn't God retain His anger on His people forever? Not because of anything His people do, but because of Who He is! Micah ended the last section of his book with the question, *"Who is a God like you?"* This is a play on Micah's name. Micah means, "Who is like Yahweh?"[20]

---

20   *Wikipedia*, s.v. "Micah," accessed June 27, 2019. https://en.wikipedia.org/wiki/Micah.

Chapter 12

ISRAEL AND JUDAH IN EXILE

In this chapter, all of the prophets we will look at began their ministry while the Northern nation of Israel and/or the Southern nation of Judah were being controlled by an enemy nation.

NAHUM

You may recall in the book of Jonah that God sent Jonah to preach to the people of Nineveh so that they would repent. When they did, God forgave them and did not bring destruction upon the city. You may also recall Jonah was none too happy about it. We don't know when Jonah died; but if he lived another sixty years after his visit to Nineveh, he may have heard Nahum's prophecy and felt vindication. Nahum, who received his message from the Lord around 697 B.C., was from a town in Judah, but considered a prophet of the nation of Israel because his message was against Israel's captors, the Assyrians. Like Obadiah, whose whole book was judgement on Edom, Nahum's whole book is a series of judgements against the Assyrian Empire represented by its capital, Nineveh. Why would God have gone to all of the trouble to get Nineveh to repent only to later pronounce His plan to destroy it? The simple answer is because it suited His purpose to do so! There are many who do not like to hear that answer, especially to some of the harder questions the Bible presents, but it is always the truth. Sometimes, God gives us the privilege of seeing what He is up to in Scripture, and sometimes, He doesn't. The bottom line is always that the almighty, sovereign Creator may do as He wishes with all of His Creation.

Nineveh's repentance after Jonah's visit was short-lived. Assyria overthrew the Northern nation of Israel, ruled over those Israelites who were allowed to stay in their land, and sent others into exile and captivity. As we looked at earlier, it was God Who raised Assyria up to conquer and oppress the nation of Israel. God empowered Assyria and then worked through their sin for His purpose. Once they saw that they had become powerful and Israel was vulnerable, they moved in with a vengeance. Because of this, God held them accountable for their actions against His people.

In the book of Nahum, we see God using some strong language against Assyria. Like in the book of Hosea, the metaphors are graphic and vivid. **Nahum 3:5-6** says, *"Behold, I am against you, declares the LORD of hosts, and will lift up your skirts over your face' and I will make nations look at your nakedness and kingdoms at your shame. I will throw filth at you and treat you with contempt and make you a spectacle."* The King James Version is even more graphic, saying, *"And I will cast abominable filth upon thee, and make thee vile"* **(Nahum 3:6, KJV).** How's that for a picture?!

ZEPHANIAH

The tiny book of Zephaniah is one of those books you can never seem to find when flipping through your Old Testament. Nestled between Habakkuk and Haggai and with only three chapters, it's easy to pass over. But its small size does not negate its worth. Zephaniah prophesied around 638 B.C. during the reign of King Josiah in Judah. A contemporary of Jeremiah, Zephaniah's message helped pave the way for King Josiah's reform and revival in Judah.

Like Joel and Isaiah, Zephaniah uses "day of the Lord" language. Unlike them, though, he uses the literary device of hyperbole to this language to show just how cataclysmic the day of the Lord will be for some. We see an example of this in **Zephaniah 1:2-3**: *"'I will utterly sweep away everything from the face of the earth,' declares the LORD. 'I will sweep away man and beast; I will sweep away the birds of the heavens and the fish of the sea, and the rubble with the wicked. I will cut off mankind from the face of the earth,' declares the LORD."* Zephaniah used exaggeration to urge the people of Judah to get right with God before the day of the Lord comes. For those who don't, a horrific reality awaits them on that day. **Zephaniah 1:15** says, *"A day of wrath is that day, a day of distress and anguish, a day of ruin and devastation, a day of darkness and gloom, a day of clouds and thick darkness."*

However, for those who repent of their unfaithfulness and turn back to God, there is nothing to fear. Zephaniah told the faithful of their fate in **3:13b**, *"For they shall graze and lie down, and none shall make them afraid."*

Like many of the prophetic books, Zephaniah ends with amazing future blessings God has in store for His children. **Zephaniah 3:17** declares, *"The LORD your God is in your midst, a mighty one who will save; he will rejoice over you with gladness; he will quiet you by his love; he will exult over you with loud singing."*

JEREMIAH

Our journey through the books of the prophets now takes us to Jeremiah. The longest of all of the prophetic books, Jeremiah began his ministry in 627 B.C. and served for over forty years. During his years of being a prophet, he saw the continued Assyrian control of Israel, as well as the destruction of Jerusalem and capture of Judah by Babylon. Jeremiah has been dubbed "the weeping prophet." While this is mostly because of his writings in the book of Lamentations (which we will get to next), Jeremiah had a difficult life, maybe the most difficult of all of the prophets. He prophesied during the most difficult time of Judah's existence—during their major moral decline and disobedience to God and during their siege by Babylon. His messages of covenant unfaithfulness and call to repentance were not well-received by the people of Judah. Added to that, the government hated him; he was considered a traitor; his hometown wanted to kill him; and false prophets were running around giving "good and happy" messages to the people, which made the people dislike Jeremiah and his "doom and gloom" messages even more.

As with the book of Isaiah and with all of the major prophetic books, only an in-depth study would do Jeremiah the justice it deserves. But we will give a summary, hit some of the important themes, and highlight some of the unique and familiar passages in Jeremiah. One thing to note when you read through the book of Jeremiah is that the chapters are not in chronological order. We have seen this before in the books of the Law and Judges and will see it again in some of the other prophets, like Daniel.

Jeremiah was a faithful servant to God; but initially, he was reluctant to accept the call from the Lord. He told God he could not speak because he was young. Obviously, Jeremiah can speak; he just didn't think he was up for the task God had called him to do. God responded to Jeremiah in **Jeremiah 1:9**: *"Then the LORD put out his hand and touched my mouth. And the LORD said to me, 'Behold I have put my words in your mouth.'"* Kind of hard to refuse after that! Maybe God's putting His hand on Jeremiah's mouth was why Jeremiah became such an eloquent speaker even when he had to explain vast negative changes and dramatic political developments that would be happening in the nation of Judah and that God was behind them all.

Like some of the other prophets, Jeremiah told Judah that they had been unfaithful to God and because of that, they would be punished. He was not the first prophet to foretell of the Babylonian siege, but he was the first to tell the Judahites that their captivity would last for seventy years. This was significant because while Judah was being told they were being punished, they were also being told that the punishment would not last forever. Prophets who were in exile in Babylon, like Ezekiel and Daniel, took Jeremiah's prophecy of seventy years very seriously. For them, the year 516 B.C. (the conclusion of the seventy years) became a target date. Also unique to Jeremiah's message was that he told the people of Judah how to behave while they were captives. Chapter twenty-nine is a letter to the exiles. In it, he told them:

> *"Build houses and live in them; plant gardens and eat their produce. Take wives and have sons and daughters; take wives for your sons, and give your daughters in marriage, that they may bear sons and daughters; multiply there, and do not decrease. But seek the welfare of the city where I have sent you into exile, and pray to the LORD on its behalf, for in its welfare you will find your welfare"* **(Jer. 29:5-7).**

God was telling them to have hope that He would eventually deliver them. In the meantime, they were to continue carrying on with life as usual and to do good to their captors (i.e. "love your enemies"). God gave them a promise to help them hold onto that hope in **Jeremiah 29:11**: *"For I know the plans I have for you, declares the LORD, plans for welfare and not for evil, to give you a future and hope."* The meaning of this verse for believers today is fulfilled in Jesus. The "prospering and not harming" means that we have been saved and will not spend eternity in hell. Thus, the "hope and future" is an eternal life spent with God.

While Jeremiah was telling the people to settle in for a seventy-year exile, there were false prophets saying something quite different. Their messages were more positive and encouraging than Jeremiah's. One claimed that God told him that the exile of Judah would not last long and that God would break the yoke of Babylon and deliver Judah back home within two years. This message was obviously not from God, but trying to convince the people of that was one more hurtle Jeremiah had in front of him.

While it is probable that many of the prophets' messages were not well-received, Jeremiah was threatened with death because of his. An example of one such instance occurs in chapter twenty-six when he spoke the words of the Lord at the temple, telling the priests, prophets, and people that God's judgement was coming if they did not repent. Their response was, *"You shall die"* **(Jer. 26:8b)**. Jeremiah's excellent oratory skills (and the sovereignty of God!) saved Jeremiah, and the people gave up their quest to kill him.

As if having the priests, other prophets, and people angry at you isn't enough, Jeremiah even managed to enrage the king of Judah, Jehoiachin. Jehoiachin called Jeremiah's prophecy of the sin and punishment of Judah treason. Showing no fear of God, Jehoiachin threw the scroll containing Jeremiah's prophecy into the fire. After, God told Jeremiah to write another scroll and give it to the king, telling him that Jehoiachin's dead body would be cast out and laid exposed to the elements. Furthermore, God also punished Jehoiachin's family and servants for his rebellion.

Throughout his life, Jeremiah was surrounded by people who hated him. His only true allies were his scribe and friend, Baruch, and God. The life of Jeremiah should be a lesson to us that not everything God calls us to will have a happy ending this side of Heaven. While we look back and appreciate Jeremiah's service and words, such was not the case during his lifetime. We aren't sure exactly when and how Jeremiah died, but most scholars agree that it was probably in Egypt after the siege in Jerusalem. Through Jeremiah, God told the people of Judah not to fight the overthrow from Babylon. They were to accept it as punishment and wait for God's deliverance. Not all heeded this, though. There were some who attempted to start an uprising by assassinating the Babylon-appointed governor in Judah. When that plan failed, they made an escape to Egypt. Jeremiah's last service as God's prophet was to follow these Judahites, trying to convince them to turn around and go back. Jeremiah's ministry ended as he followed the people down to Egypt.

LAMENTATIONS

The book of Lamentations is often credited to Jeremiah, but we don't actually know who the author is. Its detail of Babylon's destruction of

Jerusalem dates it as having been written around the time of Babylon's siege (586 B.C.). This date indicates that Jeremiah certainly could have written it. There are other arguments for naming Jeremiah as the author. Its lament style is similar to what we see in the book of Jeremiah, and both the Septuagint (the Greek version of the Old Testament) and the Vulgate (the Latin version of the Old Testament) list Jeremiah as the author. Finally, there is a reference in **2 Chronicles 35:25a** that could indicate Jeremiah is the author: *"Jeremiah also uttered a lament for Josiah."* Whether the author was Jeremiah or someone else, we know for sure that they were an eyewitness to the fall of Jerusalem because of the specific and detailed historical events it contains. It was written in Palestine for the benefit of the people of Judah who had endured the siege of Babylon.

It is hard for us to imagine what the siege of Jerusalem would have been like for the people of Judah. The people had been in the Promised Land for eight hundred years with David capturing Jerusalem and Solomon building the temple roughly four hundred years earlier. When Babylon attacked, Judah was hoping that Egypt would intervene to help, but it never happened. Instead, they were betrayed by their allies. Babylon demolished Jerusalem, destroying and desecrating the temple. The book of Lamentations is a corporate lament expressing God's people's sorrow, repentance, and plea for deliverance.

The book of Lamentations is made up of five poems that mesh to form one huge lament. Although it is impossible to see in our English Bible, in the original Hebrew, Lamentations was an acrostic which used each letter of the Hebrew alphabet in order in each chapter. It was also written in what is called a chiastic form. This structure looks like ABCBA. Applying this to Lamentations, chapters one and five are a summary of the state of the Judahites because of what had befallen them. **Lamentations 1:7** is a good example: *"Jerusalem remembers in the days of her affliction and wandering all the precious things that were hers from days of old. When here people fell into the hand of the foe, and there was none to help her, her foes gloated over her; they* *mocked at her downfall."* Chapters two and four give more explicit detail of the tragedy that befell Judah, as we see in **Lamentations 4:10-11**: *"The hands of compassionate women have boiled their own children; they became their food during the destruction of the daughter of my people. The LORD gave full vent to his wrath; he poured out his hot anger, and he kindled a fire in Zion that consumed its foundations."*

And finally, chapter three is the centerpiece and the most intense part of the lament. It starts out saying things are as bad as they can possibly be. As we see in **Lamentations 3:4-5**: *"He has made my flesh and my skin waste away; he has broken my bones; he has besieged and enveloped me with bitterness and tribulation; he has made me dwell in darkness like the dead of long ago."* But it ends with hope and encouragement as we see in the very familiar verses of **Lamentations 3:22-23**: *"The steadfast love of the LORD never ceases; his mercies never come to an end; they are new every morning; great is your faithfulness."*

Lamentations is a beautiful poem that can be used in our prayer life to help us express anguish and point us to the hope only found in Jesus. God's ways may be different than ours, but they are always right! Lamentations also gives us a glimpse into the meaning of tragedy. When we remain loyal to God, even in the midst of tragedy, He will not fail us. Out of the broken pieces of our lives, He will create something beautiful, even if we never live to see it.

HABAKKUK

A contemporary of Jeremiah and Zephaniah, Habakkuk, from Judah, received his message from God beginning around 625 B.C. The book of Habakkuk is an unusual book in that Habakkuk never directly addresses the people of Judah. Instead, the book is a conversation between Habakkuk and God. Habakkuk issued two complaints to God, and the Lord answered them. Then Habakkuk prayed and praised God, and the book ends. Habakkuk is a nice, simple, easy-to-understand book!

Habakkuk's first complaint comes in chapter one. His complaint is one we can all probably relate to. **Habakkuk 1:2-4** says:

> *O LORD, how long shall I cry for help, and you will not hear? Or cry to you "Violence!" and you will not save? Why do you make me see iniquity, and why do you idly look at wrong? Destruction and violence are before me; strife and contention arise. So the law is paralyzed, and justice never goes forth. For the wicked surround the righteous; so justice goes forth perverted.*

Habakkuk asked an excellent question! God gave him an even more excellent answer in **1:5b**: *"For I am doing a work in your days that you would not believe if told."* Habakkuk's question to God had to do with the sin that was rampant in Judah, and the Lord's answer was to tell him that He is at work doing things Habakkuk could not see, specifically in raising up Babylon to punish Judah for their sin. However, the big picture lesson for us is that we see injustice, wickedness, violence, and evil all around and wonder why God is allowing it and how long He will let it continue. Through God's answer to Habakkuk, we get our answer from Him. Although we cannot see it, God is working all things out in ways we would not believe if He told us!

After God told Habakkuk that He is raising up the Babylonians to punish Judah, Habakkuk had another complaint. Was God going to allow His people to perish at the hands of the pagan nation, Babylon? He asked him in **Habakkuk 1:13b**: *"Why do you idly look at traitors and remain silent when the wicked swallows up the man more righteous than he?"* It's not that Habakkuk thinks the people of Judah are better than the Babylonians, but they *are* God's people, whereas Babylon is His enemy. God answered Habakkuk that the nation of Babylon can expect destruction for the sins they would commit on Judah, but God's message was for the people of Judah: *"The righteous shall live by his faith"* **(Hab. 2:4b)**. Habakkuk called the *physical nation* of Judah God's people and righteous. God was correcting him, saying His people are not His people simply because they are part of a geographical nation. His people are the ones who live by faith in Him alone. In other words, not everyone from the nation of Judah (and Israel) are the people of God. It is only the chosen remnant who live by faith whom God will save.

Habakkuk ends with a beautiful prayer and praise to God. He concludes with this encouraging truth in **3:19**: *"God, the Lord, is my strength; he makes my feet like the deer's; he makes me tread on my high places."*

DANIEL

After the short reprieve of Habakkuk, we are back to another major and complex prophet, Daniel. The book of Daniel contains so much history that we may not realize it is a prophetic book, but it is! It was written in what is called a bifid structure. This means it has two parts. Chapters one through six are the historical chapters that contain narratives about Daniel and his friends; and chapters seven through twelve tell of the messages Daniel received from God, both by oracle and visions.

As you may remember from the previous chapter, the complete conquest of Judah by Babylon took place in 586 B.C., but Babylon had launched two prior campaigns on the Southern nation. It was during the first campaign in 605 B.C. that Daniel was most likely taken captive and sent to Babylon. Being one of the "best and brightest" young men from the royal families of the conquered nation, Daniel—along with his three friends, Hananiah, Mishael, and Azariah— were taken from their homes in Judah and sent to Babylon to serve King Nebuchadnezzar. When they arrived, they were given the Babylonian names of Belteshazzar, Shadrach, Meshach, and Abednego, respectively.

As we said, the first six chapters of Daniel are stories about the events that took place while these men were in Babylon. From the very beginning, we see that not only were these four young men faithful followers of Yahweh, but God was protecting them and blessing them. The four refused to eat the royal food given to them because it would defile them. Most of us know the story.

The guard agreed to let them eat fruits and vegetables for ten days; and at the end of that time, Daniel, Shadrach, Meshach, and Abednego were healthier-looking than all of the others who had eaten the royal food. This narrative is not a commercial for becoming a vegetarian. The four were not in excellent health because they didn't eat meat. Their superior physical state was because God was with them and blessed them for their obedience to His commands. **Daniel 1:20** shows us just how blessed they were by God: *"And in every matter of wisdom and understanding about which the king inquired of them, he found them ten times better than all the magicians and enchanters that were in all his kingdom."*

The good things continued to come for Daniel. King Nebuchadnezzar had a dream that was impossible for any of his magicians, enchanters, or sorcerers to interpret. When the king was ready to kill them all (including Daniel, Shadrach, Meshach, and Abednego), Daniel and his friends prayed for God to give Daniel the interpretation. He did, and even though it is not a favorable interpretation for King Nebuchadnezzar, he was so impressed with Daniel that he promoted him to ruler of the whole province of Babylon and chief over the wise men. Shadrach, Meshach, and Abednego were also promoted through a request by Daniel.

Right after this grand victory, Shadrach's, Meshach's, and Abednego's faith was put to the test when they refused to bow down to a ninety-foot gold statue King Nebuchadnezzar made of himself. For their offense, the king threatened to throw them into a fiery furnace unless they bowed. Their response showed how much they trusted their sovereign God. **Daniel 3:17-18** says, *"'Our God whom we serve is able to deliver us from the burning fiery furnace, and he will deliver us out of your hand, O king. But if not, be it known to you, O king, that we will not serve your gods or worship the golden image that you have set up.'"* The young men knew that Almighty God could easily save them from a fiery death, but they also recognized that He might choose not to. They were willing to accept either outcome. Most of us can probably finish the story. They were thrown in, but it was noticed that a fourth man was also in the furnace walking around with them. This fourth man was the preincarnate Jesus. The three came out so unscathed, their clothes didn't even smell like smoke! While not converted to becoming a follower of Yahweh, King Nebuchadnezzar was greatly awed, bowed down to worship God, and ordered all of Babylon to do the same.

The king had a second dream that Daniel interpreted for him. King Nebuchadnezzar would lose his mind and become animal-like for seven years. He would be removed from power and live amongst the animals. At the end of the seven years, though, his reason would be returned to him, and he would be restored to power. Think this sounds far-fetched? Historical records of the reigns of kings were, for the most part, accurately kept—even as far back as Nebuchadnezzar's time. During the records of the reign of King Nebuchadnezzar, there is a period of seven years where there is no recorded activity of him from 582-575 B.C.[21]

Chapter six closes out the historical portion of Daniel with the very familiar story of the lions' den. By this time, Babylon had been overthrown by the Medo-Persian Empire, and King Darius was now on the throne. Like Nebuchadnezzar, he was very fond of Daniel and put him over all of the other wisemen. Because of their jealousy, the wisemen tricked King Darius into signing an order that would snare Daniel and cause him to be punished by being thrown into a den of lions. Again, we see God's sovereignty and protection as He shut the mouths of the lions while Daniel was in the den. He did not do the same, though, for Daniel's accusers and their families who were thrown in the den the following day as they were overpowered and killed by the lions.

Chapter seven begins the apocalyptic portion of Daniel. We've already defined apocalyptic, but the book of Daniel is an excellent place to point out a few additional characteristics of apocalyptic literature. In apocalyptic

---

21   Eric and Jess Hall, "Lesson 16 on the Book of Daniel," ThyWordIsTruth.com, accessed March 30, 2019, www.thywordistruth.com/Daniel/Lesson-16-on-Daniel.html#.XJ_sYphKjIU.

literature, there is a distinct contrast between the present circumstances dominated by evil and the age of change that is coming. It is usually made clear that any positive change can only happen by God's radical intervention. There is little or nothing humans can do to change their current circumstances. In the case of the book of Daniel, the Judahites were being held captive by the powerful nation of Babylon. They had no hope of being able to free themselves. Only God's involvement could accomplish that.

Grasping apocalyptic literature requires a lot of study of the Scriptures and history. It is generally written using unusual imagery. For example, evil is depicted in grotesque forms and figures. Sometimes, this imagery is hard to understand. The reason for this imagery is to *both* reveal and conceal. If the vision blatantly spelled out who the evil kingdoms were, it would mean big trouble for Daniel or others who told of the visions. The images were given in a way that they were concealed to the outside world but revealed and understood by the writers and the people of God.

There are a lot of parallels between the books of Daniel and Revelation. While, again, it would take an in-depth study to unpack all that is contained in the book of Daniel, we will give a brief summary of each of Daniel's prophecies.

Daniel's first vision was of four beasts, each one more hideous than the last. These beasts represented the kingdoms that would rise up and oppress God's people. In order, they are: Babylon, Media-Persia, Greece, and Rome. This vision was followed by another vision of a courtroom over which God the Father presides. **Daniel 7:13** gives us a powerful image of what takes place in that courtroom:

> *"And behold, with the clouds of heaven there came one like a son of man, and he came to the Ancient of Days and was presented before him. And to him was given dominion and glory and a kingdom that all people, nations, and languages should serve him; his dominion is an everlasting dominion which shall not pass away, and his kingdom one that shall not be destroyed."*

The important take-away from this vision is that the beasts got progressively fiercer, illustrating to the people Daniel was prophesying to that things would get worse before they got better. But they should not lose hope. Jesus is the sovereign, ultimate Authority over everything. He will always prevail, and through Him, His people would prevail.

Daniel received a vision that came to him in a dream. It is one of the most specific in all of Scripture. It named the king of Greece as its subject. This prophecy was about Alexander the Great, who came to power in the Greek Empire in 336 B.C. The vision showed how Alexander would oppress the people of God and how upon his death, his kingdom would be divided into four smaller kingdoms. If you know your Greek history, you know that is exactly what happened!

As we said, some of the visions in Daniel are parallel to the visions in Revelation. An example of this is in chapter twelve. Daniel received a vision of Jesus' Second Coming and the simultaneous raising up of God's elect and the damning of those who are not. **Daniel 12:1b-2** says, *"But at that time your people shall be delivered, everyone whose name shall be found written in the book. And many of those who sleep in the dust of the earth shall awake, some to everlasting life, and some to shame and everlasting contempt."* In Revelation 20:12-15, John had a similar vision. Those whose names are written in the book—or "book of life," as John calls it—are God's elect. When Jesus comes back, He will divide the elect and non-elect. His people will be raised to everlasting life. Those who aren't will go to everlasting contempt. John cites the book of Daniel thirty-four times in Revelation.[22]

EZEKIEL

Just when you thought that we had seen it all in the book of Daniel, we come to the book of Ezekiel! Ezekiel is another apocalyptic book written

---

22   "The Revelation to John," Rel 101: Understanding the Bible: Revelation, accessed April 09, 2019, www4.westminster.edu/staff/brennie/rel101/revelati.htm.

beginning in 593 B.C., while Ezekiel was in exile in Babylon. Ezekiel was taken captive during the second siege of the Babylonians in 597 B.C. A contemporary of Daniel and Jeremiah, Ezekiel spoke to the people of his generation, who were both sinful and hopeless. He tried to bring them back to faith in Yahweh by repentance and confidence in the future. He told them that even in defeat and despair, God is sovereign and should be worshipped and praised. You can imagine that his message was not a popular one. Like Jeremiah, Ezekiel faced opposition.

The book of Ezekiel opens with Ezekiel receiving a vision of a fiery cloud, creatures, wheels, a chariot, a jeweled throne, and a man with the appearance of gleaming metal and fire. While each item represents something specific, Ezekiel summed up the vision in **Ezekiel 1:28b**: *"Such was the appearance of the likeness of the glory of the LORD."* God began Ezekiel's ministry by showing Ezekiel His sovereignty and glory!

Remember we said that God sometimes had His prophets do some bizarre things? God gave Ezekiel a scroll with His Word on it, telling Ezekiel to eat the scroll. God didn't just want Ezekiel to hear His Word; He wanted him to receive, internalize, and digest it before he went out to prophesy and preach to others. Ezekiel most likely did not physically eat the scroll. He probably saw himself doing it in a vision. This is an important metaphor for us, especially for those who teach the Word of God. Are we taking the time to study and meditate on the Word of God before we attempt to teach it to others? When Ezekiel did this, he found God's Word to be *"as sweet as honey"* **(Ezek. 3:3b)**.

Another bizarre command of God's is found in chapter four. God told Ezekiel to lie on his side, placing the punishment of Israel and Judah on himself. He was to lie for 390 days, representing the years of Israel's punishment, and another forty days, representing the years of Judah's punishment. There are many different theories on what the 390 days and forty days symbolize. It would take pages and pages to flesh out all of the theories and their supporting arguments. Since this is just a summary of the book, suffice it to say that the days represented a finite amount of time Ezekiel was to lie on his side placing the nations' punishments on himself. It is very unlikely that Ezekiel laid non-stop on his side for a total of 430 days. It is more likely that God was telling him to get into the prone position of supplication and spend many hours a day, for a set number of days, praying for Israel and Judah. The "taking the punishment on himself" was God making Ezekiel a priest who was to pray and atone for the sins of the people.

While not quite as bizarre as the previous two, God told Ezekiel to give Judah an object lesson showing the fall of Jerusalem, the destruction of the temple, and the resulting devastation that would take place. In an effort to sear the image of what was about to happen in the people's minds, Ezekiel reenacted the impending siege and destruction by using clay models.

Later, Ezekiel was given an oracle about two sisters, Oholah and Oholibah. **Ezekiel 23:5** tells us, *"Oholah played the whore while she was mine, and she lusted after her lovers the Assyrian, warriors."* And **Ezekiel 23:11** says, *"Her sister Oholibah saw this, and she became more corrupt than her sister in her lust and in her whoring, which was worse than that of her sister.'"* God was again using sexual immorality as a metaphor for covenant unfaithfulness and idol worship. Oholah represented the nation of Israel, while Oholibah represented Judah. This would have been a sobering message for the people of Judah as God was saying Judah had become as sinful as Israel, whom God crushed by the siege of the Assyrians.

Chapter twenty-eight contains a very unique passage. Amongst the prophecies of what God would do to enemy pagan nations, Ezekiel was given the vision of the original fall of Satan from Heaven. **Ezekiel 28:12b-13a** says, *"You were the signet of perfection, full of wisdom and perfect in beauty. You were in Eden, the garden of God; every precious stone was your covering."* Satan began as a beautiful angel created by God, but sinful pride got the best of him. **Ezekiel 28:17** continues, *"Your heart was proud because of your beauty; you corrupted your wisdom for the sake of your splendor. I cast you to the ground;*

I exposed you before kings, to feast their eyes on you.'" His eventual doom had already been decided on as we see in **Ezekiel 28:18b-19**: *"All who know you among the peoples are appalled at you; you have come to a dreadful end and shall be no more forever."*

Another unique vision found in Ezekiel is in chapter thirty-seven. God took Ezekiel to a valley full of bones and told Ezekiel to prophesy over the bones. He did, and the bones not only came to life, but they also began to turn fully human, except that there was no breath in them! Ezekiel was then told to pray to bring the Holy Spirit unto the bones to give them breath. God took people who were so dead that they were mere bones, and through the preaching of His Word and the Holy Spirit reviving them, brought them back to life. Could there be any clearer picture of how we are dead in our sin, useless and dried up, and only by the regeneration of the Holy Spirit and the saving power of God's Word are we brought back to life?! This is further confirmed in **Ezekiel 36:26**: *"And I will give you a new heart, and a new spirit I will put within you. And I will remove the heart of stone from your flesh and give you a heart of flesh."* For God's elect, both in the Old Testament and the New Testament, God removes their dead, stony heart and replaces it with a regenerated, live heart that is able to respond to the calling of God.

Chapter 13

POST EXILIC BOOKS

Up until now, all of the books we have looked at are recorded events that take place either before the exile of Israel and Judah or during them. All of the remaining books we will look at in this chapter record events that occur after the captives from Judah were freed by King Cyrus of Persia. These are called post-exilic books. King Cyrus was the pagan king prophesied about in the book of Isaiah. **Isaiah 44:28** says, *"Cyrus, 'He is my shepherd, and he shall fulfill all my purpose'; saying of Jerusalem, 'She shall be built,' and of the temple, 'Your foundation shall be laid.'"* God raised Cyrus up and used him to overthrow the Babylon Empire and to free His people, so they could return to the Promised Land and rebuild the temple.

You may wonder what happened to the Northern nation of Israel, which was made up of ten of the twelve tribes. Secular history and tradition tell us the Northern nation, with the exception of a remnant from each tribe, was lost due to their intermarrying with surrounding pagan nations and getting swallowed up into other people groups. After the people of Judah were freed, all those who remained from all twelve tribes went back to being unified and calling themselves "Israel" and "Israelites."

HAGGAI

Haggai prophesied in 520 B.C. He ministered in Judah to the people who had returned to rebuild the temple. All of Haggai's prophecies took place within a four-month span.

Haggai called himself the prophet of Zerubbabel, the governor of Judah, and of Joshua, the high priest. These were two godly men the Lord raised up who would later work with Ezra and Nehemiah. Upon returning in 537 B.C., Zerubbabel and Joshua had tried to start the rebuilding of the temple. The foundation had been laid, and the altar was constructed; but then the people stopped working on the temple so they could build their own houses. Seventeen years had gone by, and still no further work had been done on the temple. God was angry and told Haggai in **Haggai 1:9**, *"My house . . . lies in ruins, while each of you busies himself with his own house."* Also going on during those years were droughts and poor harvests. God told Haggai that the two were connected. The Israelites' failure to rebuild the temple caused their hardships. When Haggai relayed this to Zerubbabel, Joshua, and the people, they all repented and purified themselves. God blessed them, and the plans for rebuilding the temple began again.

ZECHARIAH

A friend of Haggai, Zechariah received his prophecies in the same year as Haggai—520 B.C. Because their ministries occurred in the same year, there are a lot of similarities in the two books. Like Haggai, Zechariah tried to encourage Zerubbabel, Joshua, and the people to get that temple built.

Unlike Haggai, Zechariah received a total of eight visions, some being similar to John's in Revelation. They are all worth taking a look at, but we will just touch on a few. One vision was of a horseman who had gone throughout the world and reported back to an angel that all was stable. The meaning of this vision was a blessing of peace from the Lord given to the people, land, and temple of Judah.

Zechariah had another vision of four horns coming at him. These horns represented Assyria, Babylon, Egypt, and Persia. Four craftsmen then appeared and threw down the horns. The meaning is that the four nations that had previously terrorized Israel and Judah would never bother them again.

The last vision we will take a look at is also Zechariah's last vision. It was four chariots drawn by horses of different colors. The chariots represented the four winds, or spirits, of Heaven. They covered every direction—north, south, east, and west. The meaning of this vision is that God is Omnipotent, and His power is seen over the whole Earth.

Besides visions, the book of Zechariah contains oracles against Israel's enemies, restoration promises for Judah and Israel, and Day-of-the-Lord language. All things we have looked at in previous books. Zechariah also contains prophecies about Jesus. We end with a haunting one. **Zechariah 12:10** declares, *"And I will pour out on the house of David and the inhabitants of Jerusalem a spirit of grace and pleas for mercy, so that, when they look on me, on him whom they have pierced, they shall mourn for him, as one mourns for an only child, and weep bitterly over him, as one weeps over a firstborn.'"*

EZRA

Time to take a break from the prophets and look at some historical books, beginning with the book of Ezra. Ezra, a priest, wrote of events that occurred in the nation of Judah after they were released by King Cyrus of Persia. These events happened almost eighty years before he arrived on the scene. We aren't sure what Ezra's source material was for these earlier years, but most likely, it was a combination of scrolls and annals (diaries) kept by others.

The book of Ezra opens with the proclamation of King Cyrus, of Persia: *"'The LORD, the God of heaven, has given me all the kingdoms of the earth, and he has charged me to build him a house at Jerusalem, which is in Judah"* **(Ezra 1:2)**. King Cyrus was not a believer. He believed in many gods, but he did recognize that Yahweh was the most powerful of gods. It is amazing when you see how often God uses pagans, or non-believers, for His purposes and to fulfill His will!

Cyrus granted permission to any of the captives who wanted to leave Babylon and return to Jerusalem to rebuild the temple that King Nebuchadnezzar had destroyed. Things did not go as smoothly as they had hoped. The nation of Judah was now inhabited by other people groups, including Samaritans. Samaritans were a mixed-race people resulting from the Jewish people, who had remained in the Promised Land under the oppression of Assyria and Babylon, intermarrying with the pagans in the land. The Samaritans, and other pagan people groups, did not want the temple rebuilt, and they did all they could to interfere with the project.

When Ezra arrived in Jerusalem eighty years later, what he found was discouraging. Not only was the temple not rebuilt, but Jerusalem was just as uninhabitable as it had been after Babylon had leveled it. To make matters worse, the Jewish people living in Judah were morally corrupt. Rather than fight the opposition they received from the other people groups, many of the returning captives divorced their Jewish wives and intermarried with pagan women. Ezra, worried that the people's unfaithfulness to God would preclude them from receiving the future blessings promised by God, began to clean house. He made it his mission to help the Israelites get right with God. He started by making them send away their second spouse and any children from the union. This was not something that would normally be done; in fact, Paul preached against it in 1 Corinthians. But because at this time, the Israelites were not permitted to divorce and remarry, the second marriages were unlawful, anyway.

Ezra finally got through to the people, and they gathered to publicly pray, confess their sins, and repent. Those who had taken foreign wives obeyed Ezra's command.

NEHEMIAH

The book of Nehemiah is a continuation of the book of Ezra. No surprise, since in the original Hebrew Bible, these two books were just one book, with

Ezra being the likely author. From the time Nehemiah arrived in Jerusalem, fourteen years after Ezra, the two began to work closely together. Both leaders in Jerusalem, they shared a passion to see the temple rebuilt and the people turn back to God. Ezra led as a priest and teacher, while Nehemiah, an excellent example of a godly leader, led as a builder and the governor.

The book of Ezra ended on a high note. The people repented, got their lives right, and turned back to God. Sadly, as is often the case, the revival was short-lived. Fourteen years later, the temple was still not rebuilt, and Jerusalem was still in ruins. Nehemiah, a prominent member of the king's court in Persia, heard of the trouble in Jerusalem. He asked the king for permission to return to Jerusalem because God had laid it on his heart to rebuild Jerusalem's walls. The king granted him permission. Upon returning, Nehemiah saw just how dilapidated Jerusalem was. While he was concerned about the declining morality of the Israelites and, like Ezra, wanted the people to get right with God, Nehemiah, as governor, made a decision that safety was the foremost concern; and he decided to rebuild the walls surrounding Jerusalem to protect the city. Just as it did previously, their building project came up against opposition. **Nehemiah 4:1-2** gives us a snapshot of what they were up against:

> Now when Sanballat heard that we were building the wall, he was angry and greatly enraged, and he jeered at the Jews. And he said in the presence of his brothers and the army of Samaria, "What are these feeble Jews doing? Will they restore it for themselves? Will they sacrifice? Will they finish up in a day? Will they revive the stones out of the heaps of rubbish and burned ones at that?"

Nehemiah and those following him prayed for protection. They put a call out to their fellow Jews in Judah to come and help. The people responded, and the rebuilding resumed. With the building under way, Nehemiah turned his attention to the moral decline of the Israelites. In particular, the poor who were being extorted. Some of the people had come upon hard times and needed money to eat. The wealthier Israelites were lending money to their fellow Jews at exorbitant interest rates, forcing them to mortgage their homes, farms, and vineyards. When they were unable to pay back what they owed because of the incredible amount of interest, the lenders took their children as slaves. The people of God had become no better than loan sharks! Nehemiah worked with the priests to stop this practice that was against Mosaic Law.

Even with the added help of fellow Israelites, those opposing the rebuilding did not quit. They plotted an assassination attempt on Nehemiah in hopes that his death would stop the building. By the grace of God, the plot failed, and the wall was finished.

Afterward, Ezra called the people together and read the Law to them. A festival was celebrated; the people confessed their sin; and everyone signed a covenant renewal rededicating themselves to the Lord. Some moved back into the city of Jerusalem to help rebuild and revitalize it.

Nehemiah made other reforms in Judah like getting rid of corrupt priests and stopping the people from giving substandard animals for sacrifice. One of his final reforms was dealing with intermarriage. It had been some years since Ezra had dealt with this sinful practice, and some of the men had once again married foreign women. Nehemiah took a different approach to dealing with them than Ezra did. Since Ezra pulling his own hair out didn't stop them, **Nehemiah 13:25a** tells us that Nehemiah *"confronted them and cursed them and beat some of them and pulled out their hair."*

ESTHER

If you like soap operas or romance novels, then the book of Esther is for you! The story of Esther takes place in Persia in 483 B.C. When Cyrus released exiles, they all should have gone back to the Promised Land; but some didn't. Some of the Jewish people chose to stay in Persia. Esther's family was among them. Orphaned as a young girl, Esther was raised by her cousin Mordecai.

The king of Persia held a banquet to show off his wealth and power before embarking on a military campaign against Greece. When his queen refused to be eye candy for him and his drunken friends, he banished her, and she was stripped of her title. The hunt for a new queen began! Esther, along with all of the other virgins in the land, was taken involuntarily and moved to the king's harem. After the girls went through a year's worth of beauty treatments, the king slept with each of them. His favorite would become queen, while the others would just be absorbed into his harem. Esther won the crown.

When the Jewish people were threatened with extermination by a decree made by the court vizier, Haman, her cousin encouraged her to use her position as queen to save her people. He told her in **Esther 4:14b**, *"Who knows whether you have not come to the kingdom for such a time as this?"* Using a mixture of humility and shrewdness, Esther brought the plot against the Jews to the attention of the king. He killed his vizier for making the decree and issued a counter-decree that ultimately saved the Jewish people.

If you recall from previous chapters, the Amalekites were enemies of Israel whom God had ordered King Saul to annihilate **(1 Sam. 15:2-3)**. While killing many, King Saul disobeyed and left some of the Amalekites alive. Haman was a descendent of the Amalekites and hated the Jews because of King Saul killing so many of his people. This is a perfect example of the far-reaching consequences of sin. Almost five hundred years later, the Jewish people were paying the price for Saul's disobedience. Had King Saul destroyed them all as he was commanded to by God, Haman would never have been born.

The book of Esther is probably best known as the book in the Bible that never mentions God. While it is true that God is never mentioned, we see God's hand throughout the entire book, working through seemingly ordinary events to cause something extraordinary to occur! Esther shows us that God is constantly at work fulfilling His sovereign plan, even when it appears He is nowhere to be found!

MALACHI

We have come to the last prophet, the last book of the chapter, and the last book of the Old Testament! It has been a long journey, but when you are finished reading this section, you will have conquered thirty-seven books in the Bible!

The book of Malachi is dated around 430 B.C. He was a contemporary of Nehemiah and Ezra. In Malachi's time, things were not great in the Promised Land. The temple had been rebuilt, and people were worshiping in it; but there was a lot of corruption, unfaithfulness, and covenant-breaking going on. Add to that a bad economy due to inflation and domination by the Medo-Persians, and you have a pretty discouraged prophet.

As the last book of the Old Covenant, the book of Malachi packs a lot into just four chapters. God knew He was about to cut off communication with His people for four hundred years. He gave them messages of judgement and warning; but in the end, He left them with promises of the coming Messiah.

Some of the last words God says to His people are found in **Malachi 4:2**: *"But for you who fear my name, the sun of righteousness shall rise with healing in its wings. You shall go out leaping like calves from the stall."*

BONUS! THE PERIOD BETWEEN THE OLD AND NEW TESTAMENT

We have all probably known the frustration and anxiety when someone we love stops speaking to us. Their silence can be deafening! We want to hear something, anything, from them. It can get to the point where we would prefer their voiced anger to their silence.

There are four hundred years between the close of the Old Testament and the opening of the New Testament. Four hundred years of silence, without a single word from God. Four hundred years of the Israelites waiting for and wondering how God would deliver them.

Knowing what happened in history during those four hundred years builds up our foundation for understanding the New Testament.

As we saw, many of the exiles went back to the Promised Land and rebuilt Jerusalem and the temple. But things did not go well for them. Because the Promised Land was so advantageously located, other nations wanted to control it. After the death of Alexander the Great, the Greek Empire was broken into four smaller kingdoms—just like God had told Daniel would happen! The four kingdoms eventually became two—the Seleucid Empire (made up of the nations conquered by the Persian Empire, including Syria and Babylon) and the Ptolemaic Empire (made up of Egypt and some surrounding neighbors). The two empires waged a series of wars against each other to gain control over the lands that included the Promised Land. For a time, control of Judah flip-flopped between the two nations; but ultimately, the Seleucids were victorious. The Seleucid ruler, Antiochus III, insisted everyone, even the Israelites, conform to Greek culture and worship their pagan gods. Wanting to wipe out the Jewish religion, Antiochus prohibited the practicing of Judaism, tried to destroy all the copies of the Torah (the first five books of the Bible), required everyone to make offerings to the Greek god, Zeus, and—the biggest slap in the face of all—sacrificed a pig to Zeus in the temple of Jerusalem.

A revolt broke out against Antiochus led by an elderly priest and his five sons called the Maccabee Revolution. This triggered a twenty-four-year war, which finally resulted in Judah's independence until Rome conquered them in 63 B.C.

When Rome took control of Judah, the emperor Julius Caesar ordered the massacre of all of the Jewish priests while they were performing their duties in the temple. This despicable act would not be forgiven by the Jews. Even though the Roman Empire allowed them to practice Judaism, the Jews cried out to God to send a king to defeat the Romans and avenge the slaughtered priests.

While it may seem like God was nowhere to be found during these four hundred years, His hand was everywhere, orchestrating events and people to ready the earth to receive His Son.

During the oppression of the Jewish people, especially during the time of Antiochus III, the Jews could not travel to the temple to worship God. They began to rely on keeping the Law and strengthening their relationship with God on their own. They were not able to have big ceremonies and celebrate festivals as they had in the past. This helped prepare for Jesus by conditioning the people that Christianity is a relationship, not a religion.

Another effect of the oppression was that the Israelites began to migrate and disperse to many different regions because of the persecution. No longer centralized in one place, this helped prepare for Jesus as it allowed the Gospel to spread faster and to more regions.

Also during this time, seventy-two Jewish scholars secluded themselves on an island, where they transcribed the entire Old Testament from its original Hebrew and Aramaic into Greek. Their translation is called the Septuagint. They chose the Greek language because Greek was the English of that day. Almost everyone who was educated had some knowledge of it. Because of the Jewish migration, many of the Jewish people no longer spoke Hebrew or Aramaic as they had when they were all together. Thanks to these scholars, the Old Testament was now readable to those Jewish people who couldn't read Hebrew and also to the Gentiles. This helped prepare for Jesus by allowing more people to read Scripture and understand why Jesus would come. In addition, it opened the door for Paul and others to preach the Gospel to the Gentiles, offering them the opportunity to become part of the family of God as was prophesied.

God raised up and used politicians during this time as well. Sadducees were the progressive liberals of the day. They only accepted the Pentateuch as legitimate Scripture and operated out of the temple. Despite discrediting the rest of the Old Testament, God used them during this period to teach the Law to people. So even while missing out on most of the prophecies about Jesus, God still used them to educate people on the Law. Since Jesus fulfilled the Law, unbeknownst to them, they were preaching about Him!

Contrasting the Sadducees were the Pharisees. These were lay people who came out of the Maccabean Revolution and became the conservative religious leaders of the synagogues. It was their job to interpret the Law and help the people remain holy and separate for God in a world that was drastically changing around them. However, their interpretations often included adding so many stipulations and requirements to the Law that it became too heavy a burden for the people to bear. Eventually, many of the Pharisees, heady with power, became corrupt and misused their authority. The Pharisees provided a perfect backdrop for Jesus preaching against corruption, legalism, hypocrisy, and insincere faith.

These are just some of the amazing things God was doing when everyone thought He had turned His back on them. He was preparing the world, and especially His people, for the New Covenant. All of the future, better-than-can-be-imagined blessings the prophets spoke of were about to culminate in one Man—Jesus Christ!

INTRODUCTION TO THE NEW TESTAMENT

Throughout the thirty-nine books of the Old Testament there's anticipation of the fulfillment of God's redemptive plan of history, planned before the creation of the world. This fulfillment was realized with the coming of the promised Messiah, God's Anointed One, Who was looked forward to and prophesied about throughout ages past. Although others claimed to be the Messiah, only Jesus fulfilled all of the Old Testament prophecies.

As Christians, we know and believe that Jesus is the Messiah through the inward witness of the Holy Spirit. But it's interesting to note that mathematical computations back that up. When calculated, the chance of one man fulfilling all the prophecies is astronomical. Peter Stoner, chairman of the mathematics and astronomy departments at Pasadena City College until 1953, researched the fulfillment of only eight of the hundreds of prophecies about the Messiah and concluded that the chance that any one man might have lived down to the present time and fulfilled all eight prophecies is one in 1017.[23] That number written out is 100,000,000,000,000,000.

Because the New Testament starts with the coming of the Messiah, we can see that it continues the story of God's redemptive plan. Therefore, we should not separate the Old Testament from the New Testament. In fact, we need the Old Testament to make sense of the New Testament! The whole Bible is God's Word to us, and we should study all of it. You will even find that the Old Testament is quoted in the New Testament quite often!

Like the Old Testament, the New Testament is made up of several books—twenty-seven to be exact—and they range in length from one chapter to many chapters. Also like the Old Testament, they are a mixed variety of genre.

23   Peter W. Stoner, *Science Speaks* (Chicago: Moody Bible Institute, 1976), http:// sciencespeaks.dstoner.net.

PART 5

THE GOSPELS
MATTHEW THROUGH JOHN

Some time passed between Jesus ascending to Heaven and the writing of the Gospels and the rest of the New Testament books. Although there may have been some history about Jesus recorded while He was here, there was no need for a written account while the eyewitnesses to the things that had happened were still alive. In that culture, oral tradition was the primary method of preserving history. It was common to memorize for the purpose of passing on. Therefore, it was not like "whisper down the lane," with accounts getting more and more skewed. They passed on facts; and, therefore, the accounts were trustworthy. They also used writing styles that made it easier to do so—like poetry, for example. Think about all of the Jewish leaders who had to memorize the entire Old Testament! They learned to memorize from an early age, and therefore, it was not a problem to pass on history using oral tradition.

However, although the oral tradition coupled with the fact that eyewitnesses were still alive sufficed for a while, eventually the Church needed a written account, especially as the Gospel spread and the Church expanded outside of Jerusalem and farther. Even certain sects of the Christian community who thought Jesus was going to return in their lifetime saw the need to have Jesus' teachings written down, as well as a written record of His genealogy, His life and death, His miracles, and what He had to say about salvation and the future.

Why are there four different Gospels, and why should we study all four of them? If you wanted to know about someone, you would ready their biography. If you really wanted to know about someone, you would read several biographies by different authors from different perspectives. The New Testament, especially the Gospels, is the biography of Jesus written from different perspectives and to different audiences. Seeing them as a collection helps to give us a clearer picture of Who Jesus is and what He means for us.

The first three Gospels—Matthew, Mark, and Luke—are referred to as the "Synoptic Gospels" because they are similar to one another. All three give many of the same events of Jesus' life, mostly in the same order, which is not often chronological, but instead are grouped by "lists" of things, such as miracles, parables, and controversies. There is even some organization that's geographic or regional. The Synoptic Gospels also contain much of the same wording and even some similar editorial comments.

The explanation accepted by most theologians is that it is very likely the book of Mark was written first and that Matthew and Luke both used Mark's book as a guide to writing their books. In addition, both Matthew and Luke's Gospel contain content from a source referred to as "Q" material. Q material is basically thought of as the sayings of Jesus. The origin of the Q material is a mystery, but it's obvious that they did use material from a source or sources other than Mark.

God worked through the ordinary, every-day lives of His people, utilizing their gifts and vocations to record His Word. Although all Scripture is divinely inspired, that does not mean that is was dictated from the heavens while pen was put to paper here on earth. Except for the prophets, the men who wrote the books of the Old and New Testaments were not secretaries taking dictation from God. All of Scripture is inspired by the Holy Spirit and is, therefore, absolute truth.

For example, Luke starts out his Gospel saying, *"Inasmuch as many have undertaken to compile a narrative of the things that have been accomplished among us ... it seemed good to me also ... to write an orderly account for you, most excellent Theophilus"* **(Luke 1:1, 3)**. God was using Luke's desire to put together an orderly account for Theophilus to write one of the books of His Word!

Chapter 14

MATTHEW

Matthew, also called Levi, was an apostle of Jesus and, therefore, an eyewitness to Jesus' ministry. Matthew is one of the most widely used Gospels for teaching, possibly because of how well it is organized into five different teaching sections:

1. The Sermon on the Mount, which includes the Beatitudes and the Lord's Prayer

2. Instructions to the twelve apostles

3. Parables about the kingdom

4. Teachings about the Church

5. Teaching about End Times judgment, often called the Olivet Discourse.

Matthew's Gospel was likely written sometime before the fall of Jerusalem and destruction of the temple in 70 A.D. because Matthew references the temple as if it was still there. He also references the Sadducees, a group that ceased to exist after that time.

Matthew was a Jewish Christian writing to his fellow Jews. We can see that by the fact that he didn't have to explain Jewish customs and that he used substitutes for the name of God, because out of reverence, the Jewish people would not say God's name. One example of this is that Matthew uses the phrase "Kingdom of Heaven" instead of "Kingdom of God."

Matthew was a tax collector when he was called by Jesus to become an apostle. The fact that he was a tax collector meant that he was thought of as one of the most despicable people of his time. The Jews who were tax collectors obtained for themselves the right from Rome to collect taxes from their own people. Then they extorted as much money as they wanted from the individuals and businesses, paying Rome what was required and keeping the rest for themselves. Upon seeing Jesus, Matthew instantly left his corrupt vocation and followed Him.

Matthew's intention with his Gospel was to show the Jews that Jesus was the promised Jewish Messiah to prove that God had fulfilled His promise to bring the Jewish Savior from the loins of Abraham, through the line of David. Matthew also points to Jesus as the promised Messiah by using the words "fulfilled" and "it is written" frequently throughout his writing, in order to emphasize the fulfillment of the Old Testament prophecies.

Matthew begins by recounting Jesus' lineage, stating that this was the genealogy of Jesus *Christ*, the Greek word meaning "anointed" that corresponds to the Hebrew word meaning "Messiah."[24] He's letting his readers know, in no uncertain terms, that this is the One Who had been prophesied about through the ages—Jesus was their much-anticipated Savior! The wait was over!

Afterward, Matthew moves on to Mary's conception of Jesus. Mary, although betrothed to a man named Joseph, was still a virgin. Betrothal in those days was almost as binding as the actual marriage. When he found out she was pregnant, he planned on divorcing her, but an angel appeared to Joseph in a dream, telling him that Mary's baby was from the Holy Spirit and to move forward with the marriage. Joseph obeyed and married her, but they did not consummate the marriage until she gave birth to Jesus.

Matthew then tells us that the new family received a visit from some Magi, or "wise men." Although the wise men are often displayed in Christmas

---

24   Strong's Lexicon G5547 "Christos," BlueLetterBible.org, accessed on May 1, 2019, www. blueletterbible.org/lang/lexicon/lexicon.cfm?Strongs=G5547&t=NASB.

plays as coming to the stable right after the birth, their visit probably happened more than a year later. Their visit alerted King Herod that a King, Who was prophesied about, had been born. Not wanting any competition, Herod ordered the mass extermination of all two-year-old boys and younger in Bethlehem and the surrounding area. Before this awful event took place, Joseph was warned by God in a dream to flee with his young family to Egypt, an act that eventually resulted in the fulfillment of the Messianic prophecy of God calling His Son out of Egypt.

ARRIVAL OF THE KINGDOM

Matthew fast-forwards twenty-five years to the beginning of Jesus' ministry. His ministry that was heralded by a forerunner, Jesus' slightly older cousin, John the Baptist. John the Baptist and his ministry are described in all four of the Gospels, and from those accounts, we're told that John was filled with the Holy Spirit while he was still in his mother's womb. John's focus was calling the Jewish citizens to repent of their sin and be baptized with water, while looking forward to the One Who would baptize with the Holy Spirit. He rebuked the piously-religious Pharisees and Sadducees, calling them a brood of vipers and warning them, *"Even now the axe is laid to the root of the trees. Every tree therefore that does not bear good fruit is cut down and thrown into the fire"* **(Matt. 3:10)**.

John was a strange dude, wearing clothes of camel hair and eating locusts and wild honey. Despite his quirkiness, **Matthew 3:5-6** tells us, *"Then Jerusalem and all Judea and all the region about the Jordan were going out to him, and they were baptized by him in the river Jordan, confessing their sins."* One day, as John was baptizing in the Jordan, Jesus came to be baptized. Confused because he knew that Jesus was sinless and not in need of baptism, *"John would have prevented him, saying 'I need to be baptized by you and do you come to me?' But Jesus answered him, 'Let it be so now, for thus it is fitting for us to fulfill all righteousness.' Then he consented"* **(Matt. 3:14-15)**.

During Jesus' baptism, as He was raised from the water, the Holy Spirit descended like a dove and rested upon Him. Just then, we're told, *"A voice from heaven said, 'This is my beloved Son, with whom I am well pleased'"* **(Matt. 3:17)**.

Following His baptism, Jesus was led into the wilderness by the Holy Spirit to be tempted by the devil. After fasting for forty days and forty nights, Satan tempted Jesus with the same kind of temptations that every human being experiences—namely physical temptations, prideful temptations, and the temptation to acquire possessions. Satan laid out each temptation with a special taunt, saying, *"If you are the Son of God, then . . . "* Satan knew exactly Who Jesus was, and Jesus answered him by Who He is . . . He answered him with the Word of God!

Jesus began His ministry by preaching, healing the sick, and calling His apostles. He called two sets of brothers—Simon Peter and his brother, Andrew, and James and his brother, John. All four men were fishermen in their family businesses, and all four left their nets immediately at Jesus' call.

THE SERMON ON THE MOUNT

After introducing the beginning of Jesus' ministry, Matthew presents us with the first of Jesus' five teachings called the Sermon on the Mount. In it, Jesus lays out God's ethical standards for His Kingdom. **Matthew 5:2-10** says:

> *And he [Jesus] opened his mouth and taught them, saying: "Blessed are the poor in spirit, for theirs is the kingdom of heaven. Blessed are those who mourn, for they shall be comforted. Blessed are the meek, for they shall inherit the earth. Blessed are those who hunger and thirst for righteousness, for they shall be satisfied. Blessed are the merciful, for they shall receive mercy. Blessed are the pure in heart, for they shall see God. Blessed are the peacemakers, for they shall be called sons of God. Blessed are they who are persecuted for righteousness' sake, for theirs is the kingdom of heaven."*

Jesus is talking to the people who will be part of His Kingdom someday. He's talking to *believers*. This is obvious because the first and last Beatitudes end with *"for theirs is the kingdom of heaven."* Only believers are going to receive the Kingdom of Heaven.

In light of this, Jesus was not teaching the crowd *how to be saved*. In fact, just by reading the Beatitudes, we can see that no one but Jesus could ever live them out perfectly enough to merit Heaven. These "qualities" are in the context of the believers' spiritual condition *in relationship to God*. The effects may spill over into the believer's relationships with other people, but the focus here is on the believer's relationship with God.

For instance, those *"who mourn"* are not those who mourn over a loss of someone or something. They are believers who mourn over their sin because of its offense to our perfectly holy God. Therefore, the comfort they receive is the forgiveness of their sins and peace with God through Jesus Christ.

The rest of the Beatitudes should be read the same way. The "meek" are those who have an attitude of humility and submission toward God. Only a believer will "hunger and thirst" for God's righteousness and not be confident in their own. A believer has already been given mercy, therefore, will "be merciful." The "pure in heart" will see God because the only way to be pure of heart is to have Christ's righteousness. "Peacemakers" are those who've made peace with God through Christ. Those persecuted for righteousness are persecuted for the sake of the Gospel because the only true righteousness a person can have is Christ's. Jesus' teaching about Kingdom life continues through the end of chapter seven of Matthew's Gospel.

As we travel on in the book of Matthew, beginning in chapter eight, we're given multiple examples of Jesus performing miracles. Jesus' miracles of healing demonstrated His power over sickness. Casting out demons from those who were possessed showed His authority over Satan. Calming storms showed His authority over nature. And His power over death was demonstrated by His raising a girl from the dead.

One of those who was healed is the servant of a Roman centurion. As soon as Jesus was told about the servant's suffering, He was willing to go to the house and heal the man. Instead, the Roman soldier demonstrated his great faith in Jesus by stating, *"Lord, I am not worthy to have you come under my roof, but only say the word, and my servant will be healed"* **(Matt. 8:8)**. Jesus used the example of this man's faith to rebuke Israel for their lack of it and to tell them that many in Israel would not be saved and that the Kingdom would include Gentiles.

INSTRUCTIONS TO THE TWELVE APOSTLES

This second teaching section begins as Jesus is getting ready to send out His twelve apostles to do the work of the Kingdom. To begin, He gave them the authority to drive out demons and heal the sick. This was not something Jesus gave all His followers; He only gave this ability to the Twelve.

Before the Twelve departed, Jesus gave them instructions about the Kingdom's work and mission. He told them not to go to the Gentiles or Samaritans, only to the "lost sheep of Israel." This was only for the time being; later, they were to spread the Good News to everybody. If they were welcomed somewhere, they were to offer them the Gospel message, but were told, *"If anyone will not receive you or listen to your words, shake off the dust from your feet when you leave that house or town"* **(Matt. 10:14).** This was a symbolic gesture severing connection with, and all responsibility for, the guilt of the people for rejecting the Gospel message.

Jesus warned them that they would be like sheep among wolves; they would be hated, arrested, and suffer persecution and torture because of the Gospel message. But despite all this, they were not to be afraid, because God knew every hair on each of their heads. He takes care of the sparrows and knows when even one of them falls to the ground in death, and His followers are worth more than many sparrows. In light of that, the apostles, and all believers for all time, are to proclaim the message from the rooftops without fear.

Jesus finished His teaching by stating that His coming was not going to bring peace between men, even within the same family. In **Matthew 10:34-36**, Jesus says, *"Do not think that I have come to bring peace to the earth. I have not come to bring peace, but a sword. For I have come to set a man against his father, and a daughter against her mother, and a daughter-in-law against her mother-in-law. And a person's enemies will be those of his own household."* He came to save His people; and because of that, He is to have supreme importance in the believer's life. Those of us who are His should never deny Him. In fact, we should acknowledge Him before all, regardless of the consequences! Jesus doesn't promise that the Christian life will be a "rose garden." In fact, there will be many thorns. Anyone who promises roses without any thorns is teaching a lie from the devil. If you ever find yourself under this kind of teaching, flee and read your Bible!

Matthew illustrates this stark reality in chapter eleven, where we find out that John the Baptist was in prison. He was eventually beheaded, not because of any crime he committed, but for proclaiming the Word of God.

PARABLES ABOUT THE KINGDOM

Starting in chapter thirteen, Matthew groups together some of Jesus' teachings done in the form of parables. A parable is a story based on everyday life situations used to make a point. While the stories may seem easy to understand because they're based on well-known situations, they aren't. Even the disciples had to ask Jesus to explain them. Therefore, we need to be very careful when interpreting them. For example, Jesus explains the parable of the sower in the form of allegory, but not all of them can be explained this way.

Parables are intentionally divisive, separating believers from unbelievers. They both reveal and obscure truths. When the disciples asked Jesus why He taught the crowd in parables, He said, *"To you it has been given to know the secrets of the kingdom of heaven, but to them it has not been given"* **(Matt. 13:11)**. To the elect, the meaning of parables will be revealed, and it will enrich their understanding of the Kingdom; but to everyone else, they will seem like silly stories and likely increase their ignorance. This was to fulfill the prophecy in **Isaiah 6:9-10** that some would *"keep on hearing,"* but not understand, just as they would "keep on seeing," but not perceive.

THE TRANSFIGURATION

One day, as the group was traveling, Jesus took Peter, James, and John to the top of a high mountain and transfigured before them, making His face shine like the sun and His clothes gleam white. At the same time, according to the Gospel of Luke, Moses and the prophet Elijah appeared before them, and the two began to talk with Jesus about His death. Peter, being nervous and unsure what to do, proposed the idea of putting up three shelters to cover Jesus, Moses, and Elijah! But before he could finish laying out his idea, they were surrounded by a bright cloud, and a Voice from the cloud said, "'This is my beloved Son, with whom I am well pleased; listen to him'" **(Matt. 17:5b).** This terrified the apostles and caused them to fall on their faces! When Jesus told them to get up, He was the only One still with them. As they headed back down the mountain, Jesus told them to keep silent about what had just happened *"until the Son of Man is raised from the dead"* **(Matt. 17:9b)**.

Continuing to do miracles as they traveled, Jesus walked on water, healed the daughter of a Canaanite woman, and a little while later, healed a boy possessed by a demon. One of the quirkier miracles Jesus did was to make a coin appear in the mouth of a fish that Peter caught, which they used to pay the temple tax. All of these were demonstrations of Jesus' Divinity. Despite all of these miracles, the apostles were still far from understanding completely Who Jesus was or what He was here to do.

TEACHINGS ABOUT THE CHURCH

Sometime in the last year of His ministry in 29 A.D., "the disciples came to Jesus, saying, *'Who is the greatest in the kingdom of heaven?' And calling to him a child, he put him in the midst of them'"* **(Matt. 18:1-2)**. So, Jesus began his fourth round of teaching, this time about the Kingdom of Heaven. As King, Jesus is Ruler and, therefore, has all authority to make the rules. In response to their questions about who is the greatest in the Kingdom—probably thinking He will name one of them—He told them they wouldn't even be able to enter the Kingdom unless they become like little children.

Jesus used a little child as an example—not because children are innocent (because they aren't) but because they are dependent, and they know it. They come in humble recognition that they can't do anything for themselves. Jesus was using the "little child" as an example for a believer. Jesus further warns that anyone who causes one of these "little ones" (another believer) to sin, that person would be better off dead!

Jesus completed His teaching on family life within the Kingdom with three parables: one showing the importance of each of His people, including the fact that the angels watch over and minister to them; one giving instruction about how to treat a fellow Christian who sins against you; and one that teaches forgiveness.

As Jesus drew closer to Jerusalem, He was being followed by large crowds, and many people were being healed. As usual, amongst the crowd were the Pharisees, who intended to try to catch Him saying something opposite of Scripture. They should have known better than to think they would accomplish their task. No matter what test they tried to throw at Him, Jesus taught about the subject more fully than they expected, challenging their own view of the Law.

One day, a rich young man came to Jesus and asked, *"'Teacher, what good deed must I do to have eternal life?' and he said to him, 'Why do you ask me about what is good? There is only one who is good. If you would enter life, keep the commandments'"* **(Matt. 19:16-17)**. In the same way as many Christians think about wealth today, many of the Jews at the time looked at wealth as evidence of God's approval and blessing. The man told Jesus that he had kept the commandments but wanted to know if there was anything else he lacked. Jesus told him to sell all his possessions, give the money to the poor, and follow Him. The man walked away discouraged because he didn't want to give up his money.

Was Jesus telling all His followers to sell all their possessions and give them to the poor? No. That would never merit anyone eternal life. This whole section of Scripture is an answer to the initial question asked by the young man—*what must I do to get eternal life?* The young man wanted to know how "good" he must be and if there was anything else he must do to earn his salvation. Jesus answered the man's question in the first part of their conversation—*there is only One [Jesus] who is good.* To be "good enough," the commandments must be kept. In other words, no human could ever be good enough to earn salvation.

The young man thought he'd been keeping the commandments, but he hadn't. This was what Jesus was showing him by telling him to sell everything. The young man needed to become poor—not in money, but in spirit. Just like the first Beatitude says, this man needed to see his need for God's merciful salvation.

The disciples overheard the conversation. Jesus told them, *"'Truly, I say to you, only with difficulty will a rich person enter the kingdom of heaven. Again I tell you, it is easier for a camel to go through the eye of a needle than for a rich person to enter the kingdom of God'"* **(Matt. 19:23-24)**. Jesus was using an exaggerated parallelism here to make this same point to His disciples. Jesus wasn't saying that being rich makes it harder to become a believer. It is God Who does the saving from start to finish! He can save a rich man just as easily as a poor man.

We see His point in the second line. Can a camel ever fit through the eye of a needle? No! It's impossible. Likewise, no human being can ever do enough, be good enough, or behave well enough to earn their way into Heaven. The disciples got it then, as we see in **Matthew 19:25-26**: *"When the disciples heard this, they were greatly astonished, saying 'Who then can be saved?' But Jesus looked at them and said, 'With man this is impossible, but with God all things are possible.'"*

Jesus told another parable, this time about a king who invited people to his son's wedding banquet. The original invitees rejected the invitation, and some even killed the messengers who were sent to invite them. The king ordered his troops to destroy them and their city. He then sent more servants out to invite anyone and everyone they could find, filling the hall with guests! However, when the king arrived at the banquet, he noticed someone without wedding clothes. When asked how he got into the banquet without the right clothes, the man had no answer. The parable ends with, *"Then the king said to the attendants, 'Bind him hand and foot and cast him into the outer darkness. In that place there will be weeping and gnashing of teeth.' For many are called but few are chosen"* **(Matt. 22:13-14)**. In this parable, the original invitees represent the Jewish people who rejected Jesus as their Messiah. The other invitees represent the Gospel going out to the Gentiles; but as shown by the lack of wedding clothing, Jesus was teaching that although the Gospel message is to go out to everyone, not all of those who hear it are God's chosen people. God's elect will indeed be clothed correctly – with Jesus' imputed robe of righteousness!

THE TRIUMPHAL ENTRY

Jesus took His twelve apostles aside and explained to them that He was moving toward Jerusalem, where He would be killed, laying down His life as a ransom for many, but that on the third day, He would be raised to life. At this point, there were still large crowds following Jesus. Many believed Jesus was there to rid them of their Roman oppressors. Jesus gave two of His apostles instructions to go to a place where they would find a donkey and her colt tied and bring the colt to Jesus. This was in fulfillment of the prophecy in **Zechariah 9:9** that says, *"Behold, your king is coming to you; righteous and having salvation is he, humble and mounted on a donkey, on a colt, the foal of a donkey."* Jesus rode the colt into Jerusalem the Sunday before He was crucified as the crowds shouted "Hosanna" to Him, which means "Save!"

TEACHING ABOUT END TIMES

During His last week on Earth, Jesus began His fifth round of teaching for His disciples. This final block of teaching had to do with judgment. He told them that the temple buildings, the place revered by Jews as the dwelling of God's presence, would be destroyed (something that happened several years later during the destruction of Jerusalem in 70 A.D.) He then gave them several signs of the coming of the end of the age. While there are many ideas— some of them outlandish—about the specifics of what Jesus told them, it's important not to get too caught up in speculation about them. The apostles understood the "last days" to be the time between Jesus' First Coming and His Second Coming. Remember, the whole Bible is about God's plan to redeem a remnant of people for Himself through Jesus' perfect life, His death, and His resurrection. Satan has and will continue to make war with God's people throughout all of history until Jesus returns; but no matter what he does, Satan is already defeated! God's people should live holy lives that are pleasing to God, always looking forward to Jesus' Second Coming—something that Jesus tells us in this passage will be at a date and hour unknown to man.

Then Jesus began to teach by using parables again, this time as warnings. He used a parable about ten virgins waiting for the bridegroom, some of whom were prepared and had everything they needed to enter and enjoy the wedding banquet, while others did not have what they needed, even though they thought they did. There are a lot of people sitting in churches all over the world Sunday after Sunday who believe they are saved. And they might be— but only if they've repented and made Jesus their Savior and Lord. Everyone should examine themselves in light of this!

Next Jesus launched into teaching about sheep and goats. This was anything but a lesson in farm husbandry. At the end of the age, Jesus will return and separate those who are saved (the sheep) from the unbelievers (the goats). Then He will tell His sheep, *"Come, you who are blessed by my Father, inherit the kingdom prepared for you from the foundation of the world"* **(Matt. 25:34).** And He will say to the goats, *"Depart from me, you cursed, into the eternal fire prepared for the devil and his angels"* **(Matt. 25:41).** This ended the last of the five discourses of Jesus' teachings recorded in Matthew.

JUDAS, THE BETRAYER

Who's to blame for Jesus' death? Some blame the Jews for killing Jesus. Some blame the Roman government at the time—the only ones who could order someone to be killed. The truth of the matter is that Jesus' death was something that had to happen to fulfill God's plan of salvation for His people. Jesus had to die. If you'll remember back to chapter one, this was God's sovereign plan from before the foundations of the earth. Jesus was the perfect, spotless Lamb Who would be the final sacrifice for sin. This was the work He came to do. No human being could take Jesus' life from Him. Jesus willingly submitted to the Father and laid down His life for His people. The King had to die so that His people would live.

In the year 30 A.D., three years after Jesus' ministry began, the chief priests and religious leaders had had enough of Jesus, so they plotted to have Him arrested and killed. This took place during the time of the Passover feast, an event that drew tens of thousands of Jews to Jerusalem from all over. The crowds were still enamored with Jesus, obvious from His triumphal entry into Jerusalem where they'd shouted "Hosanna!" Being afraid of causing a riot, the leaders decided to wait until after the feast to put their plan into action. They didn't have to look far for a recruit to help. Judas Iscariot saw the opportunity to make a lucrative deal and willingly went to the chief priests with an offer to deliver Jesus into their hands. His reward was thirty pieces of silver—silver that caused him so much guilt that instead of spending it, he committed suicide.

Judas is a figure who's been the cause of much discussion. His plight is the subject of books and television specials, and it's the subject of the musical *Jesus Christ Superstar*. As one of the twelve apostles, he heard Jesus' teaching, saw the miracles He'd performed, broke bread with Him, spent days and nights at His side, and yet, at this moment, decided to be His betrayer. Being this close to Jesus leads to the debate about whether Judas is in Hell for his actions, or whether he is saved, regardless of his egregious sin against the King.

John makes it clear in his Gospel that Judas was not only the betrayer, but was also a thief in **John 12:6**: *"He said this, not because he cared about the poor, but because he was a thief, and having charge of the moneybag he used to help himself to what was put into it."* **Luke 22:3** tells us, *"Then Satan entered into Judas called Iscariot, who was of the number of the twelve."* We also see that Jesus knew He was going to be betrayed and who was going to do it, which He made clear at the Passover meal, as we see in **John 13:21b and 26**: *"'Truly, truly I say to you, one of you will betray me . . . It is he to whom I will give this morsel of bread when I have dipped it.' So when he had dipped the morsel, he gave it to Judas, the son of Simon Iscariot."*

If God ordained Judas to be the betrayer, is Judas responsible for his sin? If he was possessed by Satan, is Satan the one responsible? And does the fact that he returned the money and took his own life because of the weight of guilt lead us to believe that he's at Jesus' side right now and not in Hell? Judas, just like everyone else since the Fall, is responsible for his own sin. Although Satan deceives us, tempts us, and may even plant an idea in our head, he is not responsible for our sin. Although God ordained everything that happened or will happen in the future, He is not responsible for our sin. God doesn't ever have to make us sin; we do it willingly and, thus, bear the responsibility for it. Judas eventually felt the weight of his sin. But feeling guilt and remorse over sin is never enough. To be forgiven requires repentance, and there is no mention in the Bible that Judas Iscariot ever repented of his sin. Judas betrayed the King of the world.

At some point, all of Jesus' apostles had doubts about Him and had moments of weak faith, and one of them even denied knowing Jesus three times. But in the end, we see there's evidence that they were sheep all along by their repentance. They belonged to Jesus from before the foundation of the world, and Jesus never loses any of those who are His, something that Judas never was.

THE LAST SUPPER

On the first day of the feast, when it's time to make plans and prepare for the Passover meal, Jesus had His disciples go to a certain man inside the city and tell him, *"'The Teacher says, My time is at hand. I will keep the Passover at your house with my disciples'"* **(Matt. 26:18)**. The disciples did as Jesus said and prepared the meal for all of them to share together. As the evening meal progressed, Jesus made it known that Judas would betray Him.

> *Now as they were eating, Jesus took bread, and after blessing it broke it and gave it to the disciples, saying, "Take, eat; this is my body." And he took a cup, and when he had given thanks he gave it to them, saying, "Drink of it, all of you, for this is my blood of the covenant, which is poured out for many for the forgiveness of sins. I tell you I will not drink again of this fruit of the vine until that day when I drink it new with you in my Father's kingdom"* **(Matthew 26:26-29)**.

This is why we practice the sacrament known as Communion. It is a remembrance of Jesus' body and blood poured out for those who believe and trust in Him.

When the meal was finished, they sang a hymn and then went out to the Mount of Olives. It was at this familiar spot, where Jesus taught His disciples many things, that Jesus gave them some shocking news about themselves. He told them that later that very night, they would all "fall away" from Him. In other words, they would abandon Him! This news sounded incredulous to Peter. He just could not fathom that the group would do such a thing; and even if the rest did, he believed that there was no way he would ever do it. But just like the rest of us who are Christians, Peter had no idea the depth of sinfulness and the possibilities for blatant, gross sin that still lurked in his heart!

Jesus continued with some very hard words for Peter to hear: *"Truly, I tell you, this very night, before the rooster crows, you will deny me three times'"* **(Matt. 26:34).** The NIV Bible (2011) uses the word "disown," and this is exactly what Peter did three times that night. He "disowned" Jesus, saying that He didn't know Him and wasn't one of His followers.

The book of Matthew leaves the story there; but in Luke's Gospel, we learn that Satan had asked Jesus' permission to sift all of the apostles—another example showing Satan cannot act outside of the boundaries God sets for him. We also learn from Luke that Jesus told Peter about Satan's request, but then He encouraged Peter by telling him that He prayed for him. Jesus further told Peter that he would indeed repent of the sin he was about to commit; and when he does and is forgiven, he should strengthen the rest of the group. Peter did betray Jesus three times, as recorded later in the same chapter of Matthew. And just as Jesus told him, he did turn in repentance and was forgiven.

THE GARDEN OF GETHSEMANE

Later that night, Jesus and His disciples headed to a place called the Garden of Gethsemane, where Jesus went off a little way from the rest of the group in order to pray. Jesus was so stressed about what was about to happen to Him that, *"His sweat became like great drops of blood falling down to the ground"* **(Luke 22:44)**. He asked His disciples to pray for Him, but they fell asleep instead. Three times Jesus prayed to the Father *"if it be possible, let this cup pass from me; nevertheless, not as I will, but as you will"* **(Matt. 26:39)**.

Something important to remember here is that Jesus is both fully God and fully Man. He has two complete natures. It was Jesus' Divine will to go to the cross and be the Substitute Sacrifice for the ransom of His people. As we said at the beginning of this book, the Trinity had made what is referred to as the "Covenant of Redemption" before the foundation of the world. This was the plan They made. He was not saying here that it was not His will to go to the cross. His distress lay in knowing the agony that was coming to Him in experiencing the Father's wrath. Yet, as the Second Adam, He fulfilled all of the Law perfectly, which Adam did not, and submitted to the punishment Adam, and all the rest of us, deserve.

JESUS' ARREST

It was not long after He finished praying that Judas showed up to betray Him; He was arrested and was taken before the high priest. Jesus claimed to him and the rest of the elders and teachers of the Law that He was indeed the Christ. The priests cried "blasphemy" and pronounced that Jesus deserved to die because of it. Then the leaders spit in His face, struck Him with their fists, and slapped Jesus. However, they had a problem because they could not put Him to death themselves. That was something only the Roman government could do, and so they must bring Jesus before Pilate, who was the local governor.

JESUS' TRIAL

Pilate knew that the real reason the Pharisees wanted Jesus dead was because He was a threat to them; however, he could not dissuade them from the idea of Jesus dying. Pilate even sent Jesus back to His hometown to go before Herod for a ruling, but Herod, frustrated by Jesus' silence before him, sent him back to Pilate. Pilate then offered the religious leaders and the crowd the opportunity to have one prisoner released to them. They picked a man who was an insurrectionist and a murderer, not Jesus. So, Pilate, surrendering to their shouts, had Jesus flogged with a whip. Not just a leather whip, but a whip of nine strands with pieces of bone tied on the strands in order to rip the skin to shreds. The prophet Isaiah spoke these words about Jesus' post-flogging appearance in **Isaiah 52:14-15a**, *"His appearance was so marred, beyond human semblance, and his form beyond that of the children of mankind—so shall he sprinkle many nations."* Capitulating to the crowd, Pilate handed Jesus over to be crucified.

The soldiers inflicted further cruelty on Jesus. They mocked Him, draped Him in a purple robe, and drove a crown of twisted vine covered with six-inch thorns into His head. Over and over, they struck Jesus on the head with a staff and spit on Him. When they finished with their abuse, they put Jesus' own clothes back on Him and led him out to be crucified. As they went, the soldiers forced a man named Simon to carry the cross for Jesus.

JESUS' CRUCIFIXION

When they reached the top of the hill called Golgotha, they offered Jesus wine mixed with gall—something that would help to lessen the pain—but Jesus refused to drink it. Then they spread out His arms and nailed Him to the cross through both His hands or wrists and through his feet. Over His head, they hung a sign that read, "THIS IS JESUS, KING OF THE JEWS." Then they divided up His clothes by casting lots and sat down to keep watch over Him. Through all of this, rulers and soldiers still mocked and taunted Him.

Jesus wasn't the only One dying on a cross that day. Two criminals were on their own crosses, one on either side of Him. Matthew recorded in his Gospel that both of these men were also heaping insults on Jesus. But Luke records something further—at some point, one of them realized Who Jesus is. He realized that Jesus is, in fact, the Messiah, and he rebuked the other criminal. Luke recorded what happened in **Luke 23:41-43**, which we'll talk about in Luke's Gospel overview.

From noon until three in the afternoon that day, darkness covered the land. At the end of that time, Jesus cried out, *"'Eli, Eli, lema sabachthani?' that is, 'My God, my God, why have you forsaken me?'"* **(Matt. 27:46b)**. Jesus' excruciating cry was not from the physical pain, but from the pain of what it would be like being separated from God—left alone in something worse than the most unbearable agony imaginable—forsaken: judgement we deserve for our sin. These words He cried come from **Psalm 22:1-2**, which says, *"My God, My God, why have you forsaken me? Why are you so far from saving me, from the words of my groaning? O my God, I cry by day, but you do not answer, and by night, but I find no rest."* Jesus didn't have the comfort of the Holy Spirit, but He had not lost the Spirit, and it's also important to note that Jesus' two natures were not separated during this time, nor was the Trinity separated during this time, nor did Jesus cease to be God at any point. But the Father did pour out His wrath on Jesus in all of its fullness—something that was agonizing to Jesus, Who had been in a constant, loving relationship with the Father from all of eternity. The next time Jesus cried out, He gave up His spirit, showing that Jesus made the decision when He would die. The moment of His death, the curtain of the temple outside of the Holy of Holies was torn in two from top to bottom. This happened because Jesus had opened the way between God and man. He is the Great High Priest, and we can go directly to the Father through Him! We no longer need an earthly priest to go to God for us!

JESUS' BURIAL

A rich man named Joseph went to the authorities and asked to have Jesus' body taken down. He wanted to bury Jesus in his own tomb that had not been used by anyone yet. Pilate ordered the body to be given to Joseph, and he wrapped the dead, lifeless body of the King of kings in clean, linen cloth and laid it in the tomb, rolling a large stone in front of the entrance. It had been a long day for Jesus' followers. Weary and worn, feeling defeated, afraid for their lives, and unsure of what to do next, the apostles went into hiding.

The next day, remembering that Jesus had claimed He would rise in three days, the chief priests and Pharisees requested that Pilate secure the tomb to avoid anyone stealing the body. Pilate agreed; the tomb was sealed; and a guard was placed in front of it until the three days passed.

HE IS RISEN!

At dawn of the first day of the week, Mary Magdalen and the other Mary went to look at the tomb. There was a violent earthquake caused by the Angel of the Lord, who came down and rolled the stone away from the entrance. This terrified the guards so much that they became "like dead men." The women arrived to see the stone rolled away and the angel seated upon it, and He said to them, *"Do not be afraid, for I know that you seek Jesus who was crucified. He is not here, for he has risen, as he said. Come, see the place where he lay. Then go quickly and tell his disciples that he has risen from the dead, and behold, he is going before you to Galilee; there you will see him"* **(Matt. 28:5-7)**. And after seeing the empty tomb, they ran with joy to tell the rest of disciples. On their way, they met Jesus! They fell down and worshiped Him. Their Savior was alive, just as He had said, and He instructed them to send apostles to Galilee to meet with Him there!

Meanwhile, the guard who saw the angel reported back to the chief priests everything that happened. To keep people from knowing the truth, the guards were given some "hush money" and told to explain that they fell asleep and the body was stolen by Jesus' disciples. They were protected from getting in trouble with Pilate for "falling asleep," as the chief priests would pay Pilate, too, to keep the secret, if need be. The Bible tells us, *"So they took the money and did as they were directed. And this story has been spread among the Jews to this day"* **(Matt. 28:15)**.

There was worship in Galilee that day as the eleven disciples met with their risen Savior. There were some who "doubted," or at least didn't know what to think about the situation. Regardless, this is where they—and, in fact, all believers for all time—got their marching orders. Matthew's Gospel ends with these words from Jesus: *"'All authority in heaven and on earth has been given to me. Go therefore and make disciples of all nations, baptizing them in the name of the Father and of the Son and of the Holy Spirit, teaching them to observe all that I have commanded you. And behold, I am with you always, to the end of the age'"* **(Matt. 28:18-20)**.

Chapter 15

THE GOSPEL OF MARK

As we said earlier, it's believed that Mark must have been the first Gospel written. He was writing to a mostly Gentile audience, and it was likely written in Rome or somewhere else in Italy. Therefore, you will see him explaining things that have to do with Jewish customs and also see him using Latin terminology. While we aren't sure Mark was an eyewitness to any of Jesus' ministry, it is possible Mark saw and heard Jesus speak while he was a teenager. In any event, Mark's accounts came from Peter, who was an eyewitness to everything.

The book of Mark is not in chronological order. It's a simple historical record of facts of the life, death, and resurrection of Jesus that is laid out in three basic parts, which we will follow:

1. The Inauguration of the Gospel

2. His Ministry in Galilee

3. His Ministry in Judea and Jerusalem

Some things that Mark imparts to his audience are that Jesus is the Divine Son of God, that the Gentiles are included in God's salvation plan, that Jesus wanted His identity as Messiah kept secret for the first part of His ministry, and that Jesus' twelve apostles had trouble understanding what His mission was.

THE INAUGURATION OF THE GOSPEL

Mark didn't start his Gospel off at the beginning of Jesus' life. Instead, he fast-forwarded to the beginning of John the Baptist announcing Jesus' ministry in 26 A.D. Because we dealt with so much of the same material in the book of Matthew and because this is such a short part of Mark's Gospel, we won't go into further detail about it.

MINISTRY IN GALILEE

Not long after He was baptized, Jesus headed to the northern regions of the land to an area known as Galilee. Although this had been the northernmost part of the Promised Land long ago, it was now vastly filled with Gentiles. Jesus came, proclaiming, *"The time is fulfilled, and the kingdom of God is at hand; repent and believe in the gospel"* **(Mark 1:15)**.

While Jesus was preaching in this Gentile region, He attended worship on the Sabbath, teaching in the synagogues while He was there, something usually reserved for rabbis. **Mark 1:22** tells us that the people *"were astonished at his teaching, for he taught them as one who had authority, and not as the scribes."* It's not clear exactly what was different about the teaching, except that when Jesus taught, it was with authority!

One day while Jesus was in the synagogue, a man with an evil spirit came in. Seeing Jesus, he cried out, *"What have you to do with us, Jesus of Nazareth? Have you come to destroy us? I know who you are—the Holy One of God"* **(Mark 1:24)**. Jesus ordered the unclean spirit to be silent and come out of the man. It obeyed but came out with a loud cry. The people were amazed that Jesus commanded evil spirits, and they obeyed Him! The reason Jesus ordered the demon to be silent was to keep it secret for the time being that He's the Messiah, something that you will see throughout the first part of Mark's Gospel.

Later that day, Simon and Andrew took Jesus and the other two apostles to their house, where Simon's mother-in-law was in bed with a fever. Jesus healed her, and she began to wait on them. By that evening, the whole town had landed on her doorstep. Everyone wanted to see Jesus and be healed by Him! Jesus healed many of them and cast out many demons, once again forbidding them to speak because they knew Who He is.

Jesus continued traveling throughout Galilee preaching and performing miracles. After returning to the town of Capernaum sometime in 28 A.D., Jesus was preaching in a house, likely that of Simon and Andrew, and a large crowd gathered to hear what He had to say. Among the crowd were Pharisees and teachers of the Law who had come from all over. On this day, there was a paralyzed man who was brought to Jesus on a mat by some men from the town. Because the crowd was so thick, the men were having trouble getting their paralyzed friend in front of Jesus, so they took him to the roof, made an opening in it, and lowered the mat in front of Him. The Bible tell us, *"And when Jesus saw their faith, he said to the paralytic, 'Son, your sins are forgiven'"* **(Mark 2:5)**. Scripture doesn't say what the man thought or what his friends thought about this. They came expecting healing, but Jesus said that the man's sins were forgiven. This fact didn't escape the Pharisees' notice either! They thought Jesus was blaspheming because who can forgive sins but God? Jesus immediately knew their thoughts and said to them, *"'Which is easier, to say to this paralytic, your sins are forgiven, or to say Rise, take up your bed and walk? But that you may know that the Son of Man has authority on earth to forgive sins"—he said to the paralytic—"I say to you, rise, pick up your bed, and go home"* **(Mark 2:9-11)**. Then the man walked out fully healed—both spiritually and physically—in front of everybody. This act of healing caused everyone to praise God!

Mark's next account is of Jesus calling His twelve apostles. Jesus chose the number twelve for a reason stated in **Matthew 19:28** when He said to them, *"'Truly, I say to you, in the new world, when the Son of Man will sit on his glorious throne, you who have followed me will also sit on twelve thrones, judging the twelve tribes of Israel."* **Mark 3:16-19** gives us the names: *"He appointed the twelve: Simon* *(to whom he gave the name Peter); James the son of Zebedee and John the brother of James (to whom he gave the name Boanerges, that is, Sons of Thunder); Andrew, and Philip, and Bartholomew, and Matthew, and Thomas, and James the son of Alphaeus, and Thaddaeus, and Simon the Zealot, and Judas Iscariot, who betrayed him."* This was a *specific call.* Apostles were appointed to that office by Jesus, Himself. He gave them power to do signs, wonders, and miracles, the things that marked an apostle, according to 2 Corinthians 12:12. Paul considered himself to be the last apostle, according to 1 Corinthians 15:8.

Mark recorded many of Jesus' parables in his Gospel; and after teaching the parable of the sower to a crowd gathered at the Sea of Galilee, Jesus told them another parable about seed in the ground. This parable is found only in **Mark 4:26-29**:

> *And he said, "The kingdom of God is as if a man should scatter seed on the ground. He sleeps and rises night and day, and the seed sprouts and grows; he knows not how. The earth produces by itself, first the blade, then the ear, then the full grain in the ear. But when the grain is ripe, at once he puts in the sickle, because the harvest has come."*

Many people of that time thought that the Messiah would swoop in and grandly usher in a "new kingdom" here on earth, triumphing over the Roman government and quickly changing the status quo for them. Instead, Jesus ushered in the Kingdom quietly, coming as a baby born to a virgin, picking unlikely men and women to spread news of His Kingdom, and growing the Kingdom over unspecified millennia, until the time of Jesus' Second Coming, when *"he will send out his angels with a loud trumpet call, and they will gather his elect from the four winds, from one end of heaven to the other"* **(Matt. 24:31)**.

When Jesus was done teaching the crowd, He and the twelve apostles climbed into a boat and crossed to the other side of the sea. Jesus experienced human tiredness just like we do, so He went to the rear of the boat, found a cushion to lay down on, and nodded off. While He was sleeping, a furious storm erupted, and waves were breaking over the boat, almost to the point of sinking it. The Twelve were scared, so they woke up Jesus and said, *"Teacher, do you not care that we are perishing?"* **(Mark 4:38b)**. Then Jesus rebuked the wind and told the sea to calm down, and the storm stopped. Just like everything that happens, the storm had a purpose. As close as the Twelve were to Jesus, they still didn't fully understand Who He is. By calming the storm, Jesus was showing them that He is God. He has to be—the wind and sea don't obey anyone else!

Reaching the other side of the sea, they landed at a place called Gerasenes (also called Gadarenes), which was a burial ground. Here, Jesus demonstrated His Divinity through His authority over demons using through a man who was possessed by so many that they called themselves "Legion." This legion had caused him to be so violent that even chains on his hands and feet hadn't been able to control him. He had been in this state for some time now, living naked and making the tombs his home. When the boat reached the shore, the man rushed toward them and attacked the group. At the same time, a herd of pigs was grazing on a hillside with a lake at the bottom of it. Encountering Jesus, he fell on his knees and shouted, *"What have you to do with me, Jesus, Son of the Most High God? I adjure you by God, do not torment me"* **(Mark 5:7)**. Jesus demanded the evil spirits to come out of the man; but not wanting to leave the area, the demons begged Jesus to let them enter the pigs, so He did. When the pigs were indwelt with the demons, they ran down the hill into the lake and drowned themselves.

Crossing back to where they came from, Jesus showed them Who He is in two more ways—healing the sick and raising the dead. Having heard about Jesus, a woman in the crowd who had menstrual bleeding for twelve years pushed her way through the throng of people and touched His cloak because she thought, *"If I touch even his garments, I will be made well"* **(Mark 5:28)**. And that's exactly what happened—her bleeding immediately stopped. There was also a synagogue ruler in the crowd named Jairus, whose twelve-year-old daughter was dying, so he pled with Jesus, saying in faith, *"My little daughter* *is at the point of death. Come and lay your hands on her, so that she may be made well and live'"* **(Mark 5:23)**. But the girl died before Jesus went to her. When Jesus arrived at the house, He raised her from the dead.

After that, Jesus traveled from town to town teaching. So many people were coming for help that Jesus and the apostles didn't even have time to eat. The crowds were so relentless, when they saw Jesus get in the boat to take the Twelve for some rest, they ran on foot to get there before the boat reached the shore. By the time it did, it's a large crowd that's gathered because they came from all the towns in the area. Despite weariness and hunger, Jesus began to teach them many things. He felt compassion for them because they were like sheep without a shepherd. It was growing late in the day, and there was nowhere close by to buy food—this was a desolate place—especially for a crowd of five thousand men, plus women and children. The apostles wanted Jesus to send the crowd away to buy their own food. But Jesus told them to give them something to eat themselves. This was a radical statement! The most they could scrounge together was five loaves of bread and two fishes—not enough to feed themselves, let alone this large group! Jesus had given them an impossible task!

However, with God, all things are possible! Jesus took the meager meal, looked to Heaven, and said a blessing. Then they divided up the loaves and fishes and set the portions in front of the people. Everyone ate, and they were all satisfied. Then they picked up the leftovers and still had twelve baskets full of bread and fish. In our own strength, the tasks we are doing will many times be impossible. In those times, we need to acknowledge that we *can't* and ask God if He will!

But this is not just another one of Jesus' miracles. This whole event harkens back to Israel in the desert with many parallels, which the apostles (as well as the other people) should have picked up on. The twelve men closest to Jesus still didn't realize Who He is. On the way back across the sea, Jesus showed them one more miracle that was meant to remind them of Israel crossing the Red Sea, something else that should have clued them in—He walked on water, just like Israel crossed on dry land!

As Jesus moved on toward the Gentile region of Decapolis, He healed a deaf and mute man by sticking His fingers in the man's ears, then spitting and touching the man's tongue with his fingers, while looking toward Heaven and crying, *"Be opened!"* **(Mark 7:34b)**. This may sound strange, but it's what the Bible says!

Opposition was beginning to mount. The Pharisees began to argue with Jesus, and they wanted Him to show them a sign. But Jesus wouldn't perform signs on demand for them. Jesus had already done many miracles, and they all knew it. Jesus warned the Twelve, *"'Watch out; beware of the leaven of the Pharisees and the leaven of Herod"* **(Mark 8:15)**. Even after all they had been through with Jesus and all they had seen Him do, the apostles still had some spiritual "blindness." They thought He was saying something about the fact that they forgot to bring bread! While quietly discussing between themselves that they had forgotten the bread, Jesus interrupted them and said, *"'Why are you discussing the fact that you have no bread? Do you not yet perceive or understand? Are your hearts hardened? Having eyes do you not see, and having ears do you not hear?'"* **(Mark 8:17-18)**.

There are no coincidences. Mark records directly after this that when they got to Bethsaida, some people brought a blind man to Jesus, begging Him to touch the man and heal him. *"And when [Jesus] had spit on his eyes and laid His hands on him, he asked him, 'Do you see anything?'"* **(Mark 8:23)**. The man opened his eyes and said, *"'I see people, but they look like trees, walking"* **(Mark 8:24)**. Then Jesus laid His hands on his eyes a second time, and after that, the man could see clearly.

Did Jesus have a problem getting His healing to work the first time? Absolutely not! Did the man not have enough faith the first time that it caused Jesus to have to lay His hands on him a second time? No. Like we said, there are no coincidences. The gradual restoration of the man's sight was symbolic of the gradual understanding of Who Jesus is that the apostles were experiencing. The image would get sharper and sharper; and when it became perfectly clear (which isn't until after the resurrection), they responded like the deaf mute whose tongue was loosed, and they spread the message of Jesus far and wide.

Jesus and the apostles moved on to the villages of Caesarea Philippi. On the way, He asked them, *"Who do people say that I am?"* **(Mark 8:27b)**. Their answers were John the Baptist, Elijah, or one of the prophets. Jesus didn't address what other people thought about Him; that was not His concern here. He got straight to the point and asked them, *"But who do you say that I am?"* Peter, answering for all of them, said, *"You are the Christ"* **(Mark 8:29)**. The Twelve He chose to lay the foundation of His Church needed to know for sure Who He is.

"And [Jesus] began to teach them that the Son of Man must suffer many things and be rejected by the elders and the chief priests and the scribes and be killed, and after three days rise again" **(Mark 8:31)**. This news was such a shock to Peter that he pulled Jesus aside and started to rebuke Him. Peter was not accepting God's plan. He was still thinking from an earthly perspective. Jesus looked at the rest of the group—who very likely were thinking the same thing—and *"rebuked Peter and said, 'Get behind me, Satan! For you are not setting your mind on the things of God, but on the things of man'"* **(Mark 8:33)**. Then Jesus called the crowd over to them and started to teach them, saying, *"'If anyone would come after me, let him deny himself and take up his cross and follow me'"* **(Mark 8:34)**. Following Jesus is not a cake walk. False teachers can promise prosperity; memes can claim that your tears will stop, and doors will open; and while your best friend may have had things turn around for her after she became a Christian, the Bible never promises that. Not any of it.

For some of the time they spent in Galilee, Jesus didn't want anyone to know where they were because He wanted to teach His apostles. Jesus spent time alone with the Twelve because they had a special position of leadership and a job to do that no one else will ever have. One of the times when they found a quiet spot, Jesus told them again that He would be betrayed, killed, and would rise on the third day. They still didn't understand what Jesus was talking about, but everyone was too afraid to ask.

MINISTRY IN JUDEA AND JERUSALEM

As the group moved toward Judea, Jesus foretold His death again. After the Triumphal Entry, which we covered in Matthew's Gospel, Jesus left Jerusalem and went back to the village of Bethany for the night. The next morning, as they were heading back to the city, Jesus was hungry. Seeing a fig tree with leaves on it, Jesus went to find some fruit. A fig tree's leaves and fruit come out at the same time. But there was no fruit—only leaves! And Jesus said to the tree, *"May no one ever eat fruit from you again'"* **(Mark 11:14)**. The tree looked impressive, but it had no fruit.

The temple, which Jesus and the apostles were heading back to, was impressive also; but like the fig tree, looks aren't everything. The teaching coming from the temple wasn't producing the fruit of repentance. In fact, the Pharisees and teachers of the Law had allowed it to become a marketplace where salesmen sold animals for sacrifice and moneychangers with an exorbitant exchange rate of currency robbed the worshipers! Not only that, but this was happening in the only area of the temple specifically set aside for worship by the Gentiles.

Being righteously angry, Jesus walked into the temple and cleared it out, flipping over tables and benches. He said, *"Is it not written, My house shall be called a house of prayer for all the nations? But you have made it a den of robbers'"* **(Mark 11:17)**. The next morning, as they were passing the fig tree, they noticed it was withered to its roots! This was a picture of what would happen to the temple—not only would it be destroyed, but it also would not be needed for worship much longer! The fig tree is also a picture of the *visible* Church, which is filled with people who all look like believers, but some are bearing no fruit because they're not truly saved. Religious exercise alone is dead. It's by faith alone in Jesus' finished work on the cross will save and produce the fruit of repentance and the outward workings that follow.

In **Mark 11:23-34**, Jesus said some words to the Twelve that have been taken completely out of context by many: *"'Truly, I say to you, whoever says to this mountain, Be taken up and thrown into the sea, and does not doubt in his heart, but believes that what he says will come to pass, it will be done for him. Therefore I tell you, whatever you ask in prayer, believe that you have received it, and it will be yours."* This doesn't mean if you ask for a million dollars and have enough faith that you'll get a million dollars. Just as the fig tree represented a "spiritual matter," the "moving mountains" does as well, representing asking the Father in prayer for spiritual help—perseverance in trials, patience, wisdom, righteousness, discernment—*these* are the things the Father is pleased to give us. This truth is reiterated in James 1:2-8.

When they got to the temple, Jesus was questioned by the chief priests and teachers of the Law about where He had received His authority. Jesus taught the Parable of the Tenants, which is about a landowner who planted a vineyard and rented it out to some farmers to tend it. At harvest time, the owner sent a servant to collect some of the fruit, but the farmers beat the servant and sent him away empty-handed and do the same and worse to several more servants sent to collect some of the fruit. Then the owner sent his son, thinking that the farmers would show respect to him. But because he was the heir, the farmers killed him, thinking that they would inherit the vineyard if the son was dead. But the owner came and killed those farmers and gave the vineyard to others who would produce fruit. The religious leaders looked for a way to arrest Jesus because they knew that the parable was against them.

JESUS' ANOINTING

With the Passover only two days away, the chief priests and teachers of the Law were diligently looking for a way to arrest and kill Jesus. They didn't have long to wait. Judas was having a meal with Jesus and the others at the home of Simon the Leper. While they were there, a woman came with an alabaster jar of very expensive perfume that would cost more than a year's wages. As Jesus was reclining at the table, she *"broke the flask and poured it over his head"* **(Mark 14:3b)**.

Jesus was questioned about why it was acceptable to use an expensive jar of perfume like this when it could have been sold and the money given to the poor. *"But Jesus said, 'Leave her alone. Why do you trouble her? She has done a beautiful thing to me. For you always have the poor with you . . . But you will not always have me . . . She has anointed my body beforehand for burial. And truly, I say to you, wherever the gospel is proclaimed in the whole world, what she has done will be told in memory of her'"* **(Mark 14:6-9)**. The question had been asked by Judas. John tells us in his Gospel account that Judas had charge of the money bags and helped himself to the money whenever he wanted. So, the idea that a day's wages was out of his reach is infuriating to him. In fact, Judas left the dinner to make plans to betray Jesus to the chief priests and lawgivers.

Mark's Gospel continues with the accounts of Jesus' passion week that we covered in Matthew's Gospel overview, after which there is some text not found in the earliest manuscripts of his Gospel. In most Bibles, these verses are usually set apart and marked this way so that the reader knows this. The verses in question are **Mark 16:9-20**. These verses have caused some serious issues, causing some churches to engage in questionable practices. While too complex to go into in an overview, it is definitely worth looking into yourself. Although conservative theologians aren't in total agreement on the subject, one thing they are in agreement on is that the practices have been abused, faked, used in excess, and used in ways that are theologically wrong. The bottom line is, be careful how you use them!

Chapter 16

THE GOSPEL OF LUKE

As we said before, right from the beginning, we see that Luke's Gospel came about by his desire to write an orderly account to someone named Theophilus, which means "lover of God." Because Luke used the designation "most excellent" when addressing him, this was likely a real person and not just the use of the name Theophilus to imply it was for all of Jesus' disciples or "lovers of God."

Luke was not an eyewitness to the events he wrote about. The accounts were based on other written, and possibly some oral, accounts that were already out there, as well as eyewitness testimony. Luke was a doctor and a dear friend of the apostle Paul, according to the book of Colossians. He's referred to by Paul as a "fellow worker" in the book of Philemon, and we see from 2 Timothy that he was with Paul when Paul was murdered for his faith. Luke also wrote the book of Acts, his Gospel being the first of the two to be written.

The "orderliness" of Luke's account can be seen in the way he starts with events leading up to Jesus' birth, Jesus' childhood, and the beginning of His ministry, and then follows along the journey beginning in Galilee, on the way to Jerusalem, the ministry in Jerusalem, and ending with the events surrounding Jesus' death and resurrection. We will follow that same format.

Luke makes it clear that salvation is available for sinful people. In his Gospel, he shows Jesus has a loving concern for the oppressed. This is seen in Luke's references to the tax-collectors, sinners, the poor, widows, the lame, the blind, and the Samaritans. Luke also shows Jesus' high regard for women, as he follows up the telling of an event involving a man with one involving a woman.

BIRTH EVENTS

After Luke's introduction, he begins his orderly account by going back to the time when neither John the Baptist nor Jesus had been born yet. John's father, who was a godly priest named Zechariah, was visited by an angel while serving in the temple. Zechariah was afraid, but the angel said to him, *"Do not be afraid, Zechariah, for your prayer has been heard, and your wife Elizabeth will bear you a son, and you shall call his name John"* **(Luke 1:12)**. Because his wife, Elizabeth, was barren, this news was so unbelievable that Zechariah dared to question the angel by asking how he could be sure! He got more than he bargained for as an answer—he was unable to speak until the child was born!

It's also from Luke's Gospel that we get the backstory to Jesus' birth. It's here that we find the familiar story of the virgin Mary's visit from an angel announcing that she would give birth to a son and would name Him Jesus. This baby would not be born of an earthly father, even though Mary was betrothed to a man named Joseph. This baby would be born of the Holy Spirit and would be the Son of God. The angel also gave Mary the exciting news that her cousin Elizabeth was six months pregnant, which prompted her to go and visit with the expectant couple.

When Mary arrived, she greeted Elizabeth. *"And when Elizabeth heard the greeting of Mary, the baby leaped in her womb. And Elizabeth was filled with the Holy Spirit"* **(Luke 1:41)**. In response to this, Mary sang a song of praise to God. In it, she said, *"My soul magnifies the Lord, and my spirit rejoices in God my Savior, for he has looked on the humble estate of his servant'"* **(Luke 1:46-48a)**. Mary recognized her position before God—a servant. Mary was a created being, just like all of humanity. Being the mother of Jesus didn't change that. Therefore, we should not worship Mary, nor pray to her. Likewise, for any other human being who's been designated a "saint." All Christians are considered "saints" according to the Bible. Worship is reserved for God alone. No created being should be worshiped.

Luke follows up the news of both pregnancies with birth announcements first, with Zechariah's restored voice singing a song of praise upon the birth of his son. Second, several months later, in the fields near Bethlehem, where shepherds were keeping watch over their sheep:

> *An angel of the Lord appeared to them, and the glory of the Lord shone around them, and they were filled with great fear. And the angel said to them, "Fear not, for behold, I bring you good news of great joy that will be for all the people. For unto you is born this day in the city of David a Savior, who is Christ the Lord. And this will be a sign for you: you will find a baby wrapped in swaddling cloths and lying in a manger"* **(Luke 2:9-12)**.

If the shepherds were terrified at the sight of one angel appearing, it's hard to imagine how they felt when an army of them joined the first one, praising God and saying, *"'Glory to God in the highest, and on earth peace among those with whom he is pleased!'"* **(Luke 2:14)**. When the angels left the, the shepherds hurried to Bethlehem and found things just as they'd been told.

Following the Law, when Jesus was eight days old, Joseph and Mary presented Him at the temple, where he was circumcised and given the name Jesus, just as the angel had told them to do. While they were at the temple, a devout worshiper of God named Simeon was there, too. Simeon had been waiting for the Messiah and the relief and comfort that He would bring, and the Holy Spirit had revealed to him that he would not die before he had seen the One promised. Finally, Simeon did have the pleasure of holding the baby Jesus in his arms, just as it had been revealed to him. He praised God for this and said, *"'Lord, now you are letting your servant depart in peace, according to your word; for my eyes have seen your salvation that you have prepared in the presence of all peoples, a light for revelation to the Gentiles, and for glory to your people Israel'"* **(Luke 2:29-32)**.

Following the account of Simeon's prophecy, Luke gives an account of an eighty-four-year-old widow named Anna who'd been worshipping night and day at the temple, prophesying over and giving thanks for the baby Jesus.

The next picture we get of Jesus is as a twelve-year-old boy who is travelling with his family on their way to Jerusalem to celebrate the Passover feast. On the long journey home, they realized Jesus was not with the caravan. Returning to the temple, they find Him sitting amongst the teachers in the temple courts amazing the listeners with His understanding and answers. When Mary asked Jesus why He worried them for days, Jesus' answer was, *"Why were you looking for me? Did you not know that I must be in my Father's house?'"* **(Luke 2:49)**. At twelve years old, Jesus already was doing His Father's work.

Luke's Gospel continues with the accounts of John the Baptist and with Jesus' baptism, which we covered in the Gospel of Matthew. And then Luke includes Jesus' maternal genealogy that is somewhat different than Matthew's paternal genealogy of Jesus. Luke's account then moves on to Jesus' temptation in the wilderness, which we also covered already, and then begins to tell us about Jesus' ministry in Galilee.

JESUS' GALILEAN MINISTRY

In the next several chapters of Luke's Gospel, he recounts many stories of Jesus ministering mostly in the area of Galilee, whose residents included a large population of Gentiles. Being a Gentile himself, Luke shows Jesus' concern for the Gentiles in contrast to the reactions of the Jews to the news that Gentiles would be included in God's family. Luke illustrates Jesus' care for the poor and downtrodden as He ministered in the region and shows us glimpses of controversy and opposition to Jesus as the Gospel message was spread.

After His temptation in the wilderness, Jesus visited his hometown of Nazareth in Galilee. On one Sabbath, He entered the synagogue just like He'd always done and stood to read from the scroll of the prophet Isaiah. The scroll that He was handed said, *"'The Spirit of the Lord is upon me, because he has anointed me to proclaim good news to the poor. He has sent me to proclaim liberty to the captives and recovering of sight to the blind, to set at liberty those who are oppressed, to proclaim the year of the Lord's favor'"* **(Luke 4:18-19)**. This text was from the prophet Isaiah when he was proclaiming the end of the Babylonian exile. But Jesus clarifies the text further when He says, *"'Today this Scripture has been fulfilled in your hearing"* **(Luke 4:2)**. Jesus is the ultimate end of captivity—He sets His people free from death and decay and from the tyranny of sin!

Because of His gracious words, the people who'd heard Jesus declare the fulfillment of the prophecy marveled at Him and spoke well of Him, but they still didn't understand Who He was! In their minds, this was still Joseph's son, the local hometown boy they'd watch grow up. Then Jesus recounts two stories where God's prophets helped Gentiles instead of Jews—one during the prophet Elijah's ministry and a second during the prophet Elisha's. What Jesus was really telling them is that the Good News of the Gospel is also for the Gentiles, not just the Jews. When the hometown crowd heard this, their kind thoughts turned to fury and they tried to kill Jesus by throwing Him off of a cliff, but He walked right through the throng of people and escaped death that day. Opposition to Jesus was starting to show!

After the calling of His first apostles, we find teaching that is similar to the Sermon on the Mount but is most likely a different teaching event. The chapter lists some beatitudes that are like some of those in Matthew. Just like His previous sermon, Jesus started out talking to believers this time, too, so *"blessed are you who are poor,"* found in **Luke 6:20**, is not those with a lack of money, but those who recognize their spiritual need for God. Christians are beggars before God, having nothing to offer Him in exchange for salvation.

Next, Luke launches into a series of "woes" that correspond the beatitudes he just listed. A woe is a warning. In this section, Jesus was addressing the unbelievers in the crowd, which included the Jewish leaders who were "rich" in knowledge of the Old Testament yet did not recognize the Messiah. They continued to base their righteousness on their observance of the Law. They were anything but "poor in spirit" before God! They were confident in their own moral behavior, just like much of the world is today. But Jesus has higher standards than they could even imagine, and He lays it out for them in **Luke 6:27**: *"But I say to you who hear, Love your enemies, do good to those who hate you, bless those who curse you, pray for those who abuse you."* In this one statement, Jesus is showing that His Kingdom is totally opposite a sinful human being's nature! Then Jesus goes on to say, *"To one who strikes you on the cheek, offer the other also, and from one who takes away your cloak do not withhold your tunic either"* **(Luke 6:29)**.

Was Jesus saying we should never try to get away from someone who is harming us? Was Jesus saying that if someone steals from us, give them even more than they've already stolen? No. Striking meant "when someone insults you," not when someone is physically harming you. Christians should be able to stand up to insults for being Christians, but we're not required to let ourselves be physically beaten. Also, if we gave thieves even more than they originally got every time they stole from a Christian, it would go against the biblical idea that justice has a place in our world. So, what was Jesus saying? He summed it up in **Luke 6:31**, *"And as you wish that others would do to you, do so to them."*

Jesus performed more miracles as they traveled—one of which happened in a city called Nain, where they encountered a dead person being carried out of the town. It turned out that this was a man who was the only son of a widow. Now for a widow, this presented quite a problem. Widows were often destitute without a son to carry on the family name. Jesus felt compassion for the woman because of her desperate plight and touched the funeral pyre, saying, *"Young man, I say to you, arise!"* **(Luke 7:14b)**. And the dead son was given back to his mother alive. In keeping with his pattern of following the story of a man with a similar one of a woman, Luke gives the account of a daughter who is brought back to life again.

As we've said before, Luke gave special attention to the poor and lowly, women being one of those groups of people. But not all the women of Jesus' time were poor and destitute, and Luke tells us about some of them who were following behind Jesus and the apostles. These women weren't just "groupies." These women were helping to support Jesus and the apostles out of their own means. They were wealthy women who had been cured of evil spirits and diseases, one of which was Mary Magdalene, from whom Jesus had exorcised seven demons. These wealthy women helped the message be proclaimed throughout the land

As the group traveled, Jesus began to teach in parables and to show the Twelve and others His Divinity by calming the storm, casting out more demons, and healing the poor and downtrodden—in this case, a leper and a paralytic and a woman with menstrual bleeding for twelve continuous years, most of which we already covered.

FROM GALILEE TO JERUSALEM

As the time approached for Jesus to die, there was growing belief in His message, as well as growing rejection. Nonetheless, Jesus had a mission, and He resolutely set out for Jerusalem, sending messengers ahead of the group to prepare for them to stay in Samaria. We're not told why, but the people of Samaria rejected Jesus' desire to stay there. It could be that they didn't want that many Jews in their village because they hated the Jews, or it could be that they were rejecting Jesus. The apostles James and John were outraged at this and asked Jesus if He wanted them to call down fire on that town, but Jesus rebuked them. Hadn't He just taught them that revenge was not the way the citizens in His Kingdom did business? The group traveled on, looking for another place to stay.

There is a cost to following Jesus. As they were walking along the road, they met three men, each who claimed they wanted to follow Him. The first one bowed out when Jesus told him the circumstances that go along with it. The second wanted to wait until he was done taking care of his aging father. And the third wanted Jesus to wait until he said goodbye to his family. Jesus answered the remaining two men, saying, *"Leave the dead to bury their own dead . . . No one who puts his hand to the plow and looks back is fit for the kingdom of God'"* **(Luke 9:60a, 62)**. Jesus wasn't saying not to care for your family. We know that from other Scripture. Jesus was just making the point that the cost of following Him is that He must be first in our lives. Our focus is to be centered on Jesus and the work He's given us to do. We take care of the people and the things God has given us as if we were doing it for Him, but we always put Him first.

Moving closer to Jerusalem, Jesus visited with his friends Martha and Mary and some others who were at their house. Jesus taught almost everywhere He went, and one of the people listening intently that night was Mary, who was sitting at Jesus' feet, soaking in everything He had to say. Meanwhile, her sister, Martha, was busy serving the guests by herself. Feeling frustration about it and expecting Jesus to take her side, Martha said, *"Lord, do you not care that my sister has left me to serve alone? Tell her then to help me. But the Lord answered her, 'Martha, Martha, you are anxious and troubled about many things, but one thing is necessary. Mary has chosen the good portion, which will not be taken away from her"* **(Luke 10:40-42)**. Mary chose what was *needed*—hearing and learning the Word of the Lord! Actively serving the Lord isn't a bad thing, but it isn't a substitute for hearing and studying His Word. When Jesus was tempted by Satan in the wilderness, He said, *"Man shall not live by bread alone, but by every word that comes from the mouth of God'"* **(Matt. 4:4)**. The fact that Jesus used Scripture during His trials and temptations should make us realize just how important it is to know it well ourselves!

On the heels of teaching about the importance of learning Scripture, Luke gives us Jesus' teaching about prayer, known as the Lord's prayer: *"Father, hallowed be your name. Your kingdom come. Give us each day our daily bread, and forgive us our sins, for we ourselves forgive everyone who is indebted to us. And lead us not into temptation"* **(Luke 11:2-4)**. And then He launched into another parable about being boldly persistent in our prayer life, asking the Father for *spiritual* things, the things in the Lord's prayer, confident that the Father will answer those type of requests.

Facing opposition and accusations that His power was actually coming from Satan, Jesus began teaching the crowds that there are only two kinds of people—those who are with Him and those who are not. There is no middle road when it comes to Jesus. While He was talking, a woman stood up in the crowd and said, *"Blessed is the womb that bore you, and the breasts at which you nursed!"* **(Luke 11:27)**. But Jesus tells her it takes even more than being related to Him by flesh to be "blessed"—you must be united with Him in Spirit by believing and trusting in Him!

Jesus had the same message for the increasingly large crowds who were asking for a sign from Him. True faith doesn't come from being given a sign. It comes in response to the preaching of the Word. Having Jesus right there preaching to them should have been all they needed. They were seeing Him, hearing His Words, but not perceiving; and Jesus told them they were condemned, and judgement was coming—something that should be a sober warning for those enamored with the idea of seeing signs and wonders today.

As Jesus moved closer to Jerusalem, He urged the people to *be ready*, followed by a warning about feeling self-righteous compared to someone else's sin. Jesus told them that ALL need to repent! Those who don't will perish! No one can rely on their own moral superiority compared to the rest of the world for salvation. There are two options for them—repent or be burned in the fire. Like we said earlier, Jesus leaves no middle ground.

Heading on toward the city, Jesus moved through the towns and villages teaching that the door to salvation is narrow. When someone asks Him if He meant that only a few would be saved, Jesus says, *"Strive to enter through the narrow door"* **(Luke 13:24a)**. Many of the religious elite of the day followed the moral law, knew Scripture, and observed the Sabbath, but didn't recognize the Savior, nor their sin and never repented of it. Jesus said that *many* will be standing outside the door knocking, but His reply to them will be, *"'I do not* *know where you come from. Depart from me, all you workers of evil!'"* **(Luke 13:27)**. This is why it's important that churches teach their congregations that they are sinners who need to repent!

Jesus followed this by giving us a glimpse of what it looks like apart from Him. Despite what many who reject Jesus want to believe, Hell won't be a never-ending party where the sinners are having a good time, happy—maybe even elated—to be out from under the condemning gaze of God and the "saints." Jesus says, *"In that place there will be weeping and gnashing of teeth"* **(Luke 13:28)**. This, along with the other Scriptural pictures of Hell, describe it as anything but a good time!

Being invited to a ruling Pharisee's house for dinner, Jesus told more parables admonishing those who think they're deserving of honor and the rich who are unwilling to share with those who can't pay them back. As He traveled, Jesus spent time with tax collectors and others who were considered extremely sinful, and many who fit that description gathered around to hear His words. Words of salvation offered to those who have a sense of their unworthiness are like beautiful music to their ears.

But Jesus' interaction with "sinners" made the Pharisees and the teachers of the Law question just what kind of man Jesus was. He was welcoming the very people they despised. So, Jesus tells three parables about lost things. The first one was about a lost sheep whom the shepherd leaves the other ninety-nine to go after; and when he finds it, He puts it on His shoulders and brings it into the fold. Unlike the Pharisees, God goes after sinners. The Pharisees would accept someone who came to them as a repentant sinner, but God actually *goes after* those who are His. The second parable was about a lost coin, showing what the response should be over someone who repents of their sin. And the third was about a lost son and is commonly known as the story of the Prodigal Son.

This parable is often portrayed as teaching about wandering sinners coming to God. But it's about a father with *two* sons—one who obeys and is very self-righteous, and the other who squanders his inheritance, coming back as a starving beggar, with the idea he will ask his father for a paying job. But the father won't accept him as a worker. Instead, he restores him to the family, throws a feast for him, and welcomes him with open arms, even though the son came back totally empty-handed after having lived a life of debauchery! The father's reaction struck right at the heart of the Pharisees and teachers of the Law, who were like the older, rule-following, "good" brother in the story—the one who thought *he* deserved the feast.

Luke next introduces us to a man named Zacchaeus, who lived in the town of Jericho. He was a chief tax collector, making him very wealthy. Zacchaeus wanted to see Who Jesus was; but because he was short, he couldn't see over the crowd. Seeing a good climbing tree, he decided to do just that! When Jesus reached the spot where Zacchaeus was, *"He looked up and said to him, 'Zacchaeus, hurry and come down, for I must stay at your house today'"* **(Luke 19:5)**. This was the day of salvation for Zacchaeus! Jesus' statement that He *"must* stay" at the man's house shows that He saw Zacchaeus as part of His Divine mission. The people began to mutter because Jesus went to the house of someone they considered one of the worst of sinners. But Zacchaeus shows what *true repentance* looks like. He gave half of his possessions to the poor and paid back four times the amount from anybody he had cheated. Luke ends this part with Jesus telling us about His mission, *"For the Son of Man came to seek and to save the lost"* **(Luke 19:10)**.

THE JERUSALEM MINISTRY

Luke includes the Triumphal Entry, Jesus' passion week, and the events surrounding His crucifixion that we covered in Matthew's Gospel. Matthew recorded that there were two criminals being crucified with Jesus; however, Luke is the only Gospel that tells us that one of the men became a believer. In **Luke 23:39-43**, we learn that through the work of the Holy Spirit, this man suddenly became confident that death wasn't the end of Jesus, *"And he said, 'Jesus, remember me when you come into your kingdom.'* Jesus answers him, "Today you will be with me in paradise." God saves His elect—sometimes right at the end of their life.

Luke also records something for us that is only briefly mentioned in the Gospel of Mark and isn't seen in the others either. Commonly referred to as the Road to Emmaus, the account is of two of Jesus' disciples, one named Cleopas, encountering the risen Savior as they headed to a village called Emmaus, but they did not recognize Who He was. As they walked, Jesus asked what they were discussing and why they looked sad. Surprised at the question, the two of them explain. *"And [Jesus] said to them, 'O foolish ones, and slow of heart to believe all that the prophets have spoken! Was it not necessary that the Christ should suffer these things and enter into his glory?'"* **(Luke 24:25-26)**. Then He started explaining the Scriptures to them from the Old Testament, explaining everything said about Himself. Eventually, God opened their eyes, and they were totally amazed. Then Jesus disappeared from their sight. *"They said to each other, 'Did not our hearts burn within us while he talked to us on the road, while he opened to us the Scriptures?'"* **(Luke 24:32)**. This is the way some believers describe the feeling they get when they hear preaching or teaching from the Word of God that's done in an expository fashion (taking whole passages of Scripture and explaining exactly what the text means in its original context). This is the best way the Scriptures are "opened" to us – the same way Jesus does it!

When the apostles were together again later that night, Jesus showed up, gave them permission to touch Him to see that He really did have flesh and bones, then asked them for something to eat, giving them a glimpse into the Kingdom, that His risen body could still make use of food. Then He explained what He had been trying to tell them all along—that everything written about Him had to be fulfilled! The book of Luke ends with these words: *"Then he opened their minds to understand the Scriptures, and said to them, 'Thus it is written . . . You are witnesses of these things . . . But stay in the city until you are clothed with power from on high'"* **(Luke 24:45-51)**. And they did what Jesus said. They stayed in the city until they received the Holy Spirit at Pentecost, something Luke tells us about in the book of Acts.

CHAPTER 17

THE GOSPEL OF JOHN

The Gospel of John was almost certainly written by the apostle John. It's obvious that the author was an eyewitness to the things he wrote about and that he was Jewish due to his breadth of knowledge of Jewish customs, beliefs, and practices, as well as his knowledge of the geography of Israel. John does not name himself in this Gospel, but refers to himself as *"the disciple whom Jesus loved"* in several places.

The book was definitely written before 130 A.D. as evidenced by a piece of papyrus that was discovered with a few verses of John's Gospel written on it and information in the Dead Sea scrolls.

John was writing for a mixed group of Jews and Gentiles. As you read John's Gospel, look for contrasts such as *love* and *hate*, *light* and *dark*, *above* and *below*, etc. John also quotes Jesus, saying, *"I AM,"* the name God used for Himself in the Old Testament. When Jesus said this, He was telling us that He is the Great I AM—God!

We don't have to wonder why John wrote this Gospel; he makes it clear in **John 20:30-31**: *"Now Jesus did many other signs in the presence of the disciples, which are not written in this book; but these are written so that you may believe that Jesus is the Christ, the Son of God, and that by believing you may have life in his name."*

WHO IS JESUS?

In his opening sentences, John takes us all the way back into the halls of eternity to before the creation of the world. Within five verses, John gives us many important theological points that he wants us to know and which he will flesh out for us later. Those points are:

1.   That Jesus has always been,

2.   That He is the Word,

3.   That He was with God,

4.   That He *is* God,

5.   That all things were made through Him, and

6.   That in Him was life and that life was the light that darkness cannot overcome.

John goes on to tell us, *"And the Word became flesh and dwelt among us, and we have seen his glory, glory as of the only Son from the Father, full of grace and truth"* **(John 1:14)**. Just as in the Old Testament the Father showed His glory in the wilderness and met with His people in the tabernacle and the temple, Jesus "making his dwelling" among us is the same as saying Jesus *"tabernacles"* with us.

JESUS THE LAMB OF GOD

Just as we saw in the other Gospels, John gives the account of John the Baptist's baptism ministry. The Jews who were in Jerusalem wanted to know who John the Baptist was and whether he was the Messiah or not; so, they sent some priests and Levites to question him about these things. John the Baptist knew the role that God planned for his life—he was the one prophesied about by Isaiah in **Isaiah 40:3**: *"A voice cries: 'In the wilderness prepare the way* *of the LORD; make straight in the desert a highway for our God.'"* He was not the Messiah; he was the one whom the Father sent ahead to herald His Son, and he had no trouble telling the priests and Levites that!

One day as John the Baptist was dunking people in the water and calling them to repentance, he shouted out, *"'Behold, the Lamb of God, who takes away the sin of the world'"* **(John 1:29)** when he saw Jesus. John wanted his followers to know Who Jesus is; he was not interested in self-preservation and keeping his own ministry alive.

On one of these occasions, Andrew and another man, who many believe was the apostle John himself, were there when Jesus walked past. The two followed Jesus, and Andrew went to gets his brother, Peter, to introduce him to Jesus. Although this account of Andrew and the other fishermen meeting Jesus seems different from the one in the Synoptic Gospels, many commentators believe this is actually the first time they met Jesus; and later, when they were fishing, Jesus called them to follow. Since the Gospel writers focused on different aspects of Jesus and His life, this could be how it happened.

JESUS THE SON OF GOD AND KING OF ISRAEL

John continues by telling us that the three of them followed Jesus. The next day, Jesus also called Phillip, who went to find Nathanael and told him to come and see Jesus. The way that Phillip and Andrew both brought people they knew to meet Jesus is a picture of how the Gospel often spreads! When Jesus met Nathanael, He told him that He saw him under the fig tree, the place where Nathanael had been. This caused Nathanael to realize that he was standing in front of the Son of God, the King of Israel, which he exclaimed in front of everyone.

In His first year of ministry in 27 A.D., Jesus headed for Galilee, to a place called Cana, where His mother was a guest at a wedding. Noticing that the host had run out of wine, Jesus' mother informed Jesus of the situation, to which Jesus asked, *"Woman, what does this have to do with me? My hour has not yet come"* **(John 2:4)**. Jesus wasn't being snarky with his mom; He was making it clear that it's God the Father Who was in charge of the time to reveal Who He is. Nevertheless, His mother had confidence Jesus would do something to help the situation, and He did! Jesus had the servants fill the six twenty to thirty-gallon water jars that were used for ceremonial washing, and then He changed the water into the best wine that was served at the wedding feast!

JESUS SON OF GOD AND SON OF MAN

Because it was almost time for the Passover Feast, Jesus headed for Jerusalem. Living in the region was a Pharisee named Nicodemus, who was a member of the ruling council—therefore, someone who knew the Scriptures well. Nicodemus and the other council members knew about the works that Jesus had been doing and truly believed that only someone whom God sent could do these things. Under the cover of darkness, Nicodemus secretly went to Jesus to find out more. Knowing the questions in the man's heart, Jesus tells Nicodemus, *"Truly, truly, I say to you, unless one is born again he cannot see the kingdom of God"* **(John 3:3)**. Nicodemus didn't understand. How could a man enter his mother's womb again? He was starting to get the picture. In the same way that no one can cause himself to be born the first time, no one can cause themselves to be "born again," which in the Greek means "from above." Jesus was telling Nicodemus that everyone who is a believer must be born of the Spirit, which means to have the Holy Spirit regenerate their heart, something that's impossible for man to make happen.

Jesus continued to tell Nicodemus, *"And as Moses lifted up the serpent in the wilderness, so must the Son of Man be lifted up, that whoever believes in him may have eternal life. For God so loved the world, that he gave his only Son, that whoever believes in him should not perish but have eternal life"* **(John**

3:14-16). Jesus confirmed to Nicodemus that God did send Him and that He is God's Son. Jesus used the word "world" here, not to say that all of mankind will be saved, but to let Nicodemus know that salvation is not just for the Jews, but also for the Gentiles. Jesus referred to Himself as "Son of Man" in this conversation and many others. It was the name He used for Himself most often in the Gospels. By using both "Son of God" and "Son of Man," Jesus was telling Nicodemus He is fully God and fully human. The name "Son of Man" also referred to the seventh chapter of Daniel, where he prophesied the Son of Man would be given dominion, glory, and an everlasting kingdom.

I AM THE CHRIST

As they traveled through Samaria on the way back to Galilee, the disciples went into a town to buy something to eat, while Jesus stopped at the town well. It was about noon, a normal time when no one would be at the well, but Jesus encountered a Samaritan woman there getting some water. Jesus asked her for a drink. This was shocking to her because the Samaritan people were hated and despised by the Jews because they were a mixed race of Jews who, back in the Old Testament, intermarried with the pagan people who conquered them. The woman replied, *"How is it that you, a Jew, ask for a drink from me, a woman of Samaria?'"* **(John 4:9)**. After showing the woman that He knew things about her having had multiple husbands and a discussion about some worship matters, *"The woman said to him, 'I know that Messiah is coming (he who is called Christ). When he comes, he will tell us all things'"* **(John 4:25)**. Jesus answered that He is the Christ, something He hasn't said to anyone else so far! Of all the people Jesus could have revealed that to, He chose to tell a sinful Samaritan woman. After hearing her life explained to her by Jesus and knowing Who He is, the woman left her water jar and ran to the town to spread the news! Jesus stayed with the people of the town for two days, and many Samaritans believed in Jesus because of the woman's testimony and because of Jesus' words to them Himself.

JESUS THE SON OF THE FATHER, EQUAL WITH GOD

A little later in the year 28 A.D., Jesus traveled back to Jerusalem for one of the Jewish festivals. There is a pool there called Bethesda, surrounded by five colonnades supporting a covering over the pool. Many people who were blind, lame, or paralyzed laid beside the pool, hoping to be the first one to get into the water when it was "stirred." What does it mean that the waters "stirred"? Some ancient Bible manuscripts actually say these words, *"And they waited for the moving of the waters. From time to time an angel of the Lord would come down and stir up the waters. The first one into the pool after each such disturbance would be cured of whatever disease he had."*[25]

For the last thirty-eight years, a paralyzed man had been helplessly lying by the pool. With no one to help him get in the pool when the water moved, he knew how unlikely it was that he would ever be healed; someone always reached the restorative waters before him. When Jesus arrived at the pool, He asked the man, *"Do you want to be healed?"* **(John 5:5b)**. When the man explained his plight, Jesus told him to get up, pick up his mat, and walk. And the man did! When the Jewish leaders saw the man carrying his mat, they confronted him about it because it was the Sabbath, and the Law—according to them—forbid carrying a mat on the Sabbath day. The man explained that the One Who healed him told him to pick up his mat and walk. The Pharisees wanted to know who healed him, but the man didn't know. And by now, Jesus had slipped away. He wasn't healing the crowd that day. How does a man who had been an invalid for thirty-eight years have the faith to get up, pick up his

---

25   *Spirit of the Reformation Study Bible: New International Version* (Grand Rapids, MI: Zondervan, 2003).

mat, and walk just because a "Man he didn't know" said to? Jesus gave Him that faith; He gives life to whomever He pleases.

A little while later, Jesus saw the man in the temple and told him, *"'See, you are well! Sin no more, that nothing worse may happen to you'"* **(John 5:14)**. That's when the man realized Who healed him! Was Jesus saying the man's sin caused his physical ailments? Maybe something sinful the man had done led to the consequences of his physical ailments, but that's not necessarily what's being said. Jesus' point was that there is something worse than being totally helpless physically, and that is being totally helpless on Judgement Day as you stand before God. Then the man went and told the Jewish leaders Who it was Who had healed him.

Because Jesus healed on the Sabbath, the Pharisees and teachers of the Law were outraged. They persecuted Him and then tried to kill Him. **John 5:17** tells us, *"But Jesus answered them, 'My Father is working until now, and I am working.'"* By claiming to be the Son of the Father, Jesus told them that He is God and has the same authority as God. Jesus concluded by condemning them for their unbelief in **John 5:39-40**, when He said to them, *"You search the Scriptures because you think that in them you have eternal life; and it is they that bear witness about me, yet you refuse to come to me that you may have life."*

I AM THE BREAD OF LIFE

Sometime around the year 29 A.D., Jesus crossed to the far shore of the Sea of Galilee, now referred to as the Sea of Tiberius. John recounted the feeding of the five thousand and Jesus walking on water and tells us that the next morning when the crowd found out Jesus and the apostles were gone, they got into boats and went looking for them. Jesus knew why they showed up again. He told them, *"'Truly, truly, I say to you, you are seeking me, not because you saw signs, but because you ate your fill of the loaves'"* **(John 6:25b)**. Jesus gets right to the heart of the matter—the reason they wanted Him is for the earthly things He could provide for them, not unlike many people who claim to love Jesus but are always looking for their "breakthrough," their "blessing," or their "promotion." But Jesus told them not to "work" for food that perishes but for food that brings eternal life. And when the people asked what work they must do, Jesus said, *"This is the work of God, that you believe in him whom he has sent'"* **(John 6:29)**.

Jesus continues in **John 6:35-44**:

> *"I am the bread of life; whoever comes to me shall not hunger, and whoever believes in me shall never thirst . . . For I have come down from heaven, not to do my own will but the will of him who sent me, that I should lose nothing of all that he has given me, but raise it up on the last day . . . everyone who looks on the Son and believes in him should have eternal life . . . No one can come to me unless the Father who sent me draws him. And I will raise him up on the last day."*

After that, Jesus continued to teach around Galilee, purposely staying away from Judea because the Jews there wanted to take His life and He was not yet ready to give it up.

JESUS GOES BACK TO JERUSALEM

About halfway through the festival time, Jesus went to the temple courts and began to teach. The Jewish leaders were still trying to find a way to kill Him, but no one could lay a hand on Him because it wasn't Jesus' time to die yet. Many people in the crowds put their faith in Him because they couldn't imagine that the Christ could do more miracles than He had already done.

In the eighth chapter of John, we have a very familiar story that is used often in preaching and teaching. However, just like the ending of the Gospel of Mark, the earliest manuscripts and many other ancient witnesses to the Gospels do not contain the last verse of chapter seven nor the first eleven verses of chapter eight. Most Bibles set these verses apart and explain this.

While Jesus was teaching, some Pharisees showed up with a woman whom they thrust before the group of people, saying to Jesus, *"'Teacher, this woman has been caught in the act of adultery'"* **(John 8:4)**. Then they "reminded" Jesus of Mosaic Law regarding adultery—that, *"Moses commanded us to stone such women"* **(John 8:5)**—and asked Him what they should do.

The Jewish leaders were hoping Jesus would demand that the woman be stoned, thus overstepping Roman law because only Roman officials could impose the death penalty for someone in their jurisdiction. The leaders also knew that to set her free would violate Mosaic Law, so they think they've caught Jesus in a no-win situation. But Jesus turned the tables on them because they already violated Mosaic Law themselves by not bringing the man who was caught in adultery as well as the woman. Both were to be stoned! Remember, they said they "caught her" in the act! Therefore, the man would have been caught in the act, too!

Without answering, He bent down and started to write on the ground with His finger. We're not told what Jesus wrote. Did He write the Laws from Leviticus and Deuteronomy saying it was both the man and the woman who were to be stoned? Did He write the full meaning of "committing adultery" the way He explained it in the Sermon on the Mount? Whatever it was, He told the crowd while He continued writing, *"Let him who is without sin among you be the first to throw a stone at her'"* **(John 8:7b)**. The Pharisees and the teachers of the Law quietly went away one at a time—the older ones first and the younger ones last—until the only one left standing was the woman. Jesus looked at the woman and asked, *"'Woman, where are they? Has no one condemned you?' She said, 'No one, Lord.' And Jesus said, 'Neither do I condemn you; go, and from now on sin no more'"* **(John 8:10-11)**.

Unlike what some would like to believe, Jesus wasn't the fun-loving, "do as you please" God of the New Testament. Jesus wasn't overlooking or "winking" at the woman's sin! He never treats sin as a "lightweight" issue, ever! He wasn't passing off the woman's sin as if it was not a big deal when

He said He didn't condemn her. He addressed her sin issue and told her not to do it anymore! The "neither do I condemn you" Jesus was referring to was legal condemnation. The woman was given no formal legal court case and no legal procedures, something required by both Roman and Mosaic Law.

I AM THE LIGHT OF THE WORLD

On another occasion when Jesus was speaking to the people, He told them, *"I am the light of the world. Whoever follows me will not walk in darkness, but will have the light of life"* **(John 8:12)**. Just as the Israelites followed God as a pillar of fire in the darkness of night, leading them out of slavery in Egypt, Jesus was claiming to be that Light, calling His people to follow Him out of the darkness of slavery to sin!

This caused the Pharisees to get upset even more because they knew He was claiming to be God. Jesus went on to say many things about His relationship to the Father, including that the Father sent Him and that they didn't know the Father. And then Jesus made two more "I AM" statements, saying, *"You are from below; I am from above. You are of this world; I am not of this world"* **(John 8:23)**. This made the Jewish leaders really upset, but they didn't seize Him yet.

As Jesus spoke that day, many made a profession of faith. However, things are not always as they seem, and many who claimed faith in Jesus had made a profession that was only superficial. To those who made the profession, Jesus said, *"If you abide in my word, you are truly my disciples, and you will know the truth, and the truth will set you free"* **(John 8:31-32)**. The fact that Jesus was talking about being set free got their attention! But Jesus told them right away He was not talking about political freedom; He was talking about freedom from being slaves to sin.

This is the freedom we sing about—freedom from our bondage to sin! The freedom Jesus came to give us is not freedom from our bad circumstances, freedom from our financial burdens, freedom from prison (as we saw with

John the Baptist), or freedom from other earthly burdens. And for these people, it wasn't political freedom Jesus came to give. It's the spiritual freedom of being restored to the position Adam and Eve were in before the Fall—having the ability to make God-glorifying choices—freedom from the weight of our guilt when we repent and ask forgiveness, freedom from death, and the freedom from experiencing God's wrath someday!

This was not the message the people wanted to hear. They weren't interested in being freed from the bondage of sin; they wanted freedom from earthly constraints. Then in **John 8:47**, Jesus claimed to be God when He said, *"Whoever is of God hears the words of God. The reason why you do not hear them is that you are not of God."* This angered the crowd further, and they picked up stones to throw at Him, but Jesus slipped away from them.

One day as they were traveling, Jesus and the apostles met a blind man. Jesus healed him by spitting on the ground, making some mud with his saliva, and putting it on the man's eyes, then telling him to go and wash in the pool of Salome. The man did what Jesus said, and his sight was restored. The twelve assumed the blindness was caused by sin—either his parents' sin, or the man's own—and asked Jesus who caused it. But Jesus told them neither of those was the right answer, but *"It was not that this man sinned, or his parents, but that the works of God might be displayed in him"* **(John 9:3)**.

This flies in the face of anyone who says that God never intends someone to be born with or to contract a sickness, disease, or disability. There are many false teachers out there who say that the devil is responsible for all sickness, illness, and disability; and in a big picture way, thinking back to sin coming into the world in the Garden of Eden, that is true. But as we see in this example, the man was born blind to serve God's purposes. This is a hard truth; but as we know from **Romans 8:28**, *"And we know that for those who love God all things work together for good, for those who are called according to his purpose."* Everything happens for the good of believers and for God's glory, though sometimes we don't understand it or see it this side of Heaven.

I AM THE DOOR FOR THE SHEEP

The story of the blind man who received his sight didn't end there. In the closing verses of John chapter nine, the Pharisees were asking Jesus if He was accusing them of being "blind." So, Jesus taught using an illustration that's very familiar to everyone—sheep and their shepherd. In **John 10:1-10**, Jesus uses this illustration to say that a legitimate shepherd is let into the pen with the sheepfolds by the gatekeeper. Anyone else would have to try to get into the sheep pen by climbing over the wall; and as everyone knows, the only kind of people who try to sneak in some way they're not supposed to are thieves and robbers! Jesus is explaining that He is the Door for the sheep. The only way into the fold is through Him. Christianity is the only true religion. No other religion, not even Judaism, will fix your relationship to God, nor lead to Heaven!

Jesus went on to say that once the true shepherd enters the sheep pen, he calls his sheep by name to come out of the pen. Once all the sheep of the flock have come out of the pen, the shepherd leads them into green pastures. The sheep follow the shepherd because they know his voice; they will not follow a stranger! In fact, they will run from a shepherd who isn't theirs.

Jesus was explaining that He is the true Shepherd. Jesus calls *His* sheep by name until His entire fold (all of the elect) is out of the pen, separated from those who are not His. Then He will lead them out to pasture, and they will follow because they know His voice. But the Pharisees did not understand what He was saying to them, so Jesus continued with the explanation.

I AM THE GOOD SHEPHERD

In **John 10:11-18**, Jesus *says*:

> *"I am the good shepherd. The good shepherd lays down his life for the sheep. He who is a hired hand and not a shepherd . . . sees the wolf coming and leaves the sheep and flees . . . I am the good shepherd. I know my own and my own know me, just as the Father knows me and I know*

the Father; and I lay down my life for the sheep. And I have other sheep that are not of this fold. I must bring them also, and they will listen to my voice. So there will be one flock, one shepherd."

Jesus is the Good Shepherd Who gave His life for His sheep. No one could take His life away from Him; He had full authority over it. He went to the cross willingly, and He rose again! He brought the Gentiles into the fold, and there is now one Church composed of Jews, who come to believe in Him as Savior, plus Gentile believers.

After hearing this, the people were divided over Who Jesus is, with some believing He was possessed. Later, as Jesus was walking through the temple, the people questioned Him, wanting to know for sure if He is the Christ or not! Jesus told them that they did not believe, even though they witnessed many miracles, because they were not His sheep. At this, they tried to stone Him, but He slipped away again.

I AM THE RESURRECTION AND THE LIFE

Jesus heard that his good friend, Lazarus, the brother of Mary and Martha, was very ill. When the sisters told Jesus about their brother, He assured them that the sickness would not end in death but that it was for God's glory, *"so that the Son of God may be glorified through it"* **(John 11:4)**. Knowing about the illness, Jesus stayed where He was two more days before heading to the home of Lazarus in Judea.

The disciples were concerned about heading back to Judea again after having escaped across the Jordan, but Jesus told them that Lazarus had "fallen asleep" and they had to go wake him up. Not understanding Jesus was speaking about death, the Twelve questioned this move, so Jesus spelled it out plainly for them—Lazarus is dead! Thomas, being not only a doubter but sometimes a Debbie Downer, said, *"'Let us also go, that we may die with him'"* **(John 11:16)**.

When Jesus arrived, Lazarus had been in the tomb four days. A lot of Jews were there comforting Mary and Martha. Stricken with grief, Martha told Jesus that if He had just been there, Lazarus would not have died. *"But even now I know that whatever you ask from God, God will give you"* **(John 11:22)**. Jesus told her Lazarus would rise again, saying, *"I am the resurrection and the life. Whoever believes in me, though he die, yet shall he live, and everyone who lives and believes in me shall never die. Do you believe this?"* **(John 11:25)**.

Having compassion on the sisters and all the people who were crying over the death of Lazarus, we get the shortest verse that's in the Bible, which says, *"Jesus wept"* **(John 11:35)**. Being deeply moved, Jesus approached the tomb, and although Martha was afraid of the bad odor caused by a decaying body, Jesus rolled the stone from the tomb. Giving the Father thanks out loud so the people hearing would believe that the Father had sent Him to Earth, Jesus called in a loud voice, *"Lazarus, come out"* **(John 11:43b)**. Lazarus stepped from within the tomb, his hands and feet wrapped in strips of linen and a cloth around his face. Jesus told them to take off the grave clothes and let him go.

Seeing Lazarus risen from the grave caused many Jews to believe in Jesus, but some of them went to the Pharisees and reported what happened. The Pharisees and the chief priests called a meeting. They were more afraid than ever that people would start believing in Jesus, causing the Romans to take away both the temple and the nation of Israel. One of the high priests named Caiaphas spoke these words: *"It is better for you that one man should die for the people, not that the whole nation perish"* **(John 11:50)**.

Jesus had a bounty on His head. The chief priests and Pharisees ordered anyone who saw Him to report to them. Because they were going to kill Jesus, He no longer moved around publicly among the people in Judea. Instead, He withdrew to a village called Ephraim and stayed there with the Twelve until it was almost time to celebrate the Passover.

I AM LORD AND TEACHER

Just before the Passover feast, Jesus and the disciples were gathered in the upper room, where Jesus gave the apostles an example of *servant leadership*. And they were to go and do likewise. Jesus used an act of hospitality to make a general point to the Twelve. At that time, because of the dusty, dirty roads, it was customary for a servant to wash your feet when you entered a home. While the rest of the body stayed fairly clean, your feet would need to be cleaned at least daily, if not more. Just before the evening meal was about to be served, and after the devil had already prompted Judas to betray Jesus, the Savior stood up, wrapped a towel around His waist, poured water in a basin, and began to wash their feet.

> *When he had washed their feet and put on his outer garments and resumed his place, he said to them, "Do you understand what I have done to you? You call me Teacher and Lord, and you are right, for so I am. If I then, your Lord and Teacher, have washed your feet, you also ought to wash one another's feet. For I have given you an example, that you also should do just as I have done to you"* **(John 13:12-15)**.

I AM THE WAY, THE TRUTH, AND THE LIFE

Jesus told His disciples that He is the Way to the Father, that His Father's house has many rooms, and that He was going to prepare a place for them. Thomas, not understanding, asked how they could know the way to where Jesus was going when they didn't even know where that was. *"Jesus said to him, 'I am the way, and the truth, and the life. No one comes to the Father except through me. If you had known me, you would have known my Father also. From now on you do know him and have seen him'"* **(John 14:6-7)**.

Then Jesus said, "'If you love me, you will keep my commandments. And I will ask the Father, and he will give you another Helper, to be with you forever'" **(John 14:15-16)**. Jesus is talking about the Holy Spirit, Who will come and live within every believer and never leave them. Not only does the Holy

Spirit regenerate the hearts of the elect so that they can respond to the Gospel message, but He also teaches God's people truth as they read the Bible and seals them for eternity, meaning they cannot ever lose their salvation.

I AM THE TRUE VINE

Jesus taught them more about Himself, saying in **John 15:1-2**, *"I am the true vine, and my Father is the vinedresser. Every branch in me that does not bear fruit he takes away, and every branch that does bear fruit he prunes, that it may bear more fruit."* Just like the branches of a vine will wither and die if they are broken from the root, anyone who is apart from Jesus withers and dies. They are not a part of the vine and will be thrown into the fire to be burned.

However, for the branches that are abiding in His salvation, the Heavenly Father will prune them. Pruning fruit trees involves not only cutting off dead or diseased branches, but also some of the buds and even some healthy shoots. This improves the size and quantity of the crop because the tree is healthier, has less stress, and is less prone to damage than if left growing wildly. The Father is the Vinedresser. He will trim off parts of us—whether it be our sin, things in our life that aren't bringing Him glory, and maybe even some good things that aren't needed to further His plan—so that we will bear even more fruit. This is often a painful process; but in the end, it brings glory to God and joy to us. Jesus ended this teaching commanding them to love one another, something they, and we, need to get through times of pruning!

ENCOURAGING WORDS AND THE PROMISE OF A HELPER

Following the news that they would be pruned, Jesus gave the Twelve a strong warning that the world would hate them. Why? *"Because you are not of the world, but I chose you out of the world, therefore the world hates you"*

(John 15:19b). A believer is no longer like the worldly sinner he once was. When a person is born again, he is a new creature with new desires. A believer won't be changed all at once. However, he will begin to hate sin, both his own and the sin of others. Instead of basking in it and boasting in it, a believer will want to repent and turn from it. Until the return of Jesus, believers live in the world but are not like the world. We're to be different, set apart, just as God wanted the Israelites to be a separate, holy people. We're God's peculiar people; and because of that, the world will hate us.

Jesus told the disciples He was leaving, but they didn't know where He was going. They were grieved that Jesus was going away, but He told them, *"Nevertheless . . . it is to your advantage that I go away, for if I do not go away, the Helper will not come to you. But if I go, I will send him to you"* **(John 16:7)**. It's hard for us to imagine that anything would be more advantageous to us than having Jesus physically right beside us, but those are the words He spoke to those closest to Him!

The apostles finally understood part of what Jesus had been saying—they understood and believed that Jesus came from God. But that's not all. Along with the baffling news that He was going away, Jesus told them something else that was going to happen—they were all going to scatter from Him, leaving Him alone, and again, they would have trouble in the world. He said, *"In the world you will have tribulation. But take heart; I have overcome the world"* **(John 16:33b)**.

JESUS' HIGH PRIESTLY PRAYER

Knowing that the time had almost come to be arrested and taken to die, Jesus looked toward Heaven and prayed a prayer that's recorded in chapter seventeen of John's Gospel and is often referred to as the High Priestly Prayer. Jesus prayed that the Father would glorify Him. Then He prayed for believers for all time saying, *"I am praying for them. I am not praying for the world but for those whom you have given me, for they are yours"* **(John 17:9)**. He prayed these things for them: protection from Satan, sanctification (being made more and more holy) through the Word, and unity. This isn't unity for unity's sake. It isn't unity that's gained by diminishing God's precepts in any way. It is unity that is based on the Word, the only type of unity that is truly God-glorifying.

MY KINGDOM IS NOT OF THIS WORLD

In chapters eighteen and nineteen, John gives us the accounts of Jesus' arrest; being questioned by the high priest, Caiaphas; Peter's denials; and Jesus going before Pilate. John recorded Pilate asking Jesus directly, *"'Are you King of the Jews?'"* **(John 18:33b)**. But Jesus told him, *"My kingdom is not of this world . . . You say that I am a king. For this purpose I was born and for this purpose I have come into the world—to bear witness to the truth. Everyone who is of the truth listens to my voice"* **(John 18:36-37)**.

John continues his Gospel by recounting Jesus' sentencing, crucifixion, death, and burial.

THE RISEN CONQUERING KING

In chapter twenty, John recounts the story of the empty tomb; Jesus appearing to Mary Magdalene and His disciples; and more on the story of "doubting" Thomas than is in the other Gospels. Thomas, who was a twin, wasn't with the other ten when they saw Jesus the first time after His resurrection. Eight days later, when they were all together again in a locked room, Jesus came and stood among them! Knowing that Thomas didn't believe Christ had risen and had said, *"Unless I see in his hands the mark of the nails, and place my finger into the mark of the nails, and place my hand into his side, I will never believe"* **(John 20:25)**. Jesus told him, *"Put your finger here, and see my hands; and put out your hand, and place it in my side. Do not disbelieve, but believe"*

(John 20:27). Thomas immediately proclaimed that Jesus is Lord and God, a recognition of His deity.

John tells us that Jesus did many other signs in the presence of them that aren't recorded in his book—there were so many, in fact, that the world itself couldn't contain the books if they were written down. He ends his Gospel with two more things: a miraculous fishing expedition with Jesus and the story of Peter's reinstatement by Jesus after having denied Him three times.

Having been so close to Jesus and having turned and disowned Him three times when things got rough likely made Peter feel sad and ashamed, and possibly like he was on shaky ground—not only with Jesus, but possibly with the other apostles. But Jesus didn't leave Peter in that condition. After they had finished eating the fish they'd caught earlier, Jesus asked Peter, *"'Simon, son of John, do you love me more than these?' He said to him, 'Yes, Lord; you know that I love you'"* **(John 21:15b-16a)**. Then Jesus asked Peter the same question two more times, and Peter answered the same. After each of Peter's three answers, Jesus gave Peter these instructions: *"Feed my lambs"*; *"Tend my sheep"*; and *"Feed my sheep."* It hurt Peter that Jesus asked him three times if he loved Him, but the three times showed that Jesus was fully restoring Peter and the rest of the group's confidence in Peter as an apostle. Then Jesus told Peter what may be one of the hardest things he would ever hear—that he was going to die by crucifixion for the Gospel message.

One more thing that John ends his Gospel with is that he once again refers to "the disciple whom Jesus loved," whom most scholars believe was John himself. *"This is the disciple who is bearing witness about these things, and who has written these things, and we know that his testimony is true"* **(John 21:24)**.

PART 6

THE EPISTLES

ACTS THROUGH REVELATION

We have arrived at our last part! It also happens to be the section that will cover the greatest number of books at twenty-three! We will cover the rest of the New Testament beginning with Acts and ending with Revelation.

You have probably heard many of the books in the New Testament called both "epistles" and "letters." An epistle is a formal letter that is meant for public viewing. Usually, the writer and the reader do not have a close, prior relationship. The writer of the epistle expects and wants his letter to be shared with everyone. A letter is more informal as the writer and reader have an established relationship. Often, letters contain things that the reader would have understood because of their relationship with the writer, information that we're not privy to. Some of the epistles we will look at could be considered letters; but since all were meant for public reading, we have lumped them into the category of "epistles." Of the twenty-three books we will look at in this chapter, twenty-one are epistles. Of the other two, the book of Revelation is part epistle, part apocalyptic; and the book of Acts is not an epistle at all. The book of Acts has been given a genre all its own called, appropriately, the "Acts of the Apostles." However, it fits perfectly into this chapter because, as we will see, Acts is the springboard for many of the epistles. We will go through the rest of the New Testament chronologically (sort of), not in the order the books appear in the Bible.

Although the epistles were written by six different authors to about fifteen different recipients over a span of fifty years, they all contain other common messages in addition to the Gospel message: God's sovereignty over everything, living in light of that reality, persevering through trials and persecution, and warnings against false teaching. The people of the first century, whether Jew or Gentile and regardless of where they were living, needed to hear these messages, as has every Christian who has lived since then and every Christian who will live until Jesus comes back!

Chapter 18

ACTS

All four of the Gospels end with Jesus' resurrection and His commissioning the apostles. The book of Acts is that commission being lived out. It is the extraordinary recording of how, through the power of the Holy Spirit, the apostles spread the Gospel throughout the known world, resulting in the formation of the Church. Written by Luke, Acts is the sequel to the Gospel of Luke, but it is the sequel to all of the other Gospels as well. Luke wrote this book in 62 A.D., but the events took place beginning in 30 A.D., forty days after Jesus' resurrection. Luke recorded Acts while visiting Paul, who was on house arrest in Rome and awaiting trial—a fact affirmed by Paul in his letter to Timothy in **2 Timothy 4:11**: *"Luke alone is with me."* You will see many "we" sections in Acts. These are the events that Luke himself was an eyewitness to.

The theme of Acts can be summed up in **Acts 1:8**: *"But you will receive power when the Holy Spirit has come upon you, and you will be my witnesses in Jerusalem and in all Judea and Samaria, and to the end of the earth."* This book is the recording of the Holy Spirit coming to and indwelling in Jesus' apostles and other believers, empowering them to go out and preach the Gospel first to the Jews (Jerusalem and Judea), but then also to the half-Jews and outcasts (Samaria) and all the way to Rome, the biggest empire in the known world at that time (the ends of the Earth), symbolizing the Gospel going to the Gentiles. The good news of salvation is not just for the Jews; God has expanded His people to now include the Gentiles. Although this was foretold about many times in the Old Testament, it was not understood by most.

Acts makes the shift from the *acts of Jesus* (as we saw in the Gospels) to the *acts of Jesus' followers* as they are empowered by the Holy Spirit. It is the story of how Christianity and the Church began. It is extremely helpful to read Acts before reading any of the epistles because it fills in a lot of the "why's." The book first focuses on Peter, but then transitions its focus to Paul. It tells of Paul's journeys, detailing the hardships, miracles, encouragements, and discouragements he faced while taking the Gospel into the Gentile world. You will recognize a lot of the names of places he went as the recipients of the letters he later writes. Since getting the foundation of Acts is so important to understanding the rest of the books in this chapter, we will spend a good amount of time in it.

There is something important to note before we delve into the content of the book. Peter, Paul, and some of the other disciples were uniquely gifted because of the mission they had at that time. While every Word of Scripture is important and helpful for us, we should never read Acts, or any of the other books, and think that everything that was applicable to the disciples at that time directly applies to us now. We will look at this in more depth as we get to specific events. It's important to make the distinction between things in Scripture that were exceptional to that time only and things that are universally true for Christians for all time. Understanding the verses within their historical context and comparing them to other Scripture is the best way to differentiate which category the passages fall into.

Like most sequels, Acts begins with a retelling of the end of the first installment. Luke repeats his telling of Jesus' ascension into Heaven while the apostles looked on. Before Jesus left them, He told them to stay in Jerusalem and wait for the Holy Spirit to come. While they were waiting, they chose a replacement for Judas Iscariot. As you may recall from the last chapter on the Gospels, the number of twelve apostles was significant, and it was important for that number to be maintained. With the help of God, they choose Matthias.

Ten days after Jesus ascended into Heaven, the people of Jerusalem were celebrating Pentecost. If you remember back from chapter two, the Lord gave Moses festivals the people were to celebrate. One of those festivals was Pentecost, or the Festival of Weeks, which was celebrated fifty days after Passover. It was on this day, when Jerusalem was filled with Jews from all over who had pilgrimed to the temple to celebrate, that the Holy Spirit descended upon the apostles. **Acts 2:1-4** paints the picture for us:

> *When the day of Pentecost arrived, they were all together in one place. And suddenly there came from heaven a sound like a mighty rushing wind, and it filled the entire house where they were sitting. And divided tongues as of fire appeared to them and rested on each one of them. And they were all filled with the Holy Spirit and began to speak in other tongues as the Spirit gave them utterance.*

Now all of us who are believers have had the Holy Spirit regenerate and fill our hearts, but no one has had the Holy Spirit come like this! That's because this was one of those events that were unique to that particular time. The coming of the Holy Spirit to the first apostles was a one-time only event never to be repeated. It was done this way to mark a new beginning. The New Covenant and the Kingdom of God were upon them, and God was letting everyone know it! Pentecost marks the beginning of the Holy Spirit permanently indwelling in believers. No longer would the Holy Spirit come and go in God's people as He had in the Old Testament. Now, believers would have the Holy Spirit living in them!

This extraordinary event also had a secondary purpose. It was a reversal on the curse at the Tower of Babel. If you remember the story, the people all spoke one language and decided to build a tower up to Heaven. As punishment, they were scattered, and God confused their speech, making them speak different languages. At Pentecost, the Holy Spirit allowed people of at least seventeen different languages to hear the apostles, who were speaking in Galilean (Aramaic), in their own language! This was a spectacular, supernatural feat of God!

Peter, who not too long ago was so afraid of repercussions that he denied Jesus and then hid in a room with the other disciples, now boldly gave a sermon to all the people gathered. He immediately quoted Old Testament Scripture to show the Jewish crowd that Jesus is the fulfillment of all of the Old Testament prophecy. (Remember, they were starting by bringing the Gospel to the Jewish people.)

All of the believers devoted themselves to the apostles' teaching. They went out and sold all of their possessions, giving the money to the apostles to distribute to anyone who was in need. They ate and prayed together at the temple. And as **Acts 2:47b** tells us, *"And the Lord added to their number day by day those who were being saved."* The Way (the early name for Christianity) had begun!

Instantaneously, the twelve apostles were emboldened and equipped by the Holy Spirit to continue the work of Jesus, including performing miracles. They healed and preached as Jesus had. They also become hated by the Jewish leaders as Jesus had been and were beaten and threatened with death if they did not stop.

Let's pause here and look at what was going on from the perspective of the Pharisees and other Jewish leaders. Jesus was a huge threat to them and their way of life; hence, they had Him crucified. Throughout history, anytime a movement arose, killing off the leader took the wind out it, and it would dissolve into oblivion. In this case, though, the exact opposite happened. They killed (or so they thought) the Leader, but the movement was multiplying at an astronomical rate. The Pharisees panicked and were desperate to stop it, but they were powerless to do so. It seemed that the more they tried to squelch The Way, the more it grew. One Pharisee tried to speak reason to his peers, telling them, *"'If this plan or this undertaking is of man, it will fail; but if it is of God, you will not be able to overthrow them. You might even be found opposing God!'"* **(Acts 5:38b-39)**. Scripture says they agreed to take his advice, but just one verse later, they beat Peter and John and told them not to speak in the name of Jesus.

Chapter six shows the start of tensions occurring within The Way between the two major groups of Jews. There were the Hebrews—those born in Palestine who, even though they may have been fluent in Greek, mostly spoke Aramaic and strictly adhered to the practices and traditions of the Old Testament. Then there were the Hellenists—those Jewish people who were the product of earlier generations scattering and leaving Jerusalem and Judea. They spoke Greek and were immersed in Greek culture. They had no ties to the old ways. Problems arose when the Hellenists accused the Hebrews of neglecting the Hellenist widows and only caring for their own. This problem was symptomatic of the many problems that soon occurred between the two groups. As the church expanded and brought in more and more Gentiles, who were also Hellenists, the Hebrew Jews felt more pushed out, grew more resentful, and eventually many left and returned to Judaism.

To solve the widow issue, though, they went to the apostles for a solution, who appointed the first deacons to handle caring for all of the widows within the church. This practice has transcended to many of today's churches, who appoint deacons to be in authority over the physical needs of their congregation.

One of these deacons, Stephen, was seized and brought before the Jerusalem Council (Jewish leaders). He gave a beautiful sermon, well worth reading in Acts chapter seven, that started off recounting Jewish history but turned as he told the Council that there was no need to hold to Jewish practices and traditions because Jesus had ushered in the New Covenant. He even told them that the temple building wasn't important anymore. He ended by calling them "stiff-necked" and murderers of the Messiah. Stephen's words would have made the Pharisees as angry as anything said by Jesus. In fact, they became so enraged, they took him out of the city and stoned him. At his stoning, we meet someone for the first time—a young Pharisee named Saul, who was watching and approving Stephen's killing.

Saul so approved of killing the followers of Jesus that he went to the high priest to get permission to go to the synagogues in Damascus and arrest followers there, with the intent of bringing them back to Jerusalem to be dealt with. What happened to Saul on his way to Damascus is probably familiar to most of us. **Acts 9:3-9** tells of the event:

> *Now as he went on his way, he approached Damascus, and suddenly a light from heaven shone around him. And falling to the ground, he heard a voice saying to him, "Saul, Saul, why are you persecuting me?" And he said, "Who are you, Lord?" And he said, "I am Jesus, whom you are persecuting. But rise and enter the city, and you will be told what you are to do." The men who were traveling with him stood speechless, hearing the voice but seeing no one. Saul rose from the ground, and although his eyes were opened, he saw nothing. So they led him by the hand and brought him into Damascus. And for three days he was without sight, and neither ate nor drank.*

Saul knew he was having an encounter with God; what he only now realized, though, is that Jesus *is* God! Jesus blinded Paul so that he could see the truth!

After blinding him, Jesus instructed Saul to go a house where a man named Ananias would meet him. In the meantime, God spoke to Ananias and told him to go meet Saul. Ananias was terrified because of Saul's reputation but trusted God and agreed. Upon Ananias restoring Saul's sight, the Holy Spirit filled Saul, and at once, he began preaching about Jesus. From this point on, Saul used the Greco-Roman version of his name—Paul; probably because his mission was ultimately to bring the Gospel to the Gentiles.

From the very beginning, Paul had a rough road of it. The disciples mistrusted him because of his past persecutions of Christians; and the Pharisees, who used to admire him and be his friends, wanted to kill him because he was preaching about Jesus. One disciple, though—Barnabas—took Paul under his wing, so to speak, and convinced the other apostles that Paul was the real deal. Paul was then sent to Tarsus for his own safety.

In the meantime, while Peter was serving God by healing a paralytic and raising a dead woman to life, he had a vision. This vision is recorded in **Acts 10:11-15**:

> *The heavens opened and something like a great sheet descending, being let down by its four corners upon the earth. In it were all kinds of animals and reptiles and birds of the air. And there came a voice to him: "Rise, Peter; kill and eat." But Peter said, "By no means, Lord; for I have never eaten anything that is common or unclean." And the voice came to him a second time, "What God made clean, do not call common."*

God gave Peter this vision three times. Peter realized that the meaning was that God's Kingdom was no longer for those considered "clean," meaning the Jewish people. God made everyone clean, meaning that the Kingdom of God now included Gentile believers. God was telling Peter to preach to the Gentiles! And Peter did, beginning with Cornelius, a Roman centurion, and all those Cornelius gathered to listen to him.

Peter may have been stoked about Gentiles joining the church, but not everyone was. Remember we said the widow issue was just the beginning of the problems between the Hellenist Christians and Hebrew Christians? Well, they were at it again. The Hebrew Christians insisted that the Gentiles had to be circumcised before they were allowed to join the church. We don't have the space in this summary to flesh this out completely, but in a nutshell, what these Hebrew Christians did not understand was that baptism had replaced circumcision as the sign of the covenant between God and His people. As we said, they were tied to the old way of doing things and could not accept the new ways.

Peter continued to have problems with the leaders in Jerusalem. King Herod, a half-Jewish king who was given power by the Roman government in exchange for being their puppet, killed one of the apostles, James, the brother of John. When he saw that it pleased the Jews (the ones against Christianity), he decided to give a repeat performance and arrested Peter. Scripture tells of the event better than we ever could!

> *Now when Herod was about to bring him out, on that very night, Peter was sleeping between two soldiers, bound with two chains, and sentries before the door were guarding the prison. And behold, an angel of the Lord stood next to him, and a light shone in the cell. He struck Peter on the side and woke him, saying, "Get up quickly." And the chains fell off his hands. And the angel said to him, "Dress yourself and put on your sandals." And he did so. And he said to him, "Wrap your cloak around you and follow me." And he went out and followed him. He did not know that what was being done by the angel was real, but thought he was seeing a vision. When they had passed the first and the second guard, they came to the iron gate leading into the city. It opened for them of its own accord, and they went out and went along one street, and immediately the angel left him* **(Acts 12:6-10)**.

An angel walked into the prison and walked out with Peter! As for Herod, shortly after this, an angel struck him dead, and he was eaten by worms.

Barnabas brought Paul back from Tarsus to Antioch. They preached for a year there, and a new name for the followers of the Way emerged, as we are told in **Acts 11:26b**, *"And in Antioch the disciples were first called Christians."*

It was during his time at Antioch that Paul's missionary journeys began, as he and Barnabas were called by the Holy Spirit to go and preach to the nations. Paul went on a total of three missionary journeys. The places and events during each of these journeys are detailed in Acts. There are a few things worth noting when you read of Paul's journeys. First, in each city, he always started off preaching in the synagogues to the Jews and then took his message to the Gentiles. Again, he was fulfilling what Jesus said about taking the Gospel first to the Jews and then to the Gentiles. Also, when he preached, he tailored his delivery to the people he was speaking to. The Gospel message he delivered never changed, but the way in which he delivered that message and the way he behaved did change according to his audience.

He was respectful of people's preconceived beliefs and customs. For example, when he was speaking in a synagogue, he didn't insult the Jewish people by explaining about sin. Knowing the Old Testament as they did, they would have known all about sin. When he was speaking to Greeks who had carved statues to their many gods, including one to "an unknown god," Paul didn't berate them or judge them. Instead, he used this unknown god to tell them that he knew Who this unknown God is. He is Jesus, and He is the one, true God.

Acts tells of many things that happened to Paul while he was taking the Gospel to the Gentile world. One time, he was stoned and left for dead. When the disciples gathered around him, he got up and went back into the city to preach some more! He was put on trial, beaten, imprisoned, and ultimately killed for bringing the good news of Jesus to the unbelieving world. Being dissuaded by nothing, he said, *"I am ready not only to be imprisoned but even to die in Jerusalem for the name of the Lord Jesus"* **(Acts 21:13b)**.

There is no way we could recount all of the amazing things found in the book of Acts, but we hope that if you have never read the entire book, you will be enticed to now!

Chapter 19

THE PAULINE EPISTLES

We now begin looking at the epistles, starting with the Pauline epistles (written by Paul). Just as other letters are meant to be read in one sitting, so should each of the epistles in the Bible. Reading the entire letter will help you get the most out of it. Also helpful is to put them into context historically, compare the contents to other Scripture, and try to grasp the big picture of what Paul is saying instead of focusing on one or two verses.

In every one of Paul's letters, there was an "occasion" that made him write. Sometimes, it was to address problems that had arisen, give encouragement in a tough situation, or to teach theology and doctrine that the church lacked. Take notice of the beautiful closings many of Paul's letter have. Often, when you hear pastors giving a benediction at the end of a worship service, it is one of Paul's epistles they are quoting. One last thing to note is that Paul spoke with authority on God's Word as God was inspiring him to do so. He even says things like, *"If anyone does not obey what we say in this letter, take note of that person, and have nothing to do with him"* **(2 Thess. 3:14)**. Paul was not full of himself. He knew that what he was saying was coming from God.

1 THESSALONIANS

The first letter Paul wrote is most likely 1 Thessalonians, written to the mostly Gentile church in Thessalonica in 51 A.D. You can read of

Paul's travels and planting of the church there in Acts 17:1-15. He wrote this letter two years after he was in Thessalonica. Paul had to leave the city in a hurry because of an uprising of some of the Jews who, due to jealousy, wanted to kill him and one of his mission partners, Silas. They had to leave Thessalonica sooner than they had anticipated, so they did not have time to teach and ground the people in Old Testament Scripture and the teachings of Jesus. Because of this, the Thessalonians, although enthusiastic and strong in their faith, were spiritually immature and had some bad theology and wrong beliefs on the Second Coming of Jesus. Paul, deeply concerned for them and the persecution they were enduring, wrote 1 Thessalonians (and 2 Thessalonians) to praise them for their strong faith in Jesus, to encourage them to imitate him and the other apostles by hanging in there during persecution, and to correct their erroneous thinking on the Second Coming and the resurrection of the dead.

Paul reminded the Thessalonians of God's sovereignty and His love for His people. He tells them in **1 Thessalonians 1:4-5a**, *"For we know, brothers loved by God, that he has chosen you, because our gospel came to you not only in word, but also in power and in the Holy Spirit and with full conviction."* You will see phrases like *"God chose you"* or *"God's elect"* throughout all of Paul's (and the other's) epistles. All of the writers are driving home the same point—God has complete control over everyone and everything. From before creation, He chose those whom He would save—not because of anything they would do or because they deserved it, but just because it pleased Him to do so. We saw this same truth in the Old Testament when He chose a remnant of the Jewish people to save and not the entire physical nation of Israel. Here in the New Testament, God has expanded His Kingdom to include Gentiles, but that doesn't change anything about Him. Just as He sovereignly chose which Israelites to save, so He chooses which Gentiles to save. We will go into much more detail when we get to the book of Romans and Ephesians, but we wanted to point out that God's absolute sovereignty is everywhere in

Scripture—from Genesis to Revelation—not just in a few selected, pulled-out verses. In the Thessalonians' case, this truth helped get them through the persecution they were facing.

If you recall from part four, some of the prophets spoke of the "day of the Lord"—the day of Jesus' Second Coming when He would judge all, separating believers from unbelievers. The Thessalonians did not understand that this was a day that could be long into the future. They believed Jesus was coming back while all the present believers were still alive. Because of this, when some of the believers in their church died, they were troubled. They thought those who had passed would miss out on seeing Jesus and spending eternity with Him.

Paul corrected their thinking in **1 Thessalonians 4:14**: *"For since we believe that Jesus died and rose again, even so, through Jesus, God will bring with him those who have fallen asleep."* Paul was educating them on what it says in Ezekiel 27. Those who are in Christ are not dead, but merely asleep, meaning they were spiritually raised in Christ. Their soul lives on in Heaven, while their physical body is temporarily incapacitated until Jesus' return. When Jesus comes back, He will physically resurrect all of those who have died. All of those who are His will be raised to glory, just as Jesus was. In light of that, while we grieve the loss of those we love, if they belong to Jesus, we *should "not grieve as others do who have no hope"* **(1 Thess. 4:13b)**.

Paul ended his letter with one of those beautiful benedictions we mentioned. In **1 Thessalonians 5:23**, he says, *"Now may the God of peace himself sanctify you completely, and may your whole spirit and soul and body be kept blameless at the coming of our Lord Jesus Christ."*

2 THESSALONIANS

Only one year after his first letter, Paul wrote a second letter to the Thessalonians. It seems Paul's clarification about the "day of the Lord" confused the Thessalonians even more. Because Paul had told the church that those who had died were already raised spiritually with Christ, some took that to mean that Jesus had already come back. They stopped working because they thought they didn't need to since Jesus has returned. They sponged money off of the wealthier believers. It was this "Second Coming fever" that Paul addressed in his second letter.

Obviously, the Thessalonians' beliefs about the Second Coming were wrong. Their mistake was in their thinking that the "end times" and "the day of the Lord" were the same thing. This is an error made by people today. The end times is not an event, but a time frame—the time between Jesus' First and Second Coming. In contrast, the day of the Lord is an event when Jesus returns to judge all people and to completely destroy sin, death, and Satan. When Paul talked of "the end times being upon us," the Thessalonians mistakenly thought he meant that Jesus had returned. To correct this, Paul told the people of three events that must occur before Jesus comes back. There is some mystery to us when we read of these events because Paul, who had been with the Thessalonians, surely taught them things that we are not privy to. As outsiders looking in, we cannot be completely sure what Paul meant, but the Thessalonians would have known for sure. The three events that must occur are:

1. **The Rebellion** – In **2 Thessalonians 2:3a**, Paul writes, *"Let no one deceive you in any way. For that day will not come, unless the rebellion comes first."* Scholars disagree on who Paul is saying will rebel. It could be the world in general rebels against God, or it could mean those who once professed to be Christians. These "Christians," who were never really Christians at all, would turn from obeying God and rebel against His Word. There is also the possibility that Paul means both! We could certainly make an argument that we see both of these happening today, but Paul is saying that there will be one final, great rebellion.

2. **The Man of Lawlessness** – Continuing the passage in **2 Thess. 2:3-4**, Paul says, *"And the man of lawlessness is revealed, the son of destruction, who opposes and exalts himself against every so-called god or object of worship, so that he takes his seat in the temple of God, proclaiming himself to be God."* The man of lawlessness, the "antichrist," of 1 John 4:3 and the beast of Revelation 13 are all one and the same. Some have defined them as one evil individual who appears shortly before Jesus returns. Some say they are symbolic of a political system (e.g. the Roman Empire). Others, especially the reformers like John Calvin and Martin Luther, define them as the Catholic papacy. Still others have viewed the man of lawlessness, beast, and antichrist as anyone who opposes the authority of Jesus Christ as Messiah and King—in other words, all non-believers. While we aren't completely sure who Paul is referring to, we will be sure before Jesus comes back because this man of lawlessness will be revealed!

3. **The Restrainer** – Paul tells us the last thing that will occur before Jesus comes back in **2 Thessalonians 2:6-7**, *"And you know what is restraining him [the man of lawlessness] . . . is already at work. Only he who now restrains it will do so . . . until he is out of the way."* Before the man of lawlessness can be revealed, the one restraining him has to be taken away. Someone or something is restraining evil now and will continue to do so until right before Jesus comes back. It could be the Holy Spirit, could be God the Father, or it could be an archangel. Paul could have also meant someone else. The people he was writing to knew who he meant so he didn't define it. We don't need to get frustrated, though, because it doesn't really matter exactly whom Paul is speaking of. Ultimately, God is sovereign over all, and whether He is restraining evil Himself or has appointed Michael, the archangel, to do it, doesn't change anything for us. Satan, sin, and evil had their fate already sealed when Jesus was resurrected. Regardless of who

is currently holding them back, it will be Jesus Who crushes and destroys them once and for all.

After this, Paul addressed the people who stopped working and were living off the generosity of the wealthier congregants. He told all of the physically able people to get to work! He entreated the people to stop enabling these lazy Christians in **2 Thessalonians 3:10b**: *"If anyone is not willing to work, let him not eat."*

Lastly, Paul asked for prayer, as he was being persecuted as much as they were. He encouraged the Thessalonians to stay strong in their faith.

1 CORINTHIANS

While it may seem like Paul was admonishing the Thessalonians, he really wasn't. He was very thankful and optimistic about their enthusiastic and strong faith. Paul had no problem admonishing when needed, though, as we see in his first letter to the church in the port city of Corinth, written in 54 A.D. Unlike Thessalonica, Paul's stay in Corinth was much longer. Three years prior to writing this letter, he had stayed there for a year-and-a-half with Aquila and his wife, Priscilla, Jewish Christians who had to flee from Rome due to a decree issued by Emperor Claudius (see Acts 18: 1-17).

In all of Paul's letters, no matter how bad things were at a church he was writing to, he almost always found something to be positive about. He always started his letters with thanksgiving to God for the people of the church to whom he was writing, and 1 Corinthians is no different. But after this, he dove right into the problems the church in Corinth was experiencing. Being a port city, with people coming in and out, Corinth had a serious morality problem; and it appears that some of the secular immorality was making its way into the church. Paul's impassioned letter has strong words as he corrected and reprimanded the Corinthians on several issues that were in conflict with the Gospel message they had heard.

This is probably the toughest of Paul's letters to summarize because he deals with so many issues within this troubled church, including division within the church, sexual immorality, believers taking each other to court, marriage, living your life as you are called to, sacrificing food to idols, other forms of idolatry, head coverings, communion, spiritual gifts, unity within the church, loving each other, prophecy, speaking in tongues, worship, and resurrection. It would take a whole book to delve into all of these issues! We are only able to give you a snapshot of this powerful epistle but hope your curiosity will be piqued and you will want to read what Paul says about all of these things for yourself!

The theme of 1 Corinthians can best be summed up in two questions: What does it mean to be wise, and what does it mean to be spiritual? Corinth was a bustling and busy port city in Greece. The Greeks were known for valuing education and intelligence over everything else, and the Corinthians were no different. However, Paul tells them there is a vast difference between being smart and being wise. "Worldly wisdom"—as the Corinthians so highly regarded—was of little value. It was spiritual wisdom that they needed to strive for. The wisdom that comes only from God through the power of the Holy Spirit. The unbelieving world not only doesn't acknowledge this wisdom, but they also think it's foolishness. But for believers, it is a manifestation of the power and love of God. Paul tells the Corinthians, *"For the word of the cross is folly to those who are perishing, but to us who are being saved it is the power of God"* **(1 Cor. 1:18)**. The church in Corinth needed to stop thinking like the world and start thinking like Jesus!

He also confronted what it means to be spiritual. Again, the church was using the worldly views of their time to define this. They falsely believed that the soul and body were completely separate and that one did not affect the other. So while they gave their soul to Jesus, their body was theirs to do with as they pleased. This led to sexual immorality throughout the congregation. Paul admonishes them, telling them, *"Do you not know that your body is a temple of the Holy Spirit within you, whom you have from God? You are not your own, for you were bought with a price. So glorify God in your body."*

Something worth mentioning about in 1 Corinthians is that it contains the "love chapter." Chapter thirteen is a favorite to quote at weddings to show what marital love looks like. There is certainly nothing wrong with this, but Paul meant these words to show what love between all believers should look like. There is no place for arrogance, impatience, unkindness, jealousy, resentfulness, spitefulness, or lying within the body of Christ. Instead, we should build each other up, sharing each other's burdens and joys. He sums up his thoughts in **1 Corinthians 13:13**: *"So now faith, hope, and love abide, these three; but the greatest of these is love."*

Paul ends his letter urging the Corinthians, *"Be watchful, stand firm in the faith, act like men, be strong. Let all that you do be done in love"* **(1 Cor. 16:13-14)**.

GALATIANS

Most likely written in 54 A.D., the same year as 1 Corinthians, while Paul was staying in Ephesus, this is a letter to a group of churches in Galatia with whom Paul had briefly visited (see Acts 18:23). In it, he emphasizes the doctrine of "Justification by Faith" by addressing a heated argument going on between the Jewish and Gentile Christians. The Jewish members were insisting that the Gentiles had to be circumcised in order to be Christians. Paul had been to visit these churches, located in modern-day Turkey, and had a close relationship with the people. Because of this, he uses some strong and angry language to criticize them for allowing false teaching that blotted out the message of the Gospel. In fact, Galatians is Paul's only letter without the thanksgiving section we mentioned in 1 Corinthians.

The last thing Jesus said when He was on the cross is *"It is finished"* **(John 19:30)**. Christ meant that the saving work He did on the cross to reconcile His people to God was finished. Nothing needed to be added to it.

In the churches in Galatia, the Jewish members were saying the Gentiles still had to follow the Law and get circumcised in order to be Christians. They were adding to what Jesus had already accomplished, thereby perverting the message of the Gospel. Paul lays into them, beginning in **Galatians 1:6**: *"I am astonished that you are so quickly deserting him who called you in the grace of Christ and are turning to a different gospel—not that there is another one, but there are some who trouble you and want to distort the gospel of Christ."*

Paul continued by showing them that forcing Gentiles to be circumcised was wrong. He cited an argument when he called Peter a hypocrite—not so he could drag Peter through the mud, but to show the people that he was willing to have a painful confrontation with even Peter over this issue. Paul ultimately showed them that the issue of circumcision was just a symptom of the bigger issue—thinking believers needed Christ *plus* adherence to Old Testament Law for salvation (i.e. they needed to have both faith *and* works). Paul is telling them salvation is only by "justification by faith." Works are not only useless in salvation, but it is also sinful to think they are a part of salvation.

Paul tries to right their thinking, showing them that Jesus' First Coming fulfilled the Old Covenant and ushered in the New Covenant. Consequently, observing Old Testament Law was no longer necessary. Paul tells the Galatians, *"Now before faith came, we were held captive under the law, imprisoned until the coming faith would be revealed. So then, the law was our guardian until Christ came, in order that we might be justified by faith"* **(Gal. 3:23-24)**.

If you remember from our chapters on the Old Testament, only twelve of the 613 laws from the Old Testament transferred to the New Testament: "Love the Lord your God with all your heart . . . soul . . . strength and . . . mind; love "your neighbor as yourself" **(Luke 10:27)**; and the Ten Commandments.

Paul spent a lot of time teaching them right theology. He tells them they are no longer to live in the flesh (their dead, sinful state before they were saved), but to live in the Spirit (their saved state governed by the Holy Spirit).

One way they could know they were achieving this is that they would begin to see in themselves the fruit of the Spirit: *"Love, joy, peace, patience, kindness, goodness, faithfulness, gentleness, self-control"* **(Gal. 5:22-23a)**. This is just as applicable to us today!

Paul shows his humorous side, using irony in **Galatians 5:12**, when he says of those who were insisting that believers be circumcised, *"I wish those who unsettle you would emasculate [castrate] themselves!"* Paul finishes his letter, giving them more warnings and telling them not to grow weary of doing good, but to do good to everyone, especially brothers and sisters in the faith.

ROMANS

Also most likely written during Paul's three-and-a-half year stay in Ephesus, the book of Romans was written in 57 A.D., to the church in Rome, where Paul was a citizen (see Acts 16:37). It is often called Paul's *magnus opus* (great work). Romans may very well be the most influential book in the entire Bible. That certainly proved to be the case for a Catholic monk named Martin Luther. Luther sacrificed and tortured himself trying to earn his way into Heaven and still found his sin so grievous that he was terrified of one day facing God for judgement. Then, he came across **Romans 1:17b**: *"'The righteous shall live by faith.'"* This one verse changed Luther's life. He realized salvation is not something that is to be earned but is a gift given by God through faith. Luther's encounter with the book of Romans propelled him to become one of the most formidable figures of the Reformation in the sixteenth century and one of the founders of Protestantism.[26]

What is so extraordinary about the book of Romans? First, this book contains the "five solas," or tenants, that came out of the aforementioned Reformation: *Sola fide* (faith alone) found in **Romans 1:17**; *sola gratia* (grace

---

26 Ligonier Ministries, "R.C. Sproul: For Justification By Faith Alone," YouTube video, 48:03, posted August 06, 2015, www.youtube.com/watch?v=DfKUxXB7_Cg.

alone) found in **Romans 3:21-31**; *sola Christus* (Christ alone), also found in **Romans 3:21-31**; *sola Deo Gloria* (to the glory of God alone) found in **Romans 11:36**; and *sola Scriptura* (Scripture alone) found in **Romans 3:23-25**. Put together, these tenants are the essence of Christianity: It is only faith in Christ alone that saves us. This faith comes only through grace given to us by God and is for His glory, not ours. Scripture is God's Word and the only authority on the things of God.

Another unique thing about Paul's letter to the Romans is that it while his other letters contain parts of the Gospel, Romans has the entire Gospel message in it:

1. **Romans 1:18-21; 3:11-18** – *All men have sinned against the Almighty God.*

2. **Romans 2:1-4; 3:5-8** – *God's wrath and judgement against us is righteous.*

3. **Romans 3:21-24, 28; 4:13-17** – *We are saved from God's wrath—not by anything we can do, but only by having faith in the saving work of Jesus Christ.*

In just a summary, we could never give Romans the time and space needed to unlock all of the incredible truths, doctrine, and theology contained in it. We will give some of the main points and highlights but strongly encourage you to do a complete study on this book!

The backdrop of this letter is the tension in the Roman church between the Jewish believers and the Gentile believers. Just as it was in Galatia, the Jewish Christians wanted Gentile believers to adhere to Old Testament Law and rituals. Paul's letter emphasizes that all believers, whether Jew or Gentile, are one in Christ; and, as we saw earlier, all that is required of believers is faith in Christ alone, given by grace through the power of the Holy Spirit. When reading Romans, it may seem that Paul was disparaging the Law, or the Old Covenant, but he was not. If you look at the context in which he was writing and compare it to his other letters, he believed, as he should, that the Law is perfect. The problem with the Old Covenant was that it was stuck with sinful humans who couldn't possibly obey it. The Trinity, knowing this would be the case before the creation of the world, already had the plan of redemption through Jesus, the New Covenant, in place to save all of His people.

Therefore, the Gospel message is the same for both the Jew and Gentile, for we are all in the same dead, sinful state before we are saved. As Paul tells us in **Romans 3:10b-18**:

> *"None is righteous, no, not one; no one understand; no one seeks for God. All have turned aside; together they have become worthless; no one does good, not even one." "Their throat is an open grave; they use their tongues to deceive." "The venom of asps is under their lips." "Their mouth is full of curses and bitterness." "Their feet are swift to shed blood; in their paths are ruin and misery, and the way of peace they have not known." "There is no fear of God before their eyes."*

That should make us all shutter! None of us wants to think of ourselves as that bad, but God, Who knows what unbelievers are like, tells us we are. Thankfully, God, in His mercy, chose a people to save unto Himself. As Paul tells the Romans in **5:8-10**, *"But God shows his love for us in that while we were still sinners, Christ died for us. Since, therefore, we have now been justified by his blood, much more shall we be saved by him from the wrath of God. For if while we were enemies we were reconciled to God by the death of his Son, much more, now that we are reconciled, shall we be saved by his life."*

Paul makes it clear in chapters eight and nine that it is God's sovereign choice whom He saves and whom He does not. **Romans 8:29-30** says, *"For those whom he foreknew he also predestined to be conformed to the image of his Son, in order that he might be the firstborn among many brothers. And those whom he predestined he also called, and those whom he called he also justified, and those whom he justified he also glorified."*

Paul then gave a specific message to the Jews and to the Gentiles. First, to the Jews, he tells them that it was not the physical nation of Israel that God was saving, but just an elect remnant: *"Israel failed to obtain what it was seeking. The elect obtained it, but the rest were hardened"* **(Rom. 11:7)**. He also told them not to think themselves better than the Gentiles because the Israelites were just as sinful. To the Gentiles, even though they were now to be grafted into the family of God, they should not be arrogant about it because Israel was still God's first people. Also, like all unbelievers, the Gentiles were desperately wicked apart from God's saving grace. Paul's intention in both of these messages was to show the Jew and Gentile that they were both dead in sin and were only saved by the grace of God—another reason they should be united and not opposed to each other.

Paul then spends a lot of time telling them how they should live in light of being saved. Now that their hearts have been regenerated, they are no longer prisoners to sin. He exhorts them, *"Do not present your members to sin as instruments for unrighteousness, but present yourselves to God as those who have been brought from death to life, and your members to God as instruments for righteousness. For sin will have no dominion over you, since you are not under law but under grace"* **(Rom. 6:13-14)**. While the people in Rome—and all of us—will certainly still sin, they—and we—are no longer enslaved to sin. We now have the power (through the Holy Spirit) to resist sin. The main way we do this, Paul tells us, is to *"not be conformed to this world, but be transformed by the renewal of your mind, that by testing you may discern what is the will of God, what is good and acceptable and perfect"* **(Rom. 12:2)**.

We will certainly never get it right until either we get to Heaven or Jesus comes back; but as we grow in God, we should be able to resist more and more sin. And when we do get it wrong and find ourselves sinning, Paul has these words for us in **Romans 8:1-2**: *"There is therefore now no condemnation for those who are in Christ Jesus. For the law of the Spirit of life has set you free in Christ Jesus from the law of sin and death."*

And if that doesn't make you fall to your knees in gratitude, Paul tells us there's even more! Once we are saved, we become joint heirs with Christ, meaning that we have an inheritance from God; so that no matter how we may be suffering on Earth, our future glory is sure. And even more glorious, as it says in **Romans 8:28**, *"And we know that for those who love God all things work together for good, for those who are called according to his purpose."* God works everything that happens in a believer's life for their spiritual good and for His glory. Nothing that occurs in our life, no matter how tragic, is ever in vain!

Paul ends with practical advice on how to live as a Christian, for it is how we live that will make people sit up and take notice that there is something different about us. Love genuinely; abhor evil; bless those who persecute you; rejoice with those who rejoice; and weep with those who weep. Never be wise in your own eyes; do not repay evil for evil, but overcome evil with good. If possible, live peaceably with everyone around you. Submit to authority, for God has put them there. Don't be sexually immoral or a drunkard. Don't pass judgment on people. Don't cause weaker Christians to stumble because of what you are doing. And most important, be an example of Christ to all around you.

2 CORINTHIANS

The same year Paul wrote to the church in Rome, 57 A.D., he wrote a second letter to the Corinthian church. Paul had previously visited Corinth on two occasions and had intended to make a third visit, but he wasn't able to, as he explained in this epistle. There are scholars who believe 2 Corinthians may actually be two letters that were combined into one. The first letter is thought to be chapters one through nine, where Paul has a positive attitude toward the Corinthians. Chapters ten through thirteen are thought to be a second letter because Paul's tone turns negative toward the people. Almost all scholars agree that something happened before chapter ten that changed Paul's tone to the people, but we aren't told what that is.

Out of all of the churches Paul wrote to, his relationship with the Corinthian church was the most intense. Paul wrote this letter after Titus, one of Paul's disciples, returned from Corinth and reported to Paul what he encountered there and how the Corinthians reacted to Paul's first letter (1 Corinthians). Titus was sent to receive the collection the church was to have ready, but it wasn't. Paul was sometimes criticized for taking these collections, accused of being greedy. But the reality was that he didn't collect the money for himself. In between the traveling, preaching, beatings, and imprisonments, Paul made tents to support himself. The collections he received from the various churches were distributed to poor Christians as they had need.

Paul began his letter by telling the people of Corinth that he, and those traveling with him, had suffered greatly—to the point where they thought they were going to die. Paul's life is a prime example of the teachings of Jesus that we looked at in part five—that Christians should expect trials and persecution. As a Pharisee, Paul had it pretty good. He was respected and powerful. From the moment he became a believer, though, his life was marked with suffering, beatings, death threats, prison, ship wrecks, and peril. Paul often pointed this out in his letters. But it was not to complain; instead, it was to show that he recognized God had purpose behind the suffering; and with the power of the Holy Spirit, he and his companions endure it. Paul understood that suffering is often to *"make us rely not on ourselves but on God who raises the dead"* **(2 Cor 1:9b)**.

Perhaps Paul started his letter with his sufferings to make the Corinthians understand what he had been up against and what they could expect to be up against as Christians. The church was upset that Paul had not visited again as he had promised, but Paul told them that his last visit there was so full of confrontation, that he decided it was in everyone's best interest that he not go back. Instead, he told them, he was sending this letter. Paul was not one to break a promise. The consensus is that Paul must have had information that made him decide he should not visit but write instead. A letter served the purpose of allowing the people to read and reread Paul's words, understanding more fully what he was communicating to them and, hopefully, causing them to turn to the Lord in repentance—things a personal visit might not be able to accomplish.

The Corinthians had lapsed back into sin, and Paul was confronting them on it. As we said, in chapters one through nine of this letter, Paul had a positive tone. He kept his reprimands general and did not point at anyone in particular. Most likely, Paul was writing to the entire church in these chapters, understanding that some were believers, and some weren't. Some would take his words to heart and repent, and some wouldn't because they had not had their hearts regenerated.

We can see Paul comparing the two groups in **2 Corinthians 2:15-16**: *"For we are the aroma of Christ to God among those who are being saved and among those who are perishing, to one a fragrance from death to death, to the other a fragrance from life to life."* This is an important point Paul makes. When we are witnessing to people, we need to realize that a person's heart status will determine their reaction to the Gospel message. For those who have been regenerated by the Holy Spirit, even if they are not fully believers yet, there will be something in the Gospel that rings true, and they will be drawn to it. For those whose hearts are still dead, even if not externally, internally they will respond defensively, angrily, or maybe even violently to the Gospel message. This is because even with an unregenerate heart, there is a subconscious level at which they understand that this message brings death to them. Is it any wonder then that they respond so aggressively?!

Paul went on to ask if the Corinthians needed a letter of recommendation for him. This may seem odd, but letters of recommendation were often used during this time. They were used to authenticate the credentials of the person who possessed it. Paul was being sarcastic here, asking if the Corinthians needed this type of letter to know that he was the "real deal" as an apostle of Christ. He told them that they and all of the other people Paul had worked with who became followers of Christ were his "credentials."

Having established that, Paul continued to tell them that in no way did he, nor his disciples, alter or tamper with the Word of God. The Gospel they preach is the authentic, true Gospel that *"has shone in our hearts to give the light of the knowledge of the glory of God in the face of Jesus Christ"* **(2 Cor. 4:6)**. He continues in **2 Corinthians 4:7**: *"But we have this treasure in jars of clay, to show that the surpassing power belongs to God and not to us."* Despite our fragile humanness (jars of clay), God works through us to accomplish His purposes for the Gospel. Although we may be "cracked and chipped", His power in us gives us the hope needed to endure hardships, which Paul illustrates beautifully in **2 Corinthians 4:8-9**: *"We are afflicted in every way, but not crushed; perplexed, but not driven to despair, persecuted, but not forsaken; struck down, but not destroyed."* Paul penned these divinely inspired words to bring hope and encouragement to Christians who were being persecuted in the first century. He had no way of knowing how his words would still be strengthening and emboldening Christians two thousand years later!

Paul continues for several more chapters, giving the church in Corinth practical and truth-filled teachings about Heaven, judgement, reconciliation, putting off our old selves and becoming new creations in Christ, not being a stumbling block to others, the dangers of marrying or going into business with unbelievers, and understanding that our bodies are a living sacrifice to God. Paul spent two chapters (eight and nine) on giving. You may have heard the phrase, *"God loves a cheerful giver"*—a direct quote from **2 Corinthians 9:7**.

As we've noted, Paul's tone changes in chapter ten. This is partly due to the false teachers that were appearing on the scene in Corinth and the people's acceptance of them. It was also because Paul was no longer speaking to the whole church, but to those in the church who were unbelievers. Some of the false teachers who appeared on the scene called themselves "super apostles," meaning they were Jewish and not a Gentile. Paul picked these messengers apart by comparing them to himself. He does some boasting, but not about himself and his triumphs. Paul boasts of his sufferings for the sake of Jesus and about Christ and what He has done. He had a message for these "super apostles" in **2 Corinthians 10:18**: *For it is not the one who commends himself who is approved, but the one whom the Lord commends."*

In the midst of Paul talking about the suffering he had endured, there is a narrative that many of you may be familiar with. Paul speaks of a "thorn in his flesh" in **2 Corinthians 12:7-9**, *"So to keep me from becoming conceited because of the surpassing greatness of the revelations, a thorn was given me in the flesh, a messenger of Satan to harass me, to keep me from being conceited. Three times I pleaded with the Lord about this, that it should leave me. But he said to me, 'My grace is sufficient for you, for my power is made perfect in weakness.'"* Paul had already said that he recognized that the Lord sent suffering as a way to keep him relying on God and not himself. Here, he takes that truth even further. We don't know what Paul's "thorn" was; we aren't even sure if it was physical, mental, or emotional. What we do know is that Paul recognized that God gave him a chronic problem to keep him humble and remind him that he needed God's grace. It was not just relying on God in a general sense but relying on His grace and mercy in order to function every minute of every day.

Paul ends his epistle with a benediction many of us have probably heard at the end of a worship service: *"The grace of the Lord Jesus Christ and the love of God and the fellowship of the Holy Spirit be with you all"* **(2 Cor. 13:14)**.

EPHESIANS

In 62 A.D., Paul was imprisoned in Rome, but instead of just sitting there languishing, he wrote four letters—three to churches in Ephesus, Philippi, and Colossae, and one to Philemon. Paul had previously visited Ephesus, promising to return for another visit (Acts 18:18–21). He not only returned but stayed for three-and-a-half years (Acts 19). While every one of Paul's letters, and every book in the Bible, stresses God's sovereignty, Paul really drove this truth home in the book of Ephesians. In fact, this epistle may not have been meant just for the church in Ephesus, but as a type of devotional to be used by all of the churches in Asia, of which Ephesus was the capital. There was a fear of the "powers of this dark world" in Asia. Paul's purpose in writing this letter was to alleviate these fears. Unlike his letters to the Corinthians and Galatians, Paul wrote as if he did not know his readers personally. His writing is much more generalized, but that does not keep this epistle from being powerful in theology, doctrine, and truth!

There are two major themes in the letter to the Ephesians. The first is that God calls His people; and the second is that God has had a plan for saving His people since before the creation of the world, which has manifested in the Person of Jesus. To help the people deal with their fear of evil forces, Paul emphasizes that Jesus is not only Lord over salvation, but over all world affairs—even the "powers of this dark world." God is bringing all things into subjection through Jesus and His people, whom He calls and equips to do His will. The heart of the whole letter can be summed up in **Ephesians 2:8-9**: *"For by grace you have been saved through faith. And this is not your own doing, it is the gift of God, not a result of works, so that no one may boast."* Paul wrote this verse to both the Jews and the Gentiles. For those Jews who were saved, that salvation did not come by anything they *had* done (i.e. keeping the rituals of the Old Testament like circumcision). For the Gentiles, who weren't adhering to circumcision and Old Testament rituals, their salvation was not in jeopardy because of anything they *hadn't* done. Paul showed the Ephesians that Christ has brought His people together, both the Jew and the Gentile, for His glory and His triumph.

Right out of the gate, Paul told his readers that it is God Who calls His people. *"He chose us in him before the foundation of the world, that we should be holy and blameless before him. In love he predestined us for adoption to himself as sons through Jesus Christ, according to the purpose of his will"* **(Eph. 1:4-5)**. This is a crucial truth! If you are a believer, this means before God created the world, before you were born, before you heard about Him, and before you "made the choice" to follow Jesus, God chose you to be one of His children! He chose us; we didn't choose Him! Friends, this would have made all of the difference in the world to the early church, and it should to us. No matter what we are facing, no matter how badly we get caught up in sin, and no matter how we are "feeling" about Jesus during a particular time in our spiritual walk, if we are one of God's elect, our salvation is assured and can never be lost because God decided on it, not us! Paul confirms this by telling his readers that they have been sealed by the Holy Spirit, Who guarantees our inheritance. But even beyond salvation, God is sovereign over every minute detail in the entire universe as we see in **Ephesians 1:11b**, *"According to the purpose of him [God] who works all things according to the counsel of his will."* Paul, wanting to be sure the people got this doctrine of election, states it again in **Ephesians 2:4-5**: *"But God, being rich in mercy, because of the great love with which he loved us, even when we were dead in our trespasses, made us alive together with Christ—by grace you have been saved."* We were dead in our sin. A dead person can't choose Jesus. A dead person can't even understand about Jesus. It is only when the Holy Spirit regenerates our dead hearts and brings us to life—opening our ears, eyes, and mind—that we can comprehend the Gospel and follow Jesus. From an earthly perspective, our accepting Jesus as our Lord and Savior is the most momentous event in our lives, and this truth does not diminish that. It just shows us that Jesus found us; we didn't find Him—He was never lost! Since we had nothing to do with our salvation, we have nothing to boast about except the saving work of Jesus Christ. It wasn't the work of Jesus plus our good choice that saved us. That would not only give us something to boast about but would be "works"—we did something to earn our salvation; we made the right choice. For some of you, this may be a new or hard truth. But we encourage you to read God's Word for yourself. You will see God sovereignly choosing people over and over again from Genesis to Revelation!

Paul reminds the people that being chosen by God is not meant to make us arrogant; in fact, it should do the opposite. Since we contributed nothing to our salvation, we owe everything to God and should want to obey His commands and be imitators of Christ Jesus. He extols his readers to *"walk in love, as Christ loved us and gave himself up for us, a fragrant offering and sacrifice to God"* **(Eph. 5:2)** and to *"walk as children of light (for the fruit of light is found in all that is good and right and true), and try to discern what is pleasing to the Lord"* **(Eph. 5:8b-10)**.

As in other letters, Paul gives his readers practical advice on living out their Christian walk. He talks about the relationships between husbands and wives, parents and children, and bondservants and masters.

Paul ended his letter telling the Ephesians to be strong in the Lord and in the strength of God's might. Believers are to put on the armor of God, which belongs to God, but is imputed to His people through the Holy Spirit, so they can stand against the devil and his schemes. Paul is showing believers how to fight spiritual warfare through God's power because in Christ, Satan and his demons are already defeated. This armor of God is truth, righteousness, the Gospel, faith, salvation, and, most importantly, the Word of God and prayer, given to us by the Holy Spirit.

PHILIPPIANS

You have probably noticed that most of Paul's letters contain a rebuke or reprimand to the church he was writing to. Philippians is a change from that. Written while he was in prison to the church he founded in Philippi (Acts 16:11-40), Paul's letter is filled with thanksgiving and encouragement. In contrast to the general and impersonal letter to the Ephesians, this letter has a warmth that is evidence of a close relationship between Paul and the church in Philippi. They have loved, supported, and prayed for him; and he was grateful.

We see this from the very beginning in **Phil 1:3-5**: *"I thank my God in all my remembrance of you, always in every prayer of mine for you all making my prayer* *with joy, because of your partnership in the gospel from the first day until now."* One verse later, Paul gives the central theme of the whole letter as he encourages the church that God would be with them, helping them to continue to spread the Gospel and conduct themselves in a manner worthy of the children of God. **Philippians 1:6** says, *"He who began a good work in you will bring it to completion at the day of Jesus Christ."*

This letter has some deep theological truths, which makes perfect sense in light of his encouraging them to keep living out their Christian walk. Living a solid Christian life is dependent upon our grasping theological truths. Paul knew this and wanted to edify his readers with some of those truths. We see this in **Philippians 2:6-7**, where Paul exhorts them to exemplify Jesus' example: *"[Jesus], though he was in the form of God, did not count equality with God a thing to be grasped, but emptied himself, by taking the form of a servant."* Paul is saying that even though Jesus is God, while He walked the Earth, He limited Himself to the confines of His physical body. That is what "did not count equality with God a thing to be grasped" means. Instead, He took the role of a servant. If Jesus (God) did that for us, how much more should we be willing to serve Him and others?! Paul tells the people to take heart because exemplifying Jesus is not something God leaves us to do on our own. **Philippians 2:13** says, *"For it is God who works in you, both to will and to work for his good pleasure."*

Paul further encourages the Philippians in their walk with God by telling them, *"Do not be anxious about anything, but in everything by prayer and supplication with thanksgiving let your requests be made know to God. And the peace of God, which surpasses all understanding, will guard your hearts and your minds in Christ Jesus"* **(Phil. 4:6-7)**. Remember, the first century church experienced great persecution. Paul's words were a soothing balm to these battered and weary Christians; and they should be to us, too! Paul continues, telling them to keep their minds on the things of God and not to be distracted by the things of the world: *"Whatever is true, whatever is honorable, whatever is just, whatever is* *pure, whatever is lovely, whatever is commendable, if there is any excellence, if there is anything worthy of praise, think about these things"* **(Phil. 4:8-9)**.

Just a few verses later, Paul writes one of the most often quoted verses from Scripture: *"I can do all things through him who strengthens me"* **(Phil. 4:13)**. This verse is a huge encouragement, for sure, but it is frequently taken out of context. This is not the "beat your chest, go out and take on the world, and accomplish anything you set your mind to" exhortation that it is often used as. If we read the verses before it, we see Paul talking about how he has endured many different situations. He had been in need, and he had had plenty. He had been brought low, and he had been extolled. When Paul said he could do all things through Him who strengthens him, he meant that he was able to persevere through whatever situation he found himself in because his fortitude came from Jesus, not from himself. In many ways, the actual meaning of the verse should give us more hope than the inaccurate, often-used meaning. We can start every day with confidence that no matter what we may have to face, Jesus will be with us, giving us the strength to endure it. As the hymn goes, "Strength for today and bright hope for tomorrow!"[27]

COLOSSIANS

Still in prison in Rome, Paul wrote a letter to the church in the small town of Colossae, a place he probably hadn't actually visited. Written to relatively new believers, Paul hit hard on Christology, the doctrine of Jesus Christ. He wanted to ground the Colossians in theology and truth to keep them from being influenced by other religious sects that were around. Paul wanted his recipients to know of the absolute authority and all-sufficiency of Jesus to forgive sins, save, and defeat the "domain of darkness." Paul wanted to leave no doubt in these young believers' minds of the magnificence and sovereignty

---

27 "Great is Thy Faithfulness," Public Domain.

of Christ. To that effect, he gives a beautiful discord on the preeminence of Christ in **Colossians 1:15-20**:

> *He is the image of the invisible God, the firstborn of all creation. For by him all things were created, in heaven and on earth, visible and invisible, whether thrones or dominions or rulers or authorities—all things were created through him and for him. And he is before all things, and in him all things hold together. And he is the head of the body, the church. He is the beginning, the firstborn from the dead, that in everything he might be preeminent. For in him all the fullness of God was pleased to dwell, and through him to reconcile to himself all things, whether on earth or in heaven, making peace by the blood of his cross.*

This passage on the doctrine of Christology shows us that God not only created the world through Jesus, but also when it went off-course because of sin, God brought it back again through Jesus. Jesus has already won the victory over creation and the earth, but He will bring it to completion upon His return. When Jesus comes back, He will establish a new earth, thereby, putting creation back as it was originally intended to be. This same truth applies to us, as well. If we belong to Jesus, He has already won the victory over our old, dead, sinful selves. We are a new creation, alive in Him, and no longer a slave to our sin nature. We are called to live in this new reality, resisting sin and evil. And while we are still sinning now, when we die or when Jesus returns, He will put us back to the state we were originally created to be—sinless.

Paul shows the Colossians what living in the new reality should look like in **Colossians 3:12-14**, *"Put on then, as God's chosen ones, holy and beloved, compassionate hearts, kindness, humility, meekness, and patience, bearing with one another and, if one has a complaint against another, forgiving each other; as the Lord has forgiven you, so you also must forgive. And above all these put on love, which binds everything together in perfect harmony."*

Paul closes, urging them to continually pray, being thankful, wise, and gracious.

PHILEMON

We now come to the very tiny book of Philemon; it's only one chapter! Philemon is not a letter to a church, but to an individual named Philemon, a wealthy Christian from Colossae. Even though it was written to one person, Paul did intend that it be read in the church, thereby qualifying it as an epistle. In this letter, Paul pleaded for the forgiveness of Philemon's runaway slave, Onesimus. Paul offered to take any wrong done to Philemon by Onesimus on himself in **Philemon 1:18**: *"If he has wronged you at all, or owes you anything, charge that to my account."* Although this seem like a very personal situation, the bigger picture Paul is eluding to in this letter is that as Christians, we need to forgive and love one another; and just as Paul was in a position to put himself out to help a weaker brother or sister, so should we.

1 TIMOTHY

Finally released from prison (for the time being), Paul wrote a letter to his protégé Timothy in 63 A.D. (Acts 16:1-3). Timothy, whose mother was Jewish and father was Greek, had traveled with Paul, but was now a pastor in Ephesus. Paul wrote this letter to encourage Timothy in his pastoral role and warn him of false teachers. First Timothy, along with 2 Timothy and Titus, are considered pastoral epistles because they give instruction on what it means to pastor a congregation and how to provide sound leadership and doctrine to the church.

Paul wrote his letter to Timothy, but he was writing to the entire church in Ephesus. Timothy was in a tough situation. He was trying to pastor a church that had false teachers embedded in it who were leading some in his congregation astray. Paul warned Timothy, *"Certain persons, by swerving from these, have wandered away into vain discussion, desiring to be teachers of the law, without understanding either what they are saying or the things about which they make confident assertions"* **(1 Tim. 1:6-7)**. Because some of these false teachers were elders of the church (or at least were leading the elders astray), Paul gives Timothy the qualifications that a pastor, elder, and deacon needed to have. A pastor or elder must be above reproach, faithful to his wife (if he's married), sensible, self-controlled, respectable, hospitable, and grounded and learned enough in Scripture and doctrine to be able to teach it. They should also not drink too much, have a bad temper, or be greedy. In addition, they should have their own family in order, not be a new believer, and have a good reputation in the community.

Sounds like an intimidating qualification list, but being the leader of a church is a huge responsibility and should only be done by someone who has their own life in order. We don't want someone who is a hot mess leading three hundred other people into becoming hot messes! Paul also addresses the office of deacon. A deacon, as we saw in Acts, cares for the physical well-being of a congregation. The qualifications for that office are not as strict as a pastor or elder since they are not in a teaching or ruling position over the congregation. A deacon needs to be dignified and truthful and not drink too much or be greedy. As with the elders, a deacon must be grounded in Scripture and doctrine, faithful in his marriage, and have his own household in order. If he has a wife, she must have the same characteristics that her husband does, but Paul adds she must not be a gossip.

Paul gives further instructions on how the church should conduct itself. He emphasizes the importance of all Christians knowing Scripture and doctrine so they will not be led astray by false teachers. This is certainly sound advice for Christians today! There is so much garbage being pedaled as "Christian" out there, it is only by being grounded in the Word that we can discern the Truth from the rubbish.

TITUS

As with Timothy, Titus was a protégé of Paul's (Gal. 2:3). Titus was originally a Gentile whom Paul converted. Paul wrote to him in 66 A.D. when

Titus was working on the island of Crete, where polytheism (belief in many gods) was prevalent. In this letter, Paul gives Titus some of the same advice he gave Timothy. He tells him the importance of and the qualification for church leaders and how teaching sound doctrine to the congregation is crucial, especially in light of the false teaching and polytheism that Titus was up against. Paul says in **Titus 1:12-13**, *"One of the Cretans, a prophet of their own, said, 'Cretans are always liars, evil beasts, lazy gluttons.' This testimony is true."*

Paul exhorts Titus about the importance of Christians, especially church leaders, to fight the good fight, stay faithful to Jesus and the Gospel, and conduct themselves in a manner worthy of a child of God. He reminds Titus in **3:5**, *"He saved us, not because of works done by us in righteousness, but according to his own mercy, by the washing of regeneration and renewal of the Holy Spirit."*

2 TIMOTHY

We now come to Paul's last letter, written in 67 A.D. to Timothy. Paul was in prison in Rome again when he wrote this letter. In his mid-sixties, Paul knew his life would end soon. *"For I am already being poured out as a drink offering, and the time of my departure has come"* **(2 Tim 4:6)**. Paul's words are exactly right. In 68 A.D., Paul was beheaded by the Roman emperor, Nero. In 64 A.D., Nero burned down the city of Rome for his own purposes and then blamed it on Christians. He brutally persecuted them as punishment for his own crime. Some Christians were doused with oil and set on fire, to be used as torches to light the streets of Rome at night. Others were torn apart by wild dogs. Sadly, Paul was a casualty of this madman. Paul wrote his last letter to his beloved Timothy, urging him to come visit him but leaving him a sort of last will and testament in case he was unable to.

He told Timothy he had no regrets as he had served God with a clear conscience and was not afraid to die. *"For God gave us a spirit not of fear but of power and love and self-control"* **(2 Tim. 1:7)**. He urged Timothy to be like-minded. He tells him to be a good solider of Christ, guarding the Truth of God and the Gospel. *"Do your best to present yourself to God as one approved, a worker who has no need to be ashamed, rightly handling the word of truth"* **(2 Tim. 2:15)**. As in his first letter, Paul warns Timothy of false teachers whose *"irreverent babble . . . will lead people into more and more ungodliness, and their talk will spread like gangrene"* **(2 Tim. 2:16-17a)**.

Paul gives Timothy a warning about the last days, and especially about the false teachers who will appear. As we said, "the last days" is the time period between Jesus' First and Second Coming. So, when Paul wrote this to Timothy, he was speaking about their present time, but also up until the time Jesus comes back. Self-centeredness, lovers of money, proud, arrogant, unholy, swollen with conceit, and having the appearance of godliness but not really being sincere are just some of the lovely characteristics of false teachers. I'm sure with a little thought, you can think of current "Christian" preachers, speakers, or authors who fit description! How do you fight these imposters? By knowing God's Word! The more Truth we know, the less likely we will fall for lies. As Paul tells Timothy in **2 Timothy 3:16-17**, *"All Scripture is breathed out by God and profitable for teaching, for reproof, for correction, and for training in righteousness, that the man of God may be complete, equipped for every good work."*

Paul's last instructions to Timothy were to preach the Word.

Chapter 20

LETTERS FROM THE OTHER APOSTLES

JAMES

We are now going to jump back in time to 45 A.D. For fluency, it made sense to put all of Paul's letters together right after Acts. James' epistle, though, is actually the first one chronologically. James was Jesus' brother and the leader of the church in Jerusalem. He was not an apostle; in fact, he didn't even become a believer until after Jesus' resurrection (Acts 1:14; 1 Cor. 15:7). Mark recounted a story where Jesus' family, including James, thought Jesus was crazy! But after James had an encounter with the resurrected Jesus, he became a central figure in the early church. James went from thinking his Brother was out of his mind, to becoming a follower to the point of martyrdom! James was martyred by being stoned and thrown off the roof of the temple.

James wrote to persecuted Jewish Christians living in poverty outside of Palestine. Focusing on the Divine nature and character of God, James urges the people to not just give God's Word lip service, but also to live it out practically in their lives. His no-nonsense, blunt tone makes this a book either people love or hate. We mentioned how Martin Luther was transformed by Paul's letter to the church in Rome. In contrast, Luther hated the book of James. He thought James was going back to the Old Covenant and insisting that people needed "good works" to be saved. In fact, Luther wanted the book of James, along with Jude, Hebrews, and Revelation removed from the Bible![28]

No disrespect to Martin Luther, but he misunderstood James' message. James does not say we need good works to be saved. What he does say is that good works are a fruit of being saved. In other words, we can know someone is saved when we see them doing the things James describes. James clearly understood that it is Jesus only Who saves as we see in **James 1:21**: *"Therefore put away all filthiness and rampant wickedness and receive with meekness the implanted word which is able to save your souls."* **John 1:1** makes it clear that the Word is Jesus: *"In the beginning was the Word, and the Word was with God, and the Word was God."*

In Luther's defense, James does say in **2:14**, *"What good is it, my brothers, if someone says he has faith but does not have works? Can that faith save him?"* The key word in this verse is "says." James' point is that someone can "say" they have faith, but if there is no fruit, they don't really have faith. Since their professed faith is false, it will not save him.

James gives practical advice on dealing with trials, temptation, taming the tongue, being wise, fighting worldliness, understanding everything we do depends on God's will, not being self-indulgent, and being patient in suffering.

He ends his letter with this exhortation in **James 5:20**: *"Whoever brings back a sinner from his wandering will save his soul from death and will cover a multitude of sins."*

1 PETER

Although Peter was the main source of information for Mark's Gospel, the Bible only contains two short books written by him directly, but both are packed with important doctrine and theology. This first one, 1 Peter, was written in 64 A.D. to mostly Gentile Christians who were scattered throughout modern-day

28 "Luther's Canon," Wikipedia.com, https://en.wikipedia.org/wiki/Luther's_canon (accessed April 24, 2019).

Turkey due to ongoing persecution from Nero. They were exiles, or sojourners, as Peter called them, feeling very much like strangers in a strange land.

He encourages them not to lose heart, that suffering for the sake of Christ should not be a surprise. That might not sound encouraging, but he reminds them that Jesus suffered for our behalf to free us from our sins. He tells his beleaguered readers that though they may have to suffer for a while, it will result in praise and glory to Christ. He extols them, *"As he who called you is holy, you also be holy in all your conduct"* **(1 Peter 1:15)**. Being holy in conduct includes being obedient to God, abstaining from sexual immorality, submitting to human authority, respecting and living in harmony with your spouse, and not repaying evil with evil. As a result, *"those who revile your good behavior in Christ may be put to shame"* **(1 Peter 3:16b)**.

Peter addresses their suffering again toward the end of his letter. Suffering is a tool that God uses to refine a believer's faith and grow them. Peter tells them that God is sovereign over their suffering, *"Therefore let those who suffer according to God's will entrust their souls to a faithful Creator while doing good"* **(1 Peter 4:19)**. Finally, Peter encourages the elders to lead the people by example in all things, including suffering.

2 PETER

Peter wrote this second letter three years after the first in 67 A.D., most likely while he was imprisoned in Rome. We aren't sure who his audience was, but the letter was written shortly before he was martyred. Tradition tells us that Peter was to be executed by crucifixion, but he did not want his death to resemble the death of Jesus because he considered himself unworthy. Therefore, he insisted on being crucified upside down. His letter was a farewell letter in which he urges Christians to continue growing and persevering. He calls out false teachers who were denying that there would be a Second Coming of Jesus. Like 1 Peter, 2 Peter is packed with crucial doctrine and theology.

Peter first affirms a believer's call and election by God. Like Paul, Peter often reminds his readers that God is sovereign over all, even salvation. He reminds his readers that he, and the other apostles, did not preach lies and make-believe stories as the false teachers were doing, but that, *"we were eye eyewitnesses of his majesty"* **(2 Peter 1:16b)**. Reading on, you see that Peter was referring to the transfiguration of Jesus that he, John, and James witnessed **(Matt. 17:1-8)**. Peter and the others heard the very voice of God the Father declaring that Jesus was His Son and was God! Further, the prophets from the Old Testament also testified to Who Jesus is. As we looked at in the introduction to the prophets, their words were God's words. To requote **2 Peter 1:21**: *"For no prophecy was ever produced by the will of man, but men spoke from God as they were carried along by the Holy Spirit."* This is important because there were many false teachers who were speaking of their own will and not of God's. These teachers, Peter says, infiltrate the church with their heresies and bring destruction. For these perverters of God's Words, judgement and damnation in hell await. And for those who have heard the truth yet still teach lies, *"It would have been better for them never to have known the way of righteousness than after knowing it to turn back from the holy commandment delivered to them"* **(2 Peter 2:21)**.

Friends, these are sobering words that should shake us. We have the Truth readily available to us in the Bible, yet so often we see Christians posting "spiritual" memes as their theology. This cannot be. We need to learn and study God's Truth and pass that onto our social media followers! Other believers, and even non-believers, do not need to be told, "God will fix everything that is broken in your life." This is not only a lie, but it is also destructive and false teaching! We need to be diligent in making sure what we share with others is actual truth!

Peter ends his letter speaking about "the day of the Lord." If you remember from our chapter on the prophets, the day of the Lord is the day Jesus comes back. Peter, like the prophets, urged people to make sure they are on the right side when that day comes.

JUDE

James wasn't the only brother of Jesus who became an ardent follower of The Way. Another brother, Jude, wrote a short letter in 68 A.D. to either Jewish Christians, or Gentile Christians who had knowledge of Jewish traditions. Jude's full name is Judas (Matt. 13:55), but English writers changed it to "Jude" so as not to confuse Jesus' brother with Judas Iscariot.

Jude's message is three-fold. First, he encourages his readers to fight for their faith and for the Gospel message.

His next message is an indication as to why they needed to fight for the message of salvation through Jesus Christ. He says in **Jude 4**, *"For certain people have crept in unnoticed who long ago were designated for this condemnation, ungodly people, who pervert the grace of our God into sensuality and deny our only Master and Lord, Jesus Christ."* Jude warns about ungodly false teachers who had crept into the church and were teaching distortions and lies. He reminded his readers that they should not be surprised by this, as they had been told many times, *"In the last time there will be scoffers, following their own ungodly passions.' It is these who cause division, worldly people, devoid of the Spirit"* **(Jude 18-19)**. In other words, from the time Jesus ascended into Heaven until the time He returns, the Church will have unsaved people in it—some being the cause of division and great strife within the church.

Jude's third and final message is to exhort his readers to keep growing in their faith, pray, and, as they wait on the return of Jesus, be merciful to the unsaved witnessing the Gospel to them so that some may be saved.

Jude's beautiful doxology at the end of his letter is one worth memorizing! *"Now to him who is able to keep you from stumbling and to present you blameless before the presence of his glory with great joy, to the only God, our Savior, through Jesus Christ our Lord, be glory, majesty, dominion, and authority, before all time and now and forever"* **(Jude 24-25)**.

HEBREWS

Also written in 68 A.D., the book of Hebrews' author is unknown. Some have attributed it to Paul because it was included in the Canon (books that made it into the Bible) the same time as Paul's epistles. It is unlikely that Paul wrote it, though. It lacks his usual style and does not have a salutation like his other letters have. It has also been suggested that it may have been written by Luke, Barnabas, or Apollos—all contemporaries of Paul. Whoever the author is, he was a skilled preacher and interpreter of Scripture, especially the Old Testament, with an excellent command of the Greek language.

The book of Hebrews has been called the most significant book in the New Testament in understanding the relationship between the Old Covenant (Old Testament) and New Covenant (New Testament). It was written to Jewish Christians who were discouraged because of the horrifying persecution they were facing. They were losing hope and had doubts about whether Jesus really took care of sin once and for all. Some were thinking of leaving Christianity and returning to Judaism because following Jesus was too hard.

The emphasis of this letter is that God has spoken His absolute, final Word through His Son. **Hebrews 1:1-3** says, *"Long ago, at many times and in many ways, God spoke to our fathers by the prophets, but in these last days he has spoken to us by his Son, whom he appointed the heir of all things, through whom also he created the world. He is the radiance of the glory of God and the exact imprint of his nature, and he upholds the universe by the word of his power."* Christ and His work are what all of the prophecies and Old Testament narratives had been leading up to. Jesus is God's final Word. To abandon Jesus, as the readers were contemplating, would be to abandon God altogether.

The author tells the people that Christ is superior to everything that went before—the old prophecy, the angelic mediators, the first exodus of the Jews out of Egypt, and the whole priestly system. Jesus fulfills everything in the Old Testament. He is the answer to our every past, present, and future need. When we are in Him, there is nothing we lack! God's people can have full confidence in God's Son—Who is not only our Lord and Savior, but also our High Priest, our King, and the one true Prophet. These three offices had been previously held, for a temporary period, by chosen men, but they are now forever perfectly and completely held by Jesus. As we see from the Old Testament, some of the men who held these offices were pretty good guys, and some weren't. But they were all human, which means they were all sinful and, therefore, flawed. Jesus, although fully Human, is not tainted with our sin nature. He lived a perfectly sinless life, and, therefore, is the perfect Man to fulfill these offices once and for all. In fact, it is because He is fully human, that He is able to hold these offices; but as the incarnate Word of God, Jesus is far better than any priest, king, or prophet who came before Him. He doesn't just reveal the *message of God* to humanity; He reveals *God* to humanity! Jesus gives all believers intimate access to God—something that, up until His death, was not possible. One of the richest, most encouraging books in the Bible, the book of Hebrews is ultimately about persevering through hard times in the grace of Jesus Christ. The book has three major parts:

Part 1 (1:4–4:13)—**Jesus is superior to angels despite (and because of) His humanity.** *"For to which of the angels did God ever say, 'You are my Son, today I have begotten you'?"* **(Heb. 1:5)**.

Part 2 (4:14–10:18)—**Jesus is the perfect High Priest**. *"Since then we have a great high priest who has passed through the heavens, Jesus, the Son of God, let us hold fast our confession"* **(Heb. 4:14)**.

Part 3 (10:19–13:21)—**Believers need to faithfully persevere.** *"Let us also lay aside every weight, and sin which clings so closely, and let us run with endurance the race that is set before us, looking to Jesus, the founder and perfecter of our faith, who for the joy that was set before him endured the cross, despising the shame, and is seated at the right hand of the throne of God"* **(Heb. 12:1b–2)**.

1 JOHN

Besides writing one of the four Gospels, the apostle John wrote three short epistles and the book of Revelation. Although there have been a few who have questioned whether the apostle is the author of these epistles, there are so many similarities in style, vocabulary, theology, and, especially, Christology, to John's Gospel, that most credible scholars agree that they had to be written by the same John. For example, just like in his Gospel, in these three epistles, John emphasizes that Jesus is the Christ and God Incarnate; and it is only through belief in Him that we can have forgiveness of sins.

The first of his letters, 1 John, was written in 90 A.D., to a Christian community John obviously knew well, for he calls them, *"My little children,"* and *"beloved"* **(1 John 2:1, 7)**. We aren't sure which community this is, but tradition tells us it was either Ephesus or a community located near Ephesus. John's letter came twenty-two years after the last epistle in the Bible. Predictably, in that time, some of the false teachers warned about by Paul, Peter, and others were challenging and questioning the practices of faithful believers. Some of these false teachers, who were never actually believers, defected from Christianity, taking their followers with them.

John opens his letter similarly to how he opened his Gospel—harkening back to Creation and affirming that Jesus was there from the beginning, that Jesus is the Word of God, and that Jesus, the Son of God, became fully Man. According to **1 John 1:1–2** (abridged), *"That which was from the beginning . . . concerning the word of life . . . was with the Father and was made manifest to us."* Like the other epistle writers, John urges his readers that it is not enough to just believe on Jesus; their lives need to reflect that belief. As he says, *"If we say we have fellowship with him while we walk in darkness, we lie and do not practice the truth"* **(1 John 1:6)**. John is taking aim at the false teachers, their followers, and others who claim to be Christian. When John speaks of "walking" in darkness, he means living in a pattern of sin. This doesn't mean that Christians do not sin, but those who have a relationship with God will continually search their hearts, repent of their sins, and turn back to God. If one doesn't see their sin or has no desire to even look at it, they may not be a believer at all.

John encourages faithful believers that they have had their sins forgiven by the work of Christ and are now children of God. In light of what Jesus did to acquire that forgiveness, we should strive to keep His commandments and not be attached to the world or worldly things. *"Whoever makes a practice of sinning is of the devil . . . No one born of God makes a practice of sinning, for God's seed abides in him; and he cannot keep on sinning, because he has been born of God. By this it is evident who are the children of God, and who are the children of the devil"* **(1 John 3:8–10 abridged).**

While many believe the term "antichrist" comes from the Book of Revelation, it doesn't. John used the term in **1 John 2:18**, *"Children, it is the last hour, and as you have heard that antichrist is coming, so now many antichrists have come. Therefore, we know that it is the last hour."* If you recall, the "last hour" began at Jesus' First Coming and will continue until He returns. There are many beliefs about who this "antichrist" is. While we do not have the space to delve into this as deeply as we would like, we will expand on what we said about this subject in 2 Thessalonians and give you a few of the more prevalent beliefs about the antichrist.

Some believe that the antichrist is a singular person who arrives on Earth right before Jesus' Second Coming to persecute His followers and challenge Jesus' authority. But look at John's words, *"so now many antichrists have come."* This seems to indicate that the antichrist is not just one singular person who appears at one specific time, but many people who appear throughout history. The definition of "antichrist" is "one who denies or opposes Christ."[29] In other words, someone who sets themselves up in place of Jesus. Given that definition, and John's words, we can conclude that the antichrist is not only one specific person, but, at least in part, many people throughout history.

---

29   *Merriam-Webster*, s.v. "Antichrist," Accessed May 14, 2019, https://www.merriam-webster.com/dictionary/Antichrist.

There are other credible scholars who believe that while there are many "antichrists" throughout history, there will also be one Antichrist who appears right before Jesus comes back. In addition, there are some scholars who argue that the Antichrist is not a person at all, but a political power, while still others say it is a destructive force set against the church. How you view the antichrist is directly related to what camp you are in when it comes to the Book of Revelation (more on that to come).

John ends with exhorting believers to be discerning so they will know false teachers from true teachers. He encourages them to love one another and to fear not for *"He who is in you is greater than he who is in the world"* **(1 John 4:4)**.

2 JOHN

Two years after his first letter, John wrote a very brief second letter to either an individual, prominent Christian woman or, more likely, to a specific church, which he called, "The elect lady and her children" **(2 John 1:1)**. If it was to a church, John probably used the "incognito" greeting because of the intense persecution surrounding the churches at that time. In this letter, John exhorts his readers to love one another and to walk in God's commandments. He again warns of false teachers and the antichrist.

3 JOHN

Two years after writing 2 John, in 94 A.D., John wrote another very short letter to a person named Gaius. We don't know who Gaius was, as this was a very common name during this period in the Roman Empire, but John called him "beloved" and one of his "children." We can confer that John knew him very well and that John probably mentored him. John praised Gaius for his faith and for the hospitality he had shown to other Christians traveling through town spreading the Gospel. He encouraged him to continue supporting these, and all other, missionaries.

Chapter 21

REVELATION

We are at the last book—the Book of Revelation. We have said several times that many books of the Bible require an in-depth study in order to gain a real understanding of its contents. Never is that truer than it is with the Book of Revelation! So, while we will not be able to dig deeply into the book, we will give you the theme, important takeaways, and some tools to use should you decide to take on reading this fascinating book (and we pray you do!).

The apostle John wrote Revelation in 95 A.D., during the reign of Domitian, emperor of Rome. Domitian required all of his subjects to refer to him as "lord and god." As you can imagine, the Christians of that time refused to do that, which led to widespread, horrible persecution of them. John wrote this book to encourage them to persevere in their faith, understanding that their perseverance would likely lead to their martyrdom. God, through John, is helping His people ultimately win their fight with the enemy, knowing that for many, their victory would come through their death.

The Book of Revelation is part epistle, part apocalyptic. Chapters two and three contain seven letters John wrote to seven churches, while the remainder of the book is apocalyptic and is prophecy John received through oracles and visions. If you recall from previous books we have looked at, apocalyptic can be defined as "forecasting the ultimate destiny of the world" or "ultimately decisive."[30] The Book of Revelation certainly forecasts the destiny of the world; and as has been the case since before the creation of the earth, God's plan for it and for His people is ultimately decisive, coming to fruition in this book!

One thing to note is that the book is called "Revelation," not "Revelations." The entire book is one revelation, not a series of many revelations. This is important because the whole book has one major theme—God is sovereign over all, and never will this be more evident than when Jesus returns and brings His victory over Satan, sin, and death to completion. **Revelation 1:17b–18** sums up this theme: *"Fear not, I am the first and the last, and the living one. I died, and behold I am alive forevermore, and I have the keys of Death and Hades."*

As we mentioned in the summary of 1 John, the camp you find yourself in will definitely influence how you interpret the Book of Revelation. Here some of the more prominent views on interpreting this book:

1. **The Historicist approach**—Also called dispensational premillennialism, the historicist approach made popular by C.I. Scofield is the approach used in the *Left Behind* series. The historicist approach says that Revelation is an overall, panoramic view of the church from beginning to end. Instead of seeing the visions and symbols as metaphorical, it sees the entire book as literal and assigns specific events in history to the visions and symbols. The problem with this approach is that it is only relevant to a people in a specific point in history and not to everyone for all time. He was writing to the Christians of that time, but God also intended it to be applicable to Christians throughout all of history who were enduring horrific persecution. Also, when John was given the prophecies, he understood what they meant. Had Jesus been talking about the United Nations, for example, John and his original readers would have had no idea

---

30   *Merriam-Webster*, s.v. "Apocalyptic," Accessed March 30, 2019, https://www.merriam-webster.com/dictionary/apocalyptic.

what he was writing about, and it certainly would not have been an encouragement to *them* to persevere in their trials. Besides, Jesus put time limits on the events listed in the book. *"They will trample the holy city for forty-two months"* **(Rev. 11:2b)**. If you are taking this verse literally, as historicists do, you could not say this event was fulfilled in 1948 when five Arab nations invaded Israel because it didn't last forty-two months. Another problem with this view is that proponents of it are vastly divided as to what events in history the symbols and visions are referring to. While this is a popular view, it has been debunked and rejected by most credible biblical scholars.

2. **The Preterist approach**—There are two schools with the preterist approach: full preterism and partial preterism. The full preterist approach is that everything in the Book of Revelation has already taken place—mostly during the first century. The problem with this approach is that first, the book itself says it is a prophecy of things to come: *"Blessed is the one who reads aloud the words of this prophecy, and blessed are those who hear, and who keep what is written in it, for the time is near"* **(Rev. 1:3)**. Second, it believes everything, even Jesus' Second Coming, has already occurred. Obviously, this is heresy, since **Revelation 1:7** says, *"Behold, he is coming with the clouds, and every eye will see him, even those who pierced him."*

3. **The Partial Preterist Approach**—Proponents of partial preterism believe that except for the Second Coming and the event surrounding it, everything else in the Book of Revelation has already occurred. They subscribe to the theory that most of the events described in Revelation culminated in the destruction of Jerusalem and the temple in 70 A.D., and therefore, most amillennialists date this book's writing early that 95 A.D. This view, sometimes linked to Amillennialism, is held by many credible scholars.

4. **The Idealist approach**—The idealist approach is that the Book of Revelation is a book of metaphors and symbols depicting the timeless cosmic struggle between good and evil. The things depicted in Revelation are not actual events, but pictures of the spiritual warfare that is going on around us. The book is meant to teach us spiritual truths, not be a factual account of what the end times will be. There are some very credible scholars who adhere to this approach. The problem with it, though, is that it ignores John's claim that the book is prophecy. As he said in **Revelation 22:7**, *"Blessed is the one who keep the words of the prophecy of this book."*

5. **The Futurist approach**—Another popular approach amongst credible scholars is the futurist approach. Futurists believe that everything after chapter three is yet to come. The events depicted describe actual events that will occur at the time of Jesus' Second Coming, the Millennium, and Final Judgement. While this view fully embraces that Revelation is prophecy, it makes what is written in the book relevant only to those who are living around the Second Coming of Jesus.

6. **The Eclectic approach**—The eclectic approach is a fairly new approach. It looks at the strengths and weaknesses of the partial preterist, futurist, and idealist approaches and meshes them into a new way of interpreting the book. The eclectic approach modifies the partial preterist view by conceding that much of what is in the Book of Revelation has already happened; however, it also modifies the futurist view acknowledging that there are still several events that have yet to occur, but much has already occurred. Finally, it amends the idealist approach recognizing that some, not all, of the passages in Revelation are metaphors that give us a glimpse of the spiritual warfare that is going on. This approach has been gaining widespread acceptance.

With the exception of the historicist and full preterist approaches, credible biblical theologians are divided amongst the other four. There is validity and problems within all four. One thing everyone can agree on, however, is that in order to understand the Book of Revelation, one needs to know the Old Testament. While the Book of Hebrews is the best book showing the link between the Old and New Testaments, the Book of Revelation is the best book that shows how God brings to fruition everything promised and prophesied about in the Old Testament. Trying to tackle Revelation without any understanding of the Old Testament is like trying to comprehend Calculus without having a working knowledge of basic math!

Another important element to interpreting Revelation is understanding that the numbers John uses are not literal, but symbolic. For example, the number seven is always used in the Bible to mean completeness and perfection. So, seven years may not literally be seven years, but a complete period God has ordained. The number twelve, a number representing the original twelve tribes of Israel, is also a number of completeness. Revelation 7 talks about the 144,000 of Israel who are sealed. There are not literally 144,000 Israelites saved. This number represents twelve thousand from each of the original twelve tribes and symbolizes the complete number of Israelites God has chosen to save. The Lord uses this number again in chapter fourteen to indicate all of those God has elected to be saved. Again, this is not literally 144,000, but twelve thousand times twelve thousand— the complete, complete number of people who belong to God. The number three, a reference to the Trinity, is also used to symbolize completeness. In contrast to these symbols, when the numbers six or three-and-a-half are used, it symbolizes a period shorter than the complete period. So three-and-a-half years may not be a literal time period, but a period less than the complete period. The last number to be aware of is four. Four is a number symbolizing creation. John says in **Revelation 7:1**, *"I saw four angels standing at the four corners of the earth, holding back the four winds of* *the earth."* In other words, God has complete dominion over all creation, including angels, the earth, and the wind.

We will wrap this up with a brief overview of the entire book. While being exiled on the island of Patmos, John received a vision of things that will take place. Like Isaiah, he was given a behind-the-curtain look into Heaven. He saw Jesus, Who tells him to write a letter to seven churches. These churches are thought to be actual churches, but the fact that there are seven indicates they are representative of all churches. This makes sense as the letters cover almost every circumstance a church can find itself in, ranging from praising one for its faithfulness to encouraging another during its tribulations, to accusing one of lukewarm faith, to Jesus declaring one church dead.

After the letters, John began to receive visions. First, he saw the throne of God; then he had a vision of a scroll with seven seals that only Jesus was worthy to open. The seals are judgements that will come upon the earth. The seals were followed by seven trumpets and seven bowls, also containing judgments. The seals, trumpets, and bowls are the same. God gives the judgements in three formats to show it is a done deal that they will occur. (Because three means complete!) In between the visions of each of these, John sees several visions involving a woman, a dragon, Satan, and two beasts **(Rev. 12-13)**. These visions are not a prophecy of the future, but a glimpse of what has been going on in the spiritual realm. The vision is a harkening back to Genesis 3:15 when God said He would put enmity between Satan and the woman's seed. There are more complexities in this vision, but space does not allow us to delve in any deeper. To sum it up though, all of these visions have one thing in common: Satan will try and destroy the people of God; but his fate has already been decided, and no one, not even the devil, can destroy those whom God has sealed to save from before the foundation of the world.

After the visions of the seven seals, trumpets, and bowls, John is shown a vision of the demise of what some believe is the Roman Empire, which was responsible for the horrific persecution of Christians. Their defeat came in

476 A.D., when they were overthrown by Germanic forces. Others believe that it is not just specifically the Roman Empire, but symbolic of many political establishments who have tortured the saints of Christ. John also saw the fate of other persecutors of the church, after which there is rejoicing in Heaven, as we see in **Revelation 19:6-7**: *"Then I heard what seemed to be the voice of a great multitude, like the roar of many waters and like the sound of mighty peals of thunder, crying out, 'Hallelujah! For the Lord our God the Almighty reigns. Let us rejoice and exult and give him the glory, for the marriage of the Lamb has come, and his Bride has made herself ready.'"* The "Bride" is the invisible church, or all believers. Jesus gathers His believers unto Himself. After that, Satan will be thrown into the fire, where he will be tormented day and night forever. Then God will issue final judgment on both believers and non-believers as we are told in **Revelation 20:12, 15**: *"And I saw the dead, great and small, standing before the throne, and books were opened. Then another book was opened, which is the book of life. And the dead were judged by what was written in the books, according to what they had done . . . And if anyone's name was not found written in the book of life, he was thrown into the lake of fire."* The book of life represents all who belong to Jesus. Everyone will be judged by what they have done, but the big difference for God's elect is that while we will be shown every sinful thing we have done, said, or thought, Jesus will step us and say, "This one is mine." Then our life's record will disappear, and it will be Jesus' perfect record God sees and not our sinful one. For unbelievers, they will stand on their own deeds, condemned by their sin.

After the final judgment, Jesus will establish a new heaven and new earth beautifully described in chapters twenty-one through twenty-three. Here is a brief snippet from **Revelation 21:3b-4**: *"'Behold, the dwelling place of God is with man. He will dwell with them, and they will be his people, and God himself will be with them as their God. He will wipe away every tear from their eyes, and death shall be no more, neither shall there be mourning, nor crying, nor pain anymore, for the former things have passed away.'"*

The Book of Revelation ends with Jesus assuring John and the readers that He is coming back and warns the readers not to add or take away anything from God's Word. Fittingly, the last word of Revelation and the entire Bible is "Amen" **(Rev. 22:21).**

CONCLUSION

We hope you have been as blessed journeying through the sixty-six books of the Bible as we have! Our prayer is that you feel more confident and have developed a hunger to dig even deeper into God's Word. Whether it's your first time or your twenty-first time, we pray you will feel encouraged and excited to read the Bible in its entirety!

God wrote a Book! As we said in the introduction, nothing can compare to It! Nothing compares to reading the actual pages of what God divinely inspired the writers to write! No other book has the saving, life-giving, life-transforming message of the Bible. Seeing God's plan to redeem His children unfold throughout history is about as exciting a read as there is!

BIBLIOGRAPHY

Calvin, John. "Calvin's Commentary on the Bible: Genesis 4." Studylight.org. Accessed DATE. www.studylight.org/commentaries/cal/genesis-4.html.

Easton, M. G., M.A. D.D. "Deuteronomy Definition and Meaning—Bible Dictionary." Bible Study Tools.com. Accessed January 26, 2019. *www.biblestudytools.com/dictionary/deuteronomy.*

Fee, Gordon D., and Douglas K. Stuart. *How to Read the Bible Book by Book a Guided Tour.* Grand Rapids: Zondervan, 2014.

Hall, Eric and Jess. "Lesson 16 on the Book of Daniel." ThyWordIsTruth.com. Accessed March 30, 2019. www.thywordistruth.com/Daniel/Lesson-16-on-Daniel.html#.XJ_sYphKjIU.

Ligonier Ministries. "R.C. Sproul: For Justification By Faith Alone." YouTube video, 48:03. Posted August 06, 2015. *www.youtube.com/watch?v=DfKUxXB7_Cg.*

"Luther's Canon." Wikipedia.com. Accessed April 24, 2019. https://en.wikipedia.org/wiki/Luther's_canon.

Merriam-Webster, s.v. "Antichrist." Accessed May 14, 2019. www.merriam-webster.com/dictionary/Antichrist.

Merriam-Webster, s.v. "Apocalyptic." Accessed March 30, 2019. www.merriam-webster.com/dictionary/apocalyptic.

Merriam-Webster, s.v. "Ex Nihilo." Accessed June 27, 2019. www.merriam-webster.com/dictionary/ex nihilo.

Merriam-Webster, s.v. "Exodus." Accessed January 26, 2019. www.merriam-webster.com/dictionary/exodus.

Merriam-Webster, s.v. "Leviticus." Accessed January 26, 2019. www.merriam-webster.com/dictionary/Leviticus.

Merriam-Webster, s.v. "Prophet." Accessed February 22, 2019. www.merriam-webster.com/dictionary/prophet.

"Micah." Wikipedia.com. Accessed June 27, 2019. https://en.wikipedia.org/wiki/Micah.

New Strong's Exhaustive Concordance, The. Nashville, TN: Thomas Nelson Publishers, 1990, 149.

Packer, J. I. *Concise Theology: A Guide to Historic Christian Beliefs.* Chicago: Tyndale House Publishers, Inc. 1993.

"The Revelation to John." Westminster.edu. Accessed April 09, 2019. www4.westminster.edu/staff/brennie/rel101/revelati.htm.

Rothwell, Robert. Ligonier Ministries. "The Everlasting Kingdom." https://www.ligonier.org/learn/articles/everlasting-kingdom/ (accessed April 7, 2019).

Spirit of the Reformation Study Bible: New International Version. Grand Rapids, MI: Zondervan, 2003.

Stoner, Peter W. *Science Speaks.* Chicago: Moody Bible Institute, 1976. www.sciencespeaks.dstoner.net/Christ of Prophecy.html (accessed April 27, 2019).

Strong's Lexicon G5547. "Christos." BlueLetterBible.org. Accessed May 1, 2019. www.blueletterbible.org/lang/lexicon/lexicon.cfm?Strongs=G5547&t=NASB.

Stuart, Douglas, Ph.D. "Lecture 6: The Law: Covenant Structure." BiblicalTraining.org. Accessed January 29, 2019. www.biblicaltraining.org/law-covenant-structure/old-testament-survey.

Stuart, Dr. Douglas. "Lecture 23: Prophetical Books." BiblicalTraining.org. Accessed March 07, 2019. www.biblicaltraining.org/prophetical-books/old-testament-survey-0.

Theopedia, s.v. "hesed." Theopedia.com. Accessed February 05, 2019. www.theopedia.com/hesed.

Thiele, Edwin R. Thiele. "Chapter Two: The Fundamental Principles of Hebrew Chronology" in *The Mysterious Numbers of the Hebrew Kings New Revised Edition.*" Grand Rapids: The Zondervan Corporation, 1983.

Valkanet, Rich and Discovery Bibles. "Bible Timeline." Bible Hub.com. *www.biblehub.com/timeline*. Accessed January 22, 2019.

NO
half-truths
ALLOWED

UNDERSTANDING THE
COMPLETE
GOSPEL MESSAGE

**CHRISTINE PAXSON
& ROSE SPILLER**

When it comes to proclaiming the Gospel message, half-truths, vague notions, and generalizations can be dangerous.

What are the important truths we need to know and share with others?

- Is it enough to believe that God loves us and wants a relationship with us?
- Is it enough to "ask Jesus into our hearts"?
- Is it enough to recite the "sinner's prayer," or do we need to repent of our sin?
- Is going to church and serving others enough?
- Is what Jesus suffered more than a gruesome death on a cross?
- If Jesus, who is fully God, was crucified, did God die on Good Friday?
- Is God mad at us when we sin and happy when we're behaving? Can we lose our salvation?

If you're not sure of the answers to any of these questions, you are not alone. There are a lot of false ideas out there about Christianity and the Gospel.

Join Christine Paxson and Rose Spiller as they explore the answers to these and many other questions about the true Gospel message in *No Half-Truths Allowed: Understanding the Complete Gospel Message.* Learn what Jesus did for you, why He did it, and how you can articulate the Gospel to others.

Also available is the companion *No Half-Truths Allowed Study Guide,* an interactive study guide with questions and Scriptures to help readers delve even deeper into understanding the complete Gospel message.

For more information about
Christine Paxson and Rose Spiller
and
The Bible Blueprint
please connect at:

www.proverbs910ministries.com
www.facebook.com/prov910
proverbs910ministries@gmail.com
@prov_910

For more information about
AMBASSADOR INTERNATIONAL
please connect at:

www.ambassador-international.com
@AmbassadorIntl
www.facebook.com/AmbassadorIntl

*If you enjoyed this book, please consider leaving us a review on
Amazon, Goodreads, or our website.*

Also check out Chris and Rose's Podcast: No Trash, Just
Truth! *Streaming now on all platforms.*

More from Ambassador International

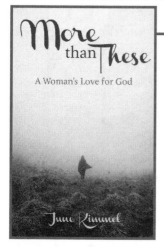

More Than These addresses the question that every woman who desires to walk with God must face: How can a woman love God as she should and keep the rest of her life in its proper place? Women are searching for the secret to balancing their lives. More Than These: A Woman's Love for God declares that loving God supremely is the answer.
More Than These
by June Kimmel

Could it be women are so busy chasing emptiness and playing the people-pleasing game, that they can't find time to live on mission? It's time to take a deep breath and do some inventory, to dig in and see what God's Word has to say about this tug-of-war between our flesh and our mission, and to figure out ways to quit chasing emptiness and take bold steps of obedience. What would happen if we said Enough of Me . . . more Jesus?
Enough of Me
by Priscilla Peters

Using her own personal journey during an adventurous move to Paris, Anne shares healing truths of Scripture and methods she found to help others find freedom from their baggage. You will be inspired and refreshed as you realize you no longer have to carry your baggage either.
Pack Your Baggage, Honey, We're Moving to Paris!
by Anne Farnum

Made in United States
Orlando, FL
26 February 2024

44156002R00189